THE
MLA
Modern Language Teacher's Handbook

by
Alan Smalley
Honorary Secretary

and
David Morris
Assistant Honorary Secretary

HUTCHINSON
London   Melbourne   Sydney   Auckland   Johannesburg

Hutchinson and Co. (Publishers) Ltd
An imprint of the Hutchinson Publishing Group
17–21 Conway Street, London W1P 6JD

Hutchinson Publishing Group (Australia) Pty Ltd
16–22 Church Street, Hawthorn, Melbourne, Victoria 3122

Hutchinson Group (NZ) Ltd
32–34 View Road, PO Box 40–086, Glenfield, Auckland 10

Hutchinson Group (SA) (Pty) Ltd
PO Box 337, Bergvlei 2012, South Africa

First published 1985
© Alan Smalley and David Morris 1985
Set in Times New Roman by Folio Photosetting, Bristol
Printed and bound in Great Britain by Anchor Brendon Ltd, Tiptree, Essex

British Library Cataloguing in Publication Data
Smalley, Alan
   The MLA modern language teacher's handbook.
   1. Languages, Modern — Study and teaching
   (Secondary) — Great Britain
   I. Title   II. Morris, David
   418′.007′1241   PB 38.G5

ISBN 0 09 161 220 9

THE
MLA
Modern Language
Teacher's Handbook

Contents

Part Three: Beyond the School

Part Four: Reference Section

Foreword

One of the great strengths of the MLA, since its foundation, has been collaboration between practising teachers of languages in schools and members of university and polytechnic faculties, in the search for ways of raising standards of performance in our very difficult métier. From the outset, at the great Cheltenham conference of 1890, from which MLA grew, university teachers played their part, in harness with devoted schoolmasters of the calibre of W. S. Macgowan and W. H. Widgery.

This book is the product of a similar cooperation. Its two authors have both given distinguished service to MLA at both branch and national levels. Alan Smalley, Principal Lecturer at Leeds Polytechnic and a former Chairman of MLA, has for some years been the Association's indefatigable Honorary Secretary. David Morris, Head of Department at Allerton Grange School, Leeds, is also a former national Chairman of MLA and in addition is Branch Secretary and an active Examination Board member.

While their work for MLA has brought them into touch with recent theoretical developments in language teaching at home and abroad, each of them has also met at first hand the practical challenges of present-day classrooms. Their earlier publications for MLA, such as *The Head of Department* and *The Probationary Teacher's Handbook*, have had a warm welcome from teachers. Now the team of Smalley and Morris offers a *vademecum* which will appeal not simply to the beginner but to many teachers with departmental responsibilities and to those who advise and train teachers.

Sheer professionalism is the key to success in the language classroom. We are lucky to have two teachers of such integrity to give us the fruits of their own professional experience. I warmly recommend this book to those who value professionalism in the classroom.

Eric Hawkins CBE
Professor Emeritus, University of York
Hon. Professor, University College of Wales, Aberystwyth.
President of the Modern Language Association, 1983–5

Introduction

The Modern Language Association was founded almost a hundred years ago to foster the growth of modern language teaching in our schools and colleges. Since its inception in 1892 it has been at the forefront of improvement and innovation in the classroom and has frequently contributed to high-level discussion of the role and function of modern languages.

In recent years the Association has made major statements to Select Committees in Parliament and to publications of the Department of Education and Science. It has, in addition, begun to publish a series of practical handbooks aimed at the teacher who works 'at the chalk face'. The present volume stems from these publications and the authors have welcomed the opportunity to expand on their earlier work to create what it is hoped will be an indispensable reference book for all teachers of languages, from student-in-training or probationer to the experienced head of department.

We stress the words 'reference book' for we have not sought to produce either a new philosophy of language teaching (though a very clear philosophy emerges) or a sustained argument in favour of one particular method, for we recognize that each individual has to develop a personal style in the classroom. To enable such a style to emerge there must be confidence and competence and we sincerely hope that this book, designed to browse through at leisure or to turn to for ideas at a moment's notice, will help these qualities to thrive even on the dullest Friday afternoon. It is a *vade-mecum* in the true sense of the word.

PART ONE

Survival in the Classroom

1 First days in school

The first few days in a new school are well known to be difficult ones for any teacher, and for the new and inexperienced teacher they can be particularly traumatic. The purpose of this book is to help *all* teachers of modern languages — and, at the outset, we especially have in mind the new entrant to the profession.

Of course, if he or she is joining a well-run school, the morning of term will certainly not be the first time he has seen the school, but unfortunately, this does happen, as more and more local education authorities are reduced to making temporary appointments at very short notice.

We hope that the suggestions made in this book will equip teachers of modern languages to face the first few days and all the other problems which, in the nature of things, confront every teacher from time to time. If the obvious is stated it is important to remember that it may not be obvious to the less experienced. If the seemingly impossible is counselled we ask that it should not be condemned without trial.

TO ALL NEW STAFF: School policy in general

School policy which transcends any single department needs to be clearly known from the start. It is useful to go to the school with a checklist to ensure all main points are covered, namely: school hours and dates of terms; dates of examinations for all years of pupils; other important deadlines in the school year, e.g. dates of meetings with parents of the different year groups, dates for completion of reports, basic facts about the school — size, intake, pupils' background, schools they are drawn from, and any particular problems.

The colleagues you will be working with need to be known as soon as possible. Not only *who* but who does *what* has to be found out at once. What is the role of the deputy heads, the year tutors, the form tutors? How is contact made with parents?

For many teachers and for all new heads of department finance is an important issue. How is money allocated to a department and within a department? What amount will be available during the current school year? Is there a contingency fund to help out in an emergency?

Examination policy is crucial to the effective running of the school. Which examination board and, more important, which syllabuses are used? Is it possible to enter pupils for examinations run by different boards? Does the school have a policy of fostering Mode 3 syllabuses?

Equipment, especially audio-visual equipment, is precious. What is the school's attitude to such equipment? Is it owned by departments or are certain items true banalities, owned in common?

Governing bodies in schools are becoming increasingly significant. What is the attitude of the governors to particular subjects and to particular teaching methods? Who are the teacher representatives? Where are the reports of the meetings they have attended?

All the above are matters of vital concern to any new member of staff taking up a post in a school. Many other vital, and some may say more immediate questions, are dealt with next.

The school and the department

As a new arrival approaching the department, refer again to the checklist. It is safe to assume in most schools these days that the department works as a team with a common policy to govern its working methods. In a modern comprehensive school the structure of courses and examinations is so comlex that there can be little scope for the individual who prefers to do things 'his way'. An agreed policy is understood.

Agreed policy usually arises from discussion at departmental meetings. This will certainly be so with regard to acceptance of methods and materials within the department. On the other hand, any matter bringing languages into contact with other subject areas will probably have been decided by an academic board or council of heads of departments.

On first entering the school, however, you will be more concerned with 'what' than with 'how' and we suggest the following checklist will be helpful:

1 *Marking*: Is there a departmental policy both as regards the system of grading (marks out of 10 or 20 or A to E or a range of comments) and a method of correction? Do pupils always do 'corrections' after a written exercise and, most important, are they checked?

2 *Assessment*: How are the term marks processed and how are they stored? Do all term marks count towards a termly grade? Is there any system of testing on a monthly, half-termly or termly basis? Are all results communicated in detail to pupils and to parents?

3 *Syllabus*: Has a full copy of the departmental syllabus been handed on? Does it cover all aspects of the work in modern languages, including attitude towards public examinations, i.e. who does what?

4 *Departmental stock*: Content and location of textbooks, visual aids, tapes, worksheets, projectors, OHP slides, tape recorders (reel-to-reel) and cassette players, radios, TV, duplicating facilities, banda, photo-copy, etc. Is there a staff reference section containing the latest books on teaching aims and methods, publishers' catalogues,

specimen copies, details of relevant courses (in-service and vacation), sets of past examination papers, both school-based and external?

5 *Departmental systems*: Central records of pupils' progress, loans recording system, procedure for recording breakages and malfunction of departmental equipment and, very important, a petty cash account to cover minor replacements urgently required, e.g. projector lamp, replacement cassettes, one or two extra course books. Do all or any of these exist?

6 *Language policy*: Which pupils do which language? Who decides which language? Do pupils opt or are they told 'Next year the second language will be Spanish'? What selection procedure is used for allocating pupils to the different languages offered? Of special concern to the newly appointed head of department should be the question of whether there are any members of staff in the department whose skills are under-used or even inefficiently deployed. How many teachers are teaching French when their first language is German or Russian? In the future could not this expertise be more effectively deployed?

7 *Public examinations*: How are pupils selected for the different public examinations? Are the graded tests in use in the school? Who is responsible for the co-ordination of graded tests? Which members of staff have public examining experience? Who serves on examination boards? And what about examination results? How do they compare with results in other subjects within the school? What reasons explain any discrepancies? Staff changes? Change of language policy?

8 *Cooperation*: What examples are there of cooperation from department to department? European Studies involving historians and geographers perhaps? Is there cooperation between schools at any level including sixth form? What is the extent of the liaison between the school you enter and the local feeder schools? Is there any staff movement between the different schools?

9 *Overseas links*: Are correspondence, visits and exchanges actively encouraged by the department? Who is responsible for such activities and how are they organized? How are pupils selected to take part in foreign visits? Is there any financial help for children from under-privileged homes? Is there a thriving town-twinning scheme? How is this exploited? Is the school linked directly to named schools abroad?

10 *Out-of-school activities*: Is there a language club? Is there any possibility of showing foreign films? Are parents able to join in with school events concerned with visits abroad? Are there visits to see foreign plays? Does the department get involved in language festivals or competitions?

11 *Support for staff*: Does the LEA employ an Adviser whose specific brief is to foster language development within the authority? Does he visit the school and when can he be seen? Does the Teachers' Centre provide support for teachers of modern languages? If so, what? Is there a language centre run by the LEA? What facilities can it offer? Is it accessible?

The points to watch for listed above are those which any conscientious new member of staff will almost automatically include in a survey of his new school. Indeed for many new staff they are points which will have been considered seriously before accepting the post. All the more reason for listing them here, for they may serve as useful points of reference for the teacher at present on the interview circuit. With all these points in mind no applicant need be stumped by that final interview question 'And now do you have any questions you would like to ask us, Mrs Jones?'

The probationary teacher

For the probationary teacher the first few days may well be even more exacting than they are for the experienced colleague simply moving into a new post and for this reason we have no hesitation in passing on the following advice to the beginner.

1 Take the first opportunity you can to talk with the member of staff who taught last year the groups which you have this year. If that teacher has left, ensure you talk to someone who had more or less the same group last year. (If they have *all* left, maybe you have accepted the wrong job!) In such a conversation it is wise to establish in your mind what the general spirit of the group is. Is there an obvious 'leader'? How is he or she best dealt with? Listen carefully to opinion and keep in mind at all times that it *is* opinion you are getting and that we are all biased in our attitudes occasionally.

2 Acquire the technique of keeping one ear open in the staffroom for remarks made by colleagues on pupils who are in one of your groups. Much useful information on pupils may be gleaned in this way, although there is doubtless in the school a formal way of passing on information about pupils and their families. General information about background, home conditions and school history may become part of the school folklore which someone forgets to pass on to new arrivals. In the early days it is certainly worth your while formalizing this knowledge by asking the year tutor or form tutor whether there is any information a teacher should have about particular pupils. In the post-Warnock era this becomes increasingly important, for we are reminded that 1 child in 5 will need remedial or special education at some time in his school career. On this point, however, beware of letting negative comments prevent you from giving a child a fair chance.

3 In the first few days the head of modern languages is bound to be the one you seek to turn to for guidance most frequently. Any beginner will be wise to take every opportunity of talking to his head of department. Through him he will become aware of the aims of the

department and precise help will be forthcoming about how to define one's objectives and how to go about achieving them. Bear in mind too that the head of department needs to get to know his staff. Only through contact with a colleague can he decide the strengths of the newcomer and how best to deploy him in the department. Finally, the head of department is the person who is most likely to pass on to the head teacher impressions that are made in the early days. In a big school, with all the goodwill in the world, the head has to be dependent on what the heads of department pass on.

4 *Qui se ressemble s'assemble* says the French proverb and its truth is often demonstrated in the staff room. It is quite remarkable how groups of teachers from the same department join together at break times to discuss progress and exchange ideas for putting across particular grammatical points. The new teacher benefits enormously from this kind of contact which may well lay the foundations of professional friendships destined to last for many years.

5 In every school one member of the staff is designated to look after the interests and the progress of the probationary teachers — hopefully someone you can have confidence in. It is important that you establish early contact with this colleague for he or she will fairly regularly want to know about work in progress and will expect to see a lesson taught on a regular basis. The more you feel at ease with such a colleague the better you will perform on these occasions.

6 It goes without saying that lesson preparation is the most vital of all tasks in the early days. It may be galling to see an experienced colleague dashing off to a class without any obvious evidence of preparation but it is easy to be deceived. Certainly as one's skills as a teacher improve, preparation time becomes shorter and what is prepared for one year may, with minor adaptations, be perfectly adequate for a following year. For the beginner there is

no such possibility. Every lesson is *ab initio* and much time has to be devoted to the making of materials as well as to the actual planning of the lesson. Much sound advice will come from more experienced colleagues and it is therefore well worth indicating to them what your future plans are. Some will lend apparatus, others may have model worksheets to pass on. (See Chapter 3.)

7 As soon as possible you should be fully familiar with school routine. The best advice which can be given is to make notes as you go along and, if in doubt, ask a colleague rather than a pupil, who will consider you 'a real wet' if you don't know what time the lesson ends or when to set homework.

8 A good knowledge of the geography of the campus is vital to efficient operation. It pays to have a good walk round in the early days to learn not only locations but also names. Though few of our pupils speak of 'big side' these days, most schools do have their own jargon and it helps to know what colleagues and pupils are talking about.

9 Other areas to become familiar with early in your career are the library (What system of loans is there? Who is the librarian? Is it possible to borrow books for class use?), the technician's room (does he or she maintain equipment for the modern languages department?), the staffrooms (which is for quiet work and which for conversation?), the school office (make a friend of the school secretary).

10 *The law of copyright*: The modern photocopier seemed like the final solution to so many teachers' problems but we quickly learnt that the copyright law prevents all copying of other people's work. It may still be a boon for producing multiple copies of original work but it must not be used to copy others' literary, dramatic, musical or artistic productions. It is important to remember also that the word 'literary' in the four categories referred to above is interpreted very broadly and may include

tables, lists, even football results. The message is simple: *no appliance can be used for making multiple copies* and any teacher who does so now runs the risk of severe penalty. Of course if permission is obtained from a publisher then that is another story. Note that some foreign news magazine publishers are known to have given permission for multiple copying to go on for class use. Where such permission exists it is usually in the form of a letter addressed to the individual who has applied.

11 *In the classroom*: The early days are crucial for establishing a good working relationship with your pupils. To start with you should avoid seeking to prove that you are 'a great guy'. Friendliness is all very well but it can be mistaken for weakness. Instead, seek to establish a good reputation for sound work, energy, activity and encouragement to do well. Any experienced teacher will confirm that it is easier to move from a firm position to a more relaxed one. It is well nigh impossible to move the other way.

12 *New pupils*: When meeting new pupils for the first time it is a good idea to take a while in the first lesson to explain the methods the teacher intends to adopt for the group. Details of homework, incidence and quantity, type of homework should be explained. Oral work sometimes causes stressful situations for pupils, so explain how it will be conducted, what its purpose is and why it is important to make an effort to contribute. Once pupils understand why we are trying to do a particular thing they usually cooperate more readily. They tend to resent what they do not understand. It is also a good idea to give clear guidance on how written work is to be set out. One way of doing this is to give to each member of the class, a model, i.e. a sheet which illustrates exactly how the ideal piece of classwork/homework should be presented. Of course, it may be that a departmental policy exists for this sort of thing. If it does, then pupils should be expected to conform. To introduce a different system will cause

confusion and, in some instances, will lead rapidly to disciplinary problems as pupils challenge the new authority.

13 *Names of pupils*: Some teachers of modern languages like to give all pupils a name characteristic of the language they teach. There is a lot of good sense in this since it helps to ensure consistency of pronunciation which phrases such as 'Je vais demander à Brian et à Tracy de se lever,' manifestly fail to do.

The idea of giving French of German names certainly appeals to younger children but it is doubtful whether it will make much of an appeal to anyone above the third form and it is probably best to put up with whatever name the pupils are blessed with in real life.

Learning names at the start is always a problem and until the teacher knows the names he is not really in charge. Pupils resent the teacher who doesn't quickly learn to recognize every individual. And they are right. Until one can put a name to each individual in the class it can hardly be said that there is any real personal contact. Any method which speeds up the name-learning process is to be welcomed. Two easy ways are: (1) have a seating plan and a preordained place for every individual or, (2) have a name card on display 'as they do at international conferences' in front of each member of the class.

The final reason for learning names quickly is that it enables the teacher to cut out masses of useless English verbiage when he tries to identify 'the girl with fair hair at the back; no, the one next to the boy in the blue pullover who's looking out of the window'.

14 *Punctuality*: It is vital to establish a reputation for being in the classroom on time to ensure a prompt start for the lesson. In many schools a period lasts forty minutes, and five minutes lost at the start on a regular basis soon cuts into progress. When pupils arrive late it is essential that the teacher finds out why. A common reason given

involves playing one member of staff off against another. If Mr X is blamed for finishing late it will be wise to check with Mr X and let him know what pupils are saying. If they are right, an enquiry will almost certainly put a stop to it. Occasionally a small group of latecomers may wander in from a far-flung annex. It is still important to check the story, even by timing movement, if necessary.

With the above points in mind you should be able to enter the classroom with confidence and, most important, feel that you have the confidence of the class. With mutual confidence real work can begin. Without it, little will be achieved.

The student on school practice

The school practice experience usually falls into two sections: the preliminary visit; and the practice proper, either 'block' practice or 'serial' practice.

The preliminary visit

First impressions count on both sides of the fence. The student should make every effort to present himself/herself in as favourable way as possible, neatly dressed and well equipped. In return he should be able to expect a courteous reception from the school staff who, knowing in advance of the visit, are able to find time to talk about classes and materials available.

At this stage the most discouraging thing for the student is to hear the regular teacher say 'Do anything you want,' since it implies that the student's contribution will have a negligible effect anyway. Much more helpful is for the teacher to take the student into his confidence, explain what he is hoping to achieve over the next month and imply that the student will be required to make a valuable contribution to this programme.

This does not restrict the student's scope. On the contrary it enables him to concentrate his attention on specific and important aims and, within that, he is free to use methods recommended to him by college and school advisers.

On this first visit the student can reasonably expect to acquire the following information:

1   classes he will teach (with names of pupils and staff responsible);
2   timetable with rooms;
3   copy of relevant syllabus;
4   precise details of present class work;
5   precise details of where the student will take over;
6   copies of all necessary textbooks;
7   list of materials and apparatus he can use.

The practice

For the first few days of a block practice the student should come to school with the intention of getting to know his future classes as well as possible by observing the regular teacher and the way he/she works with the children. This is not to say that the student will be obliged to copy slavishly all the regular teacher does, but it does mean that to be properly prepared he needs to be fully aware of how the class is used to working since too many changes cause distraction, even upset, and complicate the period of settling in that the student has to go through.

Observation: This is not sitting at the back doing nothing. The student should be equipped with a substantial notebook and should be making notes on what he sees going on. At this stage the notes should be factual and not critical and they should cover matters such as:

1   teacher's method of starting the lesson;
2   teacher's attitude to latecomers;
3   use of the foreign language for administration;
4   teacher's attitude to pronunciation accuracy;
5   teacher's attitude to pupil error — method of correction;

6 use of praise and reward (what sort?);
7 teacher's sympathy with the class — warmth and friendliness;
8 attitude of pupils to the teacher — polite, aggressive, truculent?;
9 clarity of teacher explanations — use of non-verbal clues;
10 use of materials — how varied, confidence in use;
11 activities — how varied?;
12 teacher's handling of behaviour problems;
13 extent to which the whole group is involved;
14 extent to which pupils volunteer answers;
15 extent to which teacher appears to achieve his aim;
16 sense of achievement amongst pupils;
17 content of lesson — grammar, vocabulary, civilization;
18 general note on class age and previous experience.

With such a checklist to keep in mind the conscientious student will appreciate that there is plenty to do before he begins his own teaching.

Teaching: There is little chance, other than in an infants' school, that the class will be naive enough to think that they have just acquired a new fully qualified teacher. Whilst they are not likely to enquire about the class of your degree, nor ask for your views on cognitive learning, they know a student when they see one. Nevertheless it pays to preserve some element of mystery, so introduce yourself, if the class teacher has not done so, and say what you will be doing with the class 'over the next few weeks' (avoid being too definite about when you finish). Do not put up with inquisitive enquiries about your background. Get straight down to work. See notes for the probationary teacher, page 19–25.

Classroom visitors: A number of people have the right and the duty to see a student teaching. In addition to the college supervisor there is the teacher whose class is being taught, the head of department, the teacher who has responsibility in the school for all school practice and the head teacher. Consequently, the sooner you get used to the presence of visitors the more smoothly your lessons will run.

It is always a mistake to have a dress rehearsal for an

expected visitor unless it is the same lesson with a different group of children.

When a visitor arrives you should remember that you are still the one in charge and should make that clear by showing the new arrival to a seat and then continue with the lesson.

Some visitors like to become involved in the lesson; others wish to fade into the background. As a student you should keep an eye open to detect which species you have attracted and play the game accordingly. Those who like to be involved usually want to play the part of a pupil and do not wish to interrupt the lesson with a major debate on pedagogical techniques.

Visitors usually want to see student notes, not just to ensure that they exist but to get an idea of the student's aim in order to estimate his success. No great fuss need be made. As you go around the room you should simply hand your notes as you pass by.

If anything goes wrong it is important to continue as anyone would with a visitor there or not. Ability to cope with the unexpected is part of the teacher's overall competence. This does not mean you should ignore a child bleeding to death. It means you should deal promptly and efficiently with what has occurred, even sending for assistance if necessary, and then get back to the lesson as quickly as possible.

After the visit comes the post-mortem. The visitor may be unfamiliar with particular school problems and in this case you have a duty to make the situation clear. Or again the visitor may be a non-linguist and unclear as to what you hoped to achieve. Here also you can explain. The discussion afterwards can be the most valuable part of the lesson and you should not feel you have to defend everything you do. You will have made mistakes. All learners do, and throughout your career you will continue to receive criticism of one sort or another. All the better to learn to take it gracefully. One final point: any such discussion is best conducted *away from* the staff common room.

The end of the practice: This usually means that you can go away having made your mistakes while hoping others will forget them. You, however, should not forget: after carefully looking over your classroom notes and comments you should decide what you have learnt and determine to apply it in your next school.

2 Class organization

Effective teaching begins when the teacher has 'got things organized'. Generations of pupils have recognized this simple fact. Precisely what the organization is will depend on many factors, some constants, some variables, as the following table illustrates:

Constants	Variables
Class size	Time of the lesson
Age group	Location of the lesson
Ability range	Mood of the class
Aims	Teacher energy
Teacher preferences	Specific activity
	Materials available

With all the above factors in mind the teacher has to plan to organize a series of activities which together will enable him to achieve his ultimate aim. Obviously some activities will suit the constants and the variables better than others. Some variables, with experience, will become semi-variables, i.e. the teacher can predict with some certainty what the mood of the class will be when a lesson occurs at a particular time or in a particular room. Taking all these factors into consideration the teacher then has to ensure that appropriate programmes are offered. Such programmes may be broadly grouped under the following headings:

- Oral work
- Written work
- Reading
- Class work/group work

Oral work

Ideally the use of the foreign language should dominate all activities in the modern language classroom. In using the word 'ideally' it is not intended to imply that this is unlikely to happen — rather that it must happen. The sooner classroom routine is conducted in the foreign language the more effective will all lessons become. In other words, one of the teacher's main aims will be to use the language for classroom instruction. This is much easier than the novice might imagine since many non-verbal cues can be used at the beginning and, secondly, as in real life, a request to a pupil to perform an action does not necessarily call for a verbal response. Thus 'Veux-tu bien ouvrir la fenêtre, s'il te plaît,' accompanied by a gesture implying 'too hot' followed by the simple mime of opening the window is often sufficient. Communication has begun and the pupil is already realizing the foreign language is about real things and real events.

At times, in the early stages it may be necessary for a teacher to use English to clarify a situation once and for all. 'When you hear me say: "Levez le doigt avant de répondre," what am I asking?' (with appropriate gesture) will usually result in immediate clarification and the phrase has become part of the pupils' passive vocabulary, the exact meaning of each word dawning little by little as knowledge of the language increases.

But the aim of oral work is to help the learner to move from the receptive to the productive skills and so, when such phrases as the above are used as classroom commands, the skilful teacher quickly devises ways of ensuring that they are used both by the class in chorus and by individuals. A useful way of doing this is to allow individuals in the class to take the teacher's part. Group work can also offer similar opportunities. (See below.)

Correction of oral work: It is often striking how very much more tolerant the native speaker is of errors made by foreigners straining to express themselves. Perhaps the image of the Englishman trying to say something which makes sense in a foreign tongue is similar to Dr Johnson's dog which walked on its hind legs (the wonder being not that it did it well but that it did it at all!). But this cannot be the true explanation since English mother-tongue speakers are usually equally kind to foreign speakers of English. What in fact we are probably saying is that the amateur linguist shows more common sense than generations of teachers have shown when they over-react to error in the spoken language. The effect is obvious: people who are afraid of

"En français, Jackson, en français."

Mr Punch gives encouragement to oral methods in 1959: *Pick of Punch*, 1960 being 'jumped on' as soon as they open their mouths tend to keep their mouths tight shut.

All this is not to say that we should not correct error when we hear it but that we should apply common sense. We should let the speaker finish what he has begun and, as in real life, prompt gently if necessary, in order to help the conversation along. Having taken in what the speaker is saying we conclude by saying 'Yes, and a better way of saying that is...' Then the pupil is asked to repeat the improved version.

In the earlier stages of language learning our pupils need to be aware of two grades of language error (a) the incomprehensible, where the error is so gross the listener cannot even fathom what the speaker is trying to say, and (b) the comprehensible but inaccurate. This is the category of error which we need to handle *delicately*, keeping in mind that we do not have to regard every utterance part of a formal assessment. The important thing is to get our pupils talking the language as much as possible.

The explanation for the traditional schoolmaster's demand for a hundred per cent accuracy lies in the nature of language itself. Of all school subjects only languages set before the pupil perfection as an attainable goal. The native speaker is the criterion against which all performances are measured. On the other hand, historians do not say, 'This fourth-form essay is not as good as the one A. J. P. Taylor might have written on the same subject,' and it is assessed accordingly. The wise (and successful) teacher takes a similar attitude to oral performance. Lots of encouragement, tolerance of some error and gentle correction when necessary.

Oral Methods: As a general rule

The class should **say** *only what they have* **heard**
The class should **read** *only what they have* **said**
The class should **write** *only what they have* **read**

Hear before **say** *before* **read** *before* **write**.

If we apply the rule above it follows that pupils will be asked to say what they have heard either from the teacher or from a recording. It makes sense to give pupils practice in saying what they hear before asking them to recast material in order to answer questions. For this reason the familiar four-stage approach as recommended by CREDIF more than twenty years ago is still a very sound method for establishing confidence in a class as it meets new material:

PRESENT   CLARIFY   REPEAT   EXPLOIT

PRESENT The new material orally using visual aids (picture, filmstrip, etc.) At this stage it is a good idea to warn the class the material is new and give them something specific to watch out for. 'Listen carefully and at the end tell me who arrives, who comes late, what does he bring and why does Madame X tell him to take it away.'

This kind of approach ensures listening to some purpose and stresses to learners that the very first reason for learning a language is to acquire information. With a more advanced or high ability class the introductory portion can be done in the languge. For weaker groups it makes much more sense to do it in English. If the weak linguist is so lost he does not even know why he is listening to a story the whole exercise is a pointless one.

There is no harm in repeating the *presentation* section two or three times if that is necessary to enable the majority of the class to gather the information they have been asked to find at the start.

A quick check on the extent to which the class has picked up the necessary facts leads neatly into the second stage:

CLARIFICATION: Here the teacher's skill is fully tested. The aim is to ensure that all the class comes to understand what they have been listening to and perhaps partially comprehending. As far as possible (bearing in mind the constants and the variables) this section is done in the language but with recourse to English when necessary. Over-use of the foreign languge at this stage may *mystify* when we are seeking to *clarify*. If it does have this effect it will exasperate, lead to inattention and hence disciplinary problems. In other words over-use of the foreign language with some groups will be counter-productive. Far better use a little English and be certain everyone is with the teacher at this stage which is precisely for clarification. Gradually, over the year, the teacher's professionalism will wean the class from too much English.

It is at this stage that some teachers will feel that vocabulary notes should appear on the board or on the overhead projector. In many ways this is good planning and helps to reinforce the learning of new words and phrases. However, it seems sensible to keep the writing to merely a reading exercise at this stage since the fuss and commotion caused by switching to writing in order to copy down vocabulary becomes a major distraction from oral work. It is better to keep the copying for section 4 (*Exploitation*).

REPETITION: Despite the revolution in classroom teaching aids since the fifties, examiners' reports do not suggest there has been a corresponding improvement in pronunciation. All the more reason for treating this section of the lesson in a very businesslike manner. First analyse the text being studied and isolate a few points of pronunciation which need particular emphasis. To ensure concentration it is helpful to put such phrases on an overhead projector slide and spend a few minutes on these. Note that it was a strongly held opinion at one time that by placing the written form in front of the pupil to stress the spoken form the teacher was simply compounding the difficulty. Now opinion has changed as we have come to recognize that from the age of five every single pupil has been trained to depend on the eyes for learning. So there seems little point in blindfolding the pupil in the language class.

In introducing the new vocabulary or constructions the teacher is the model. It is vital to enunciate clearly, even slowing down to an unnaturally slow pace if necessary, in order to establish correct vowel and consonant pronunciation. This, after all, is what the parent does instinctively with a small child learning the mother-tongue. It is certainly the common practice of infant teachers using words they believe to be unfamiliar to their pupils. Once the correct pronunciation is established, attention can be given to pace and intonation.

In practising the pronunciation of the new material the following should be borne in mind:

1   The whole class should practise in chorus before any individual is called upon to perform publicly. In this way every pupil has an opportunity to engage in some anonymous practice within the group.
2   The teacher should move around the room all the time since this ensures every child has the opportunity to hear the correct pronunciation from close at hand. (Classroom acoustics may well distort speech from the front just sufficiently to make the language into nonsense.) At the same time the teacher who moves around has a better chance of hearing wrong pronunciations or careless or inattentive attempts at merely humouring the teacher by looking as though serious work is going on.
3   When sloppy or inaccurate pronunciation is located it is a mistake to isolate the culprit and make him or her practise in public what he has been doing inefficiently in private. Such a tactic will simply alienate the pupil(s) in question. It is fair to assume that normally pupils will not deliberately distort what they hear. If what they say is in fact distorted they need to hear it again so the best method is to make it a class point and practise as a group a few more times.
4   Before going to individuals it is best to have small group practice and in any class there are plenty of ready-made groups:
        all the boys
        all the girls

    all this row
    all the back row
Some teachers like to have ready-made teams for such practice:
    the Blues
    the Reds; or
    the Lions
    the Tigers; or
    les Lyonnais
    les Lillois
    les Parisiens

5   To be effective the pronunciation/repetition section needs to be *brief* and *brisk* — a maximum of five minutes should be accorded to this aspect of the work. Any longer and concentration will be lost and the lesson will be killed stone dead. Far better to have two such sessions separated by twenty minutes devoted to other activities.

6   When the class is practising a long or difficult phrase, such as 'il fait du brouillard', break the phrase into manageable portions and have them repeat it in *reverse* order, i.e. 'brouillard', 'du brouillard', 'fait du brouillard', 'il fait du brouillard'. In this way the new sound is repeated first and does not overtax the memory.

7   Lavish praise for good pronunciation does wonders for any pupil's ego. It also impresses on the rest of the class that what the teacher is after is not completely unattainable. If a pupil is very successful at imitating the model there is no reason why he or she should not become a model for a group practice. (See 'Group Work', page 44.)

8   It is vital to maintain a constant standard of pronunciation from one lesson to the next or things will begin to slip. On the other hand, we have to recognize that not every pupil will reach the same standard and with some we have to be satisfied with less than perfection, as are the violin teacher and the games coach.

EXPLOITATION: | This section of the lesson makes the biggest demands of all on the teacher's inventiveness, enthusiasm, flexibility and vigilance. The more expert the teacher becomes the more important this section becomes in the lesson scheme, for it is here more than anywhere else that the teacher's creativity has full rein.

By exploitation we mean providing the class with as many opportunities as possible to *use* the material which, until this point, has been largely a passive acquisition. We move from the receptive to the productive and to the creative from the imitative. This is not to disparage the foregoing stages which are an essential part of language acquisition — witness the extensive use of imitative language amongst children still in the early stages of mother-tongue learning.

Yet the move on to this section in the lesson does not imply a sudden change in teaching strategy. The skilful teacher still ensures that there is a gradual transition from the imitative to the creative and that pupils are helped to the final stage by frequent reference back to the stages in which they have already reached a fair degree of competence.

The following techniques will help, though we recognize that individualism plays an enormous part at this stage:

1 *Sentence completion.* The teacher begins the sentence from the text and asks the class to complete it. Answer comes from an individual. Praise is given then the class as a whole completes the same sentence.
2 *Question.* The question is put for which the answer is the sentence used in (1) above. Answer from an individual. Praise. Question again to class. Class answer.
3 *Contradictions.* Teacher says the opposite to what the text says. This may involve no more than the introduction of a negative. Teacher says 'True or false?' Pupil response is part or all of the original sentence. Praise. To class. Class repeats the answer.
4 Teacher makes up other sentences about the text and finishes '*True or false?*' Individual and class response as above.
5 *Pupil takes the teacher's part.* Using the visuals used in the earlier part of the lesson a pupil makes up sentences for contradiction. Individual responses.

6 *Relay responses*. Pupil names another pupil to respond who, in turn, names another.

7 *Relay questions* on the text. When the teacher has given extensive question practice the pupils are given full opportunity to pass questions around the class. This is essential practice, as any teacher knows we need to ask more questions than we answer when we first go abroad.

8 *Pattern drills* can be very boring but remain tolerable for short periods and definitely livable with if they are dealt with in relay practice.

9 *Flash cards* are ideal for introducing new vocabulary and some structures. They need not always remain in the hands of the teacher. Hand them out for recognition practice: 'Who has the lawnmower?' Pupil response 'I have/Here is the lawnmower.' Teacher again (to the class) 'Who has the lawnmower?' Class 'Jeanne-Marie has the lawnmower.' (or appropriate pronouns). Teacher to the class 'What does Jeanne-Marie have?' Treated in a brisk and lively manner such a conversation need not sound so stultifying as it appears in cold print.

10 *Game* for the end of the lesson. Teacher says a single word from the text. Class have to put the word into a sentence. How many good sentences can we make up with this word in the last five minutes?

In these and in the many similar exercises which numerous books suggest to teachers it is very important to remember the great difference between oral work in language learning and oral work in other areas of the curriculum. In all other subjects the teacher puts questions to the class to find out who knows the answer. To the question 'In what year did Charles VIII of France invade Italy?' there is only one acceptable answer. The answers 1394, 1594 and 1694 are totally wrong. Equally inappropriate would be comments from the pupil such as 'I have no idea,' 'Ask my neighbour,' or 'I'm not sure.' In the foreign language class, however, the teacher welcomes any response in the language, for the purpose of the question is to provide the pupil with an opportunity to use the language he has acquired. Teachers would do well to stress this difference to their classes since there is no doubt that many pupils faced with a question could say something but hesitate to do so because they imagine the same rules apply in the language class as elsewhere.

What in effect we are saying is that much of the question and answer work that goes on in the modern language class is the equivalent of the musician's scale practice. Within its limited context it is meaningful. It improves agility and gives familiarity with and confidence in the instrument. It involves playing for the pupil and the teacher but very rarely for the outsider. Scale practice is not beautiful in itself but it enables the pupil to become more adept in the real musical world. And isn't question time in the language class for similar reasons?

Reading and writing

Both these activities may be regarded as extensions of the 'Exploitation' section referred to above since the reading which will be done in the first instance will be the text that has already been listened to and repeated and talked about in the earlier sections.

The class should **read** *what they have* **said**
The class should **write** *what they have* **read**.

Choral reading is often a good introduction to reading aloud which some would claim is a very artificial exercise anyway. Again it permits private practice in a public place and hence increases self-confidence which, as we well know, is ninety per cent of the battle.

Shadow reading is another form of choral reading in which the pupils are required to keep up with the pace of the teacher. It assumes phonological problems have been mastered by the majority of the class and we can now concentrate on intonation and expression. Again it permits practice without self-consciousness being involved. It is not an activity to prolong for more than a maximum of five minutes.

With lower ability groups 'reading by dictation' is a useful technique to employ since it gives a large measure of success and hence boosts confidence. Reading cards containing words and phrases from the text already listened to are prepared by the teacher. The cards should be big enough to be easily read at the back of the room. To start with, the teacher says a whole sentence and a pupil comes out to arrange the cards in the correct order. An alternative method for a restless class is to distribute the different portions of the sentence to different individuals around the class. The sentence is then repeated in full and the four or five pupils involved come out to the front and arrange themselves in the correct order. The class then reads the sentence in chorus. Variation can be introduced by deliberately missing out a word or phrase and asking the class to supply it. This leads on to:

Cloze tests. By omitting every fourth word or every verb or article or adjective pupils have to do more than repeat and yet they have a good chance of success. Such an exercise leads naturally into written work of a simple kind.

The point has been made several times that written work comes last in the skills we seek to pass on to our pupils. For some of them, written work may not go very far and we shall be very happy if reading comprehension is well established without expecting the pupil to write creatively. But for a sizeable proportion of learners the written skills are perfectly manageable if introduced gradually. Unfortunately, it is at the introduction of writing that we begin to meet our first disenchanted pupils. The reasons for this are worth summarizing:

1 teachers tend to demand one hundred per cent accuracy;
2 a pupil with a good ear may have no gifts in written work even in English;
3 writing seems less relevant to many pupils;

4   the complexities of the less phonetic languages (e.g.
     French) appear to be overwhelming;
5   teachers and examiners make little distinction between
     spellings which would change the pronunciation of the
     word and those which would have no effect;
6   correct spelling implies an understanding of sometimes
     difficult grammatical concepts;
7   if translation is done you can even lose marks for wrong
     English!

It is of course hoped that translation will not loom large in
any work below the sixth form, certainly not in any written
work but it does happen, and some examination boards still
have a translation passage in their examinations and, if it is
necessary to take such papers, pupils have to be prepared for
such tests. One would imagine, however, that candidates in
this kind of examination are of the kind who can take
written work in their stride.

The introduction of writing

The copying of vocabulary into a vocabulary notebook is
probably the first written exercise undertaken. Here the
teacher must stress the need for accuracy since this is to be a
reference book to which the pupil will have to turn
frequently. At the same time as stressing the importance of
accuracy, teachers will do well to underline the fact that the
vocabulary book has to be neat and attractive, otherwise the
learner will have no inclination to turn to it to do his
essential revision.

Copy-writing involving cloze tests such as those referred to
above ensure that the learner becomes familiar with the
written form. For lower ability classes it pays to give the
missing words for gap-filling exercises either in a box, in
jumbled order at the foot of the exercise or, possibly, a series
of three or four words at the end of each sentence from
which the correct word has to be chosen.

Sentence completion is an extension of the above. Again a
variety of possible endings may be supplied and the learner

picks the one which makes sense in the context. Such exercises are useful as homework since they are not likely to lead the pupil widely astray and they can be done without supervision but with a good chance of success.

Substitution drills are also useful for homework for they fix a pattern in the pupil's mind and, provided the preparatory work has been well done in class, they can be done at home without running the risk of forcing the learner to acquire wrong forms. Many basic grammatical forms lend themselves to this kind of reinforcement — pronouns for nouns, changes of tense, use of negatives, word order, etc.

Dictation is not the popular exercise it once was and it has certainly lost favour with the examining boards. This does not necessarily invalidate it as a useful teaching tool as opposed to an assessment procedure. A particularly useful form of dictation is one in which the pupil has a passage in front of him from which key words have been removed. The exercise then becomes gap-filling by dictation. Occasionally as a revision exercise it does no harm to dictate a complete passage from a text that has been carefully studied in class. This is quite a different proposition from the traditional O-level 'unseen' *dictée*. Its purpose is for revision and reinforcement of written forms and not for testing on a hit-and-miss basis.

Questions with multiple choice answers are as effective as dictation and have the additional virtue of offering a very valid comprehension test. They are, unfortunately, time-consuming to produce but since they are popular with some examination boards they have to be practised! There are some good collections of such tests available commercially. Almost every publisher of modern language textbooks has several on his list nowadays.

Another method is for the teacher to present the class with answers for which they have to devise questions. Such an exercise is obviously very good for oral work too. Indeed this, like most written exercises, needs to be tackled orally before being given to a class as a written exercise. If it is to be set for homework this is particularly important. When devising this type of work it is a good idea to include a fair sprinkling of questions which will have to begin with 'Why'; since pupils often find great difficulty in formulating the 'because' answer, so they need extensive practice in this area.

Sentences may be composed to describe pictures. Variations on this include questions on pictures for which the pupils have to devise answers. Alternatively you could provide statements about pictures for which pupils have to devise questions. Other variations are those involving sentence completion with multiple choice endings, or questions with multiple choice answers.

Some teachers set picture essays after very extensive oral preparation and for which lists of key vocabulary and structures are provided. This exercise and the one below can produce the most demoralizing of results for both teacher and taught. Unless a very well-established code of practice exists, pupils will fly off to the dictionary to produce the most harrowing 'franglais'.

Free composition: only to be attempted by the best of classes below the sixth form and then only when the caveats referred to above have been carefully observed.

Letter writing: a favourite with examination boards since it seems to be a more relevant exercise than either picture essays or free composition. From a teaching viewpoint it is easier to direct the practice required. The rubric can ask for the description of an incident in the past (use of past tenses) or plans for a future holiday (future tenses) or what one might do if . . . (conditionals). (See Bibliography.)

Group work

The philosophy of language teaching these days is frequently summed up by the phrase 'communicative language teaching'. By this we imply perhaps that the priorities lie with conveying meaning rather than with acquiring language forms which might or might not be used in later life to communicate. This has been implicit in what has been said so far though we acknowledge, too, that there has to be proper recognition of the more traditional, formal aspects of language learning to ensure that any communication does take place. This is particularly true of the written form of the language and has to be allowed for. However, when we turn to group work it is here that communicative competence is able to flourish for all our pupils.

First, to define a 'group': in the language class we mean any number of pupils working together independently. Group sizes will vary according to the nature of the task involved and according to the pupils' ability to cope with the task. By ability we mean not only intellectual capacity but also self-discipline and motivation.

Organization of groups

Some teachers find that a permanent arrangement of groups makes for good organization within the classroom. So the command 'Et maintenant à vos groupes' produces an immediate and known response with the minimum of fuss and commotion since every pupil knows where he has to sit and who to join with. In such a fixed arrangement there can be an appointed group leader who has won his place because of his recognized ability. He is a teacher-substitute. This system is generally efficient though it can lead to personality clashes within the group.

For various reasons many teachers prefer a more 'ad hoc' arrangement, allowing pupils to choose the partners with whom they think they can work best. A further advantage of this method is that group sizes can be varied more rapidly to suit particular needs.

The question of room arrangement also comes into the matter. In schools where teachers are fortunate enough to have their own modern language room all sorts of arrangements become possible:

1   *Desks and chairs in formal rows* are ideal for formal
    classes where only the teacher needs to see everyone's
    face. Such an arrangement inhibits all group work since
    any speaker in the class can only address the teacher
    effectively. All pupils sitting behind the speaker invariably
    complain they cannot hear. To do group work involves a
    fairly massive and noisy furniture-moving operation,
    which is time-wasting and disrupting.
2   *Desks and chairs in two semi-circles* allow for the formal
    lesson to take place with the teacher still able to see every
    individual. In addition one half of the class can see the
    other half. This facilitates team games and group
    discussions.
3   *Desks and chairs in open circles* will accommodate up to
    six pupils without any pupil needing to have his back to
    the teacher for the formal parts of the lesson. With five
    such circles, one in each corner and one in the middle,
    an average class of thirty can be seated without undue
    crowding. A big advantage of this arrangement is that
    the pupils are already in groups, which in itself is an
    encouragement to do group work.
4   *Desks and chairs randomly distributed* make teacher
    control nearly impossible and will cause endless
    complaints from cleaners.

Group activities

Work in pairs. The traditional form of group work requiring
no class movement and immediate contact. Against this
type of arrangement is the considerable disadvantage that
the teacher cannot possibly get round to all groups in the
fifteen minutes or so allowed for group work. Nevertheless
grouping of this kind permits one-to-one conversations,
dialogue practice, learning and testing together, reading and
listening, word-creation games, work together on worksheets, half dialogues in which one partner has a printed text
and the other has to respond from his previous knowledge of
the text.

Work in teams. In this situation the two teams face each other and the teacher is in the middle. This arrangement is ideal for team competition of the 'tennis' variety, i.e. question to one side, question to the other. Against this arrangement must be that it is just as inhibiting as the formal classroom situaton with the added disadvantage that weaker pupils have the strain of knowing that failure to give a correct answer involves personal humiliation and a let-down for the team. Guessing games of the 'Twenty Questions' kind are very appropriate for this type of organization.

Open circle groups. These are probably the best for most productive kinds of group work. Such work need not be competitive as in the teams above but a spirit of competition could be introduced if necessary. With a maximum of five such groups to a class there is a good chance of the class teacher being able to make a contribution in each group and keep a general eye on progress or lack of it. Where a class can be split between assistant and class teacher some very valuable work can be done.

The open circle group is sufficiently flexible to cope with fluctuation in number because of absence or withdrawal, yet it remains sufficiently dynamic for good role-playing to be developed. Assignment cards are needed in small numbers but variety is guaranteed with five groups each in turn tackling a different situation.

In addition to role-playing practice the following activities are possible:

1 dictation given by the group leader;
2 questions on a prepared text —one question per person;
3 guessing games — *Twenty Questions*; *What's my Line?*
4 spelling games;
5 counting-out games;
6 descriptions of persons — rest of the group to guess who;
7 mimes on which questions have to be asked by the group;
8 finding one's way on a street map;

9 Grandmother went to market, and there she bought . . .
   cumulative list;
10 work with individual words such as 'if'. Each group
   explores the possible consequences of a hypothetical
   situation;
11 shopping with the aid of a mail-order catalogue;
12 number practice with the aid of an authentic directory;
13 written homework preparation;
14 preparation of a text for class use;
15 learning and testing a piece of verse or prose;
16 testing knowledge of the target culture based on a book
   such as *France Quiz* (NB this gives the answers);
17 use of flashcards for verb practice, number practice,
   names of countries and/or inhabitants, general vocabulary practice. Answers can be written on the back of the
   card to enable the group leader to correct answers. This
   also means pupils can take turns to be group leader
   since they do not need to know more than anyone
   else.

Streaming and mixed ability

There are almost as many methods of pupil grouping as
there are schools.

There is *streaming*, where the pupils stay in the same ability
group for a range of subjects, though in most schools such a
rigid system has now been abandoned.

There is *banding*, where pupils are in broad ability groups
and departments are free to regroup within the band. This is
a particularly popular method for the lower classes.

There is *setting*, where pupils can be put into ability
groupings to suit a particular department.

There is *mixed ability*, which, as the name indicates, groups
pupils irrespective of their ability in the subject.

Since languages are not always included in a core curriculum
the situation becomes more complicated as a result of the

option system which operates in the school. In effect it means that even where there is a departmental attempt to set pupils according to ability it is unlikely that a narrow ability set will be possible except in the largest of comprehensive schools, i.e. a twelve-stream intake of 350 pupils or so annually.

A further complication arises because of the different educational systems used in the 105 local authorities in England and Wales. As a result pupils enter schools at age 9, 11, 13 and 16 (and a few at 12).

In a three-tier system which runs middle schools from 8 to 12 or 9 to 13 it is safe to assume that pupils entering a secondary school will already have several years of language learning behind them. Report cards are passed on to the secondary school (see Chapter 19). In theory, therefore, it would be possible to set or band pupils for languages from the start of the secondary course.

In practice the situation is different. Pupils do not enter the secondary school with a uniform language background. Quite the contrary. From a single catchment area of nine or ten schools pupils will enter with varying numbers of years of study, perhaps having followed different courses, and certainly taught by staff with widely varying expertise in languages. To classify such pupils on the strength of experience would be grossly unjust and consequently most secondary schools do have a mixed ability year, usually in French, though we actually encourage other languages.

The previous school still has its influence of course. When pupils enter at 12 or 13 an immediate start has to be made on the second foreign language and in many cases the selection is based on performance in French and English in the middle school. The pupils who embark on the second language are therefore to that extent setted if not streamed.

In 1977–78 the Modern Language Association conducted a survey into the extent to which mixed ability groups were being used in language teaching. The general results were fairly uniform from all over the country. Schools were quite content to run mixed ability groups for one year but afterwards it was felt very necessary to organize classes according to ability.

The arguments in favour of mixed ability language teaching are:

1   It prevents setting according to false criteria (e.g. ability in English) or on flimsy evidence (e.g. a short aptitude test).
2   Since language is a form of social expression, teaching a language socially should be the natural thing to do.
3   In the early stages of language learning which concentrate on oral rather than written expression the gap between the most and the least able is less apparent.
4   At the later stages (when reading and writing *are* introduced) mixed ability permits useful group work to take place in which the higher ability children act as group leaders.

Against mixed ability we may set the following:

1   While there is little doubt that the less able benefit it is not so certain that the more gifted do.
2   Many teachers instinctively, and by training, aim at the middle ability and neglect the extremes.
3   The demands on the teacher increase enormously as he/she strives to produce satisfying work for the wide ability range.
4   Increased disciplinary problems stem from failure to cope with the demands of the widening ability gap.
5   Different objectives need to be defined for the different abilities and catering for differing objectives within the same group becomes more and more difficult.
6   Better use is made of resources when teachers can confine their attention to uniform groups.
7   As public examinations draw nearer, the task of preparing pupils for examinations which make widely differing demands becomes an impossible one.
8   Pupils become increasingly frustrated and exasperated

as they are required to cope with material either above or below their natural ability.

Obviously every individual school and every department within a school has to weigh the above arguments. On balance the modern linguists have come down in favour of roughly homogeneous groups, but in saying this it is essential to add that wide ability groups still exist because of the option scheme referred to earlier. As the course progresses, so pupils are put into sets corresponding to the public examination which they will eventually sit at the end of the fifth form. The coming of the national 16+ examination with core elements and additional sections will, certainly, contribute to reducing some of the strain imposed on the system at present when pupils are prepared for discrete examinations.

3 Lesson preparation

Lesson preparation, whether short-term (one lesson or a group of lessons) or long-term (one term or one year), implies a philosophy, for without one how can we know what to prepare for? The syllabus normally expresses this philosophy and defines it in terms of aims and objectives, the aims being the ultimate achievement and the objectives being the means by which the final achievement is reached.

In planning a lesson scheme, therefore, we have to keep in mind the distant goal and define the objectives within the lesson which will enable us to achieve the aims.

In the present-day view of language teaching we generally wish our pupils to reach that level of linguistic skill which will allow them to communicate competently orally and (for some) in writing with native speakers of the language they study.

But there is no need to state this kind of aim, except in a syllabus. On the other hand, we do need to define our objectives for any particular week's work, for the objectives will be precise and clear and will ensure that the lesson has a point.

A lesson plan, then, is a list of objectives together with notes on the materials and the methods which will be used to reach those objectives.

In addition we might reasonably expect to see an indication

of why this particular objective has been selected at this time; e.g. it might arise from previous pupil error or it might be serving as an introduction to a new concept or to a new *centre d'intérêt* or to a new structure.

The conclusion to the note will indicate how the threads of the lesson will be drawn together and what precisely pupils will be told they must remember for the next lesson.

In planning a series of lessons with the aims, objectives and stages outlined above the teacher has to have in mind a whole series of questions which may be summed up as:

1   factors which influence behaviour and learning ability (e.g. time of day, location of lesson, material available, the known ability and attitude of the class); and
2   the language activities the teacher hopes to use (e.g. active oral, group, written work, etc).

As a rough-and-ready guide it is no bad thing to recall the mnemonic which states that in every lesson there must be

---

Something old (i.e. revision of past work)
Something new (i.e. presentation of new material)
Something for fun (i.e. a song, a game, role-playing)
Something to do (e.g. written work or pair work for an oral presentation)

To clarify the content still further, remember the four CREDIF stages referred to in Chapter 2 under 'Oral work':

PRESENT   CLARIFY   REPEAT   EXPLOIT

Having defined the objective of the lesson in general terms it is then no bad thing to jot down in note form how the four stages will be represented.

PRESENT: What? How much material can the class take given the factors referred to above?

CLARIFY: What will need care? What can be clarified with objects around the room, by acting, by using flashcards, by English translation? Mark the script accordingly. Are there any confusions likely to arise? Remember Monsieur Thibaut in *Voix et Images de France*? 'Oh, c'est haut. Oui c'est au troisième étage.'

REPEAT: Consider the pronunciation, new sounds, new combinations of sounds. Mark points for special attention in the script. Will regional speech differences in English cause any problems? Think of the sound é in the North of England in 'Pra*i*se him for his Gr*a*ce and f*a*vours' and the Londoner's 'Prize him for his Gr*i*ce and f*i*vers.' Will the diphthong [ai] intrude?

EXPLOIT: What activities will be used:
• question and answer
• role-playing
• repetition
• written work
• vocab. noting, etc.

What materials will be used?
• overhead projector
• blackboard
• worksheets
• flashcards
• slides
• summary charts or posters
• cassette, etc.

Before going ahead with further plans it pays to check the minor points. Is the overhead projector available for that time; is the room you are timetabled for equipped with a screen?

Check apparatus which you will use. Is there a spare filmstrip carrier which you can load up before going to the classroom? On a reel-to-reel tape-recorder have you inserted the bit of paper at the right place to enable you to find the exact part you need immediately?

Before every lesson it also pays to ensure there is a 'fallback' ready. The cassette player may not work. Is the script with you to read from? (Don't waste everyone's time going looking for a technician with a spare fuse. It's bound to be his morning at the dentist's.) What if you get through the planned lesson much more quickly than you thought? Have a 'five-minute filler' ready to switch on. It is also useful to have a written exercise up your sleeve for, occasionally, an overexcited class may be in the wrong mood for extended oral work but may settle down to appropriate written work.

Conclusion: Far too many lessons fade away as the class hears the bell ring and they begin to pack. This is an unacceptable state of affairs which every teacher can contend with by ensuring in the lesson plan that there is a proper conclusion. So, except when the hoax fire-alarm sends the class off as the teacher is in mid-sentence, it is important to draw the strings of the lesson together and to state plainly what the class is expected to retain. Finally, it is often a good lead into the next lesson if the class are told what to expect next time.

A good diary is an essential piece of equipment, and on those blank pages generously provided by printers for doodles it is very useful to have the following checklists:

Checklist for use before the lesson
Are all the following items available for the lesson?
 1 lesson notes with clear·objectives;
 2 class register/mark book;
 3 class exercise books to return;
 4 seating plan or name cards;
 5 brief note on question forms to be used;
 6 visual aids: slides, filmstrip, pictures, posters, flashcards,
       figurines, OHP transparencies;
 7 hardware — tape recorder and tape, cassette player and right
       cassette, projector, OHP;
 8 script, textbook, teacher's book;
 9 chalk, felt tips for OHP, scrap paper, pencils;
10 homework details;
11 fallback work ready on OHP or banda'd exercise.

Checklist for the end of the lesson
As the class leaves, check the following:
 1 What does this class know now that they didn't know forty
       minutes ago?
 2 What can this class do now that they couldn't do forty
       minutes ago?
 3 What can this class do *better* now that they could forty
       minutes ago?
 4 Did I attempt to do too much/too little?
 5 Did *I* do too much and the *class* not enough?
 6 Did I use pupils' errors positively?
 7 Did any individuals need special attention? Why?
 8 Did I do enough in the language?
 9 Did I allow time-wasting, a red-herring?
10 Did I set homework appropriate to the work done in class?
11 Where shall I pick up at the start of the next lesson?
12 What should I note?
13 Have I made any enemies?
14 What have I learnt?

4 Homework and marking

Homework

Of all school activities homework often appears to be the least well planned. This is a pity since, properly thought out, homework can be considered to be an essential part of the lesson because it is an extension of the lesson.

So often it is not so and children go home with something to do simply because it is 'homework night'. Perhaps the worst kind of homework that is set is the sort of activity which involves the pupil in meeting new material, new vocabulary or new structures. What teaching skill is involved here? What care with pronunciation is being taken when new words have to be looked up at the back of the book? In other school subjects it is probably easy to justify sending children enquiring into unfamiliar areas. So many teachers want their pupils to read around the subject and to come up against problems they have to solve for themselves. The linguists generally speaking do not belong to that band.

For the linguist, homework is to reinforce work done in class. Typical homeworks will involve the learning of vocabulary and structures already met in class. Written homeworks will require pupils to use recently acquired language in new combinations. Exercises involving gap filling, sentence completion, pattern drills, contradictions or use of synonyms are all possibilities. Comprehension passages are perfectly possible and composition writing based on very thorough class preparation is a possibility for fourth form and above.

General points

1 Have one written and one learning homework each week.
2 Carefully prepare the written homework in class.
3 To be sure everyone is doing the right thing it pays to let pupils start homework in the last five minutes of the lesson. At the same time the teacher can supervise layout, dates and headings.
4 All written homework must be marked by the teacher. Swapping books to correct answers called out from the front will *not* do since it leads to very slapdash work, carelessness with accents, etc.
5 All homework should be handed in. It is a mistake to adopt the attitude 'It's his loss, not mine.'
6 In addition to giving a numerical or literal grading it is helpful to add a written comment, however brief.
7 A mistake occurring in a number of exercise books indicates a need for further classwork in that area. Some teachers mark such items in the pupil's book 'Class' to indicate it will be dealt with again.
8 When the weekly learning homework is set it must be tested next lesson. This is the sort of marking for which pupils *can* exchange papers. It is always wise to collect in papers at the end and, periodically, check them carefully.
9 Not all learning homeworks need to be followed by a written test. An oral review can be just as revealing and just as effective.
10 All schools give pupils and parents an idea of the amount of time to be spent on homework. Some teachers like pupils to indicate at the foot of the exercise how long they have spent on it.
11 It is sometimes a good idea to involve parents in homework by asking for a parent's signature against the time taken.

Marking

1 Mark clearly, promptly and regularly both classwork and homework. As a general rule every exercise book should be seen once a week.

2 Before beginning to mark new work it is sensible to ensure that the corrections for the previous work have been done and that the pupil has seen where he went wrong. It is still helpful to have corrections written out in full underneath the work that is being corrected.

3 Generally it is better to add the correct version over or under a word that is wrong. However, with exercises which can be gone over in class an underlining will do. With work such as, for example, essays where each one is unique, mere underlining will not do. To leave plenty of room for corrections pupils should be asked to write on alternate lines.

4 Always insist on presentable work, especially from examination forms. Penalize scruffy presentation to bring home the point.

5 When giving back work it is often helpful to a class to show examples of work which received high marks. It sets standards and also points out that the standards set by the teacher are attainable. (But don't always use the same pupil's work!)

6 Comments on work *are* appreciated. 'Fair' is virtually meaningless and is not worth writing. Give real praise whenever possible and, if necessary, a diagnostic comment, e.g. 'Vocabulary is good but you are still careless with perfect tenses. Ask if unsure.'

7 When marking it helps to place books in piles according to the marks awarded. It is then a relatively simple matter to do a quick check on the marking standards.

8 It pays to enter all marks in the mark book as marking proceeds. It avoids the time-wasting and sometimes embarrassing practice of calling out marks in class.

9 Try not to enter into arguments about marks in class. Take the book in for a check. If an error has been made it can then easily be corrected with the minimum of fuss.

10 Examination classes will appreciate being told what the official marking scheme is. It gives them a good idea where they stand and all boards now make this information generally available.

11 Have a *positive* as well as a negative marking scheme for more advanced work: +1 for getting a difficult agreement or for a complicated use of two pronouns; +2 for the successful use of a complex structure.

12 It is important that the markbook gives a true picture of pupil progress across all four skills. This means ensuring that a mark is regularly given for oral work. If this is not done, the standing of oral skills will go down in the eyes of the class.

13 At least some of the written work done in class can be marked in class. The teacher goes round from desk to desk to do this most effectively.

14 Although it is onerous, marking should never be neglected. It helps the pupil and is equally important for the teacher since it helps him to monitor his effectiveness.

5 Question techniques

The technique of questioning is one which has to be carefully developed by the teacher of modern languages since its purpose and function is somewhat different from that required for the world outside the classroom. In real life we 'do not usually go about questioning people about what we have just told them, nor do we ask the same question three times using different words. We certainly never ask for a reply in chorus when we have already obtained a perfectly satisfactory answer from one or two individuals — except perhaps at the pantomime where the convention of repetition is readily accepted.

This same convention can easily be established in the classroom and, indeed, it has to be, to ensure that all pupils get adequate practice in speaking the language. Unreal it may be but pupils soon come to accept the process as a necessary one just as the musician accepts scale practice. True, one does have slightly lunatic conversations in language learning classes as Ionesco enjoys pointing out but we have come a long way since the days when, in linguists' folklore at least, postillions risked being struck by lightning.

And it is not just a matter of establishing the fact that questioning must take place for it is equally important that the pupils understand how the questioning operates and what exactly are the 'rules of the game'.

Rule 1, which every teacher new to a class should clearly establish, is that facts are negotiable. The important thing is to talk. If the substance of the answer is wrong it can soon be put right. If a pupil fails to speak there is little the teacher can do other than obtain the answer from another pupil and return to the one unable to reply first time round.

Rule 2 for younger classes is that if they listen carefully to the question they will often find the answer has already been supplied. 'Nous sommes aujourd'hui mardi. Quel jour sommes-nous?'

So the routine

GIVE THE ANSWER
PUT THE QUESTION
GET THE ANSWER

---

becomes a natural part of conversational give-and-take in the classroom.

Rule 3 is that a natural conversational answer may be adequate but sometimes, for the sake of practice, a slightly longer answer is the best one to give. Thus the natural answer to the question 'Where are you going?' is simply 'To school.' But the language teacher likes to hear more than that occasionally.

Some other general questioning points are:

1   In the early stages questions expressed in the affirmative with interrogative inflexion in the voice are most easily understood. This fact is noticeable even amongst native speakers in France. 'C'est Monsieur Givry qui achète encore une bouteille?'

2   *Always* put the question to the class first instead of naming an individual. Give time to think.

3   Look around. If a pupil is avoiding your gaze he/she is indicating that he does not wish to be asked. Perhaps he needs to hear the question again, so repeat it quickly.

4   Select the pupil to answer or ask for a volunteer. If the pupil can't answer don't wait. It causes embarrassment

and is unlikely to produce an adequate reply. Pass on to someone who can.

5   Then go back to the one(s) who have failed to answer, or who gave an inadequate answer. Put the same question again. Be lavish with praise.

6   Finally before leaving the question it is often a good check and an interest reviver to put the same question to the class and get back an answer in chorus.

7   It is important also to build on pupil error and very helpful if occasionally the teacher goes back to an error made and clarifies for the whole class why it was wrong.

Types of question

1   Direct questions to the class expressed affirmatively or in an interrogative form — often with the answer before the question.

2   Questions in the negative inviting contradiction.

3   Questions offering an alternative. Very useful since the substance of the answer is provided in the question, e.g. 'Ce jour-là, est-cq qu'il faisait beau ou est-ce qu'il pleuvait?' There is no reason why a third choice should not be added.

4   Questions in the third person are easiest to answer since no change of person is involved in the reply.

5   Questions in the second person require a change to first person and this bothers many beginners.

6   Do a question in the third person. Get the answer and then put the same question in the second person to the individual concerned.

7   The same question can be put in a number of different ways so that pupils become familiar with the context, the subject matter and the answer. Such a technique also avoids mere repetition of an answer as it is passed on:

(a)   Is Paris bigger than Marseille? Answer: Yes. Yes it
      is bigger. Yes it is bigger than Marseille. (Teacher
      can work towards the full answer though the first is
      an adequate response.)
(b)   Is Paris bigger than Marseille or London? (Here a
      correct Yes answer is impossible as a choice is
      offered.)
(c)   Which is the biggest city — Paris, London or
      Marseille? (Here a simple deduction has to be made
      and the text is not simply regurgitated.)

8   Factual questions are the simplest to deal with and
    should always be at the start of a questioning sequence
    but pupils will soon become bored if they do nothing but
    repeat what the text tells them.

9   Inference questions are then called for. Questions
    beginning 'Do you think that . . .?' go well into this sort of
    work.

10 Pupils must have the opportunity to formulate questions.
    One way is to put a straightforward question to the class,
    elicit the correct answer, then ask a pupil to put the same
    question again to another pupil.

11 Ask pupils to note down questions as they occur because
    someone will play the teacher's part later on. The same
    questions are then put.

12 One pupil can put a number of questions or 'question
    relay' is sometimes preferred. A puts question to B who
    questions C, etc. The important thing is that all the
    questions have already been answered.

13 Whenever possible the teacher should try to bring
    questioning round to the pupils' own lives and experi-
    ences before leaving the topic. After factual questions on
    Paris based on a text studied in class it is a good thing to
    ask 'Have you been to Paris?' 'Do you like Paris?' 'Do
    you prefer London or Paris?' This kind of work ensures
    further practice in the language and increases personal
    involvement — an important motivating factor. Where a

story is studied rather than a factual account pupils can still be invited to give their own views or opinions. After eliciting the facts of the story continue with 'What would you do if . . .?'

14 A further method of arousing personal participation and at the same time offering practice with other tenses is to invite pupils to guess what *will* happen in the story. 'Do you think the jewel thief will be caught?' 'Who do think will catch the thief?'

An important point about all questioning in the language class is that the questions can offer something for everybody. The alert teacher watches pupil behaviour and gives out questions appropriate to the ability of different individuals. Progress can, however, be quite marked and because of the intensive nature of the question practice a pupil who was quite unable to answer in the earlier part of the lesson may well cope very adequately later on. In this case a real sense of achievement is experienced by the learner.

6 Discipline in the classroom

Basic considerations and technique

In recent years the word 'discipline' appears to have taken on certain unfortunate overtones which the teacher would do well to ignore. As modern linguists let us remember instead that the origin of the word lies in the Latin *'discipulus'*, a pupil, one who learns, from *disco, discere* — to learn. There is no suggestion of a punitive element being involved and there is no need for such an idea. For the good teacher 'discipline' means quite simply the art of creating the best learning conditions possible in the circumstances. Without good learning conditions no effective teaching can take place, and every conscientious teacher gives thought as to how good conditions can be created and maintained.

Even amongst successful teachers it is seldom that two will be found to agree on what produces good discipline. Certainly physical conditions seem to have very little to do with it. Time of the day and time of the lesson appear to have some significance and any teacher who finds he has the same class last period every afternoon may justifiably protest vigorously. But even this factor is not the main one. This is why Miss Jones has a perfectly orderly class at 3.30 while her colleague next door is praying either for the end of school or the end of the world.

Whatever the secret ingredient may be it is pretty well generally agreed that before any learning can take place good order has to be established in the language classroom.

Children will not 'discover' French or German grammar despite the din in the room, though they might, admittedly, discover the products of Mozambique, the life-history of the earthworm or the loves of a pop star. What then does the modern language teacher need to have in his knapsack to ensure that learning takes place?

In *Modern Language Teachers in Action*, the report for the language teaching research project organized at York University, the researchers considered what makes up a language teacher's general proficiency.[1] The following qualities were enumerated in order of importance:

1 discipline, firmness, control;
2 humour;
3 patience;
4 enthusiasm;
5 liking for, interest in, sympathy for the pupils;
6 consistency, fairness;
7 understanding problems;
8 planning;
9 confidence.

It will not pass unnoticed that top of the list comes 'discipline' and in a sense the other eight qualities might be seen as those elements essential to securing discipline. There are, however, other qualities of professionalism which can be usefully indicated.

Voice

The importance of the voice for any teacher needs no justification here. A flat, monotonous voice will kill a lesson stone-dead and then behaviour problems will quickly follow. If the teacher fails to do anything about the voice then it is the end of the lesson and, frankly, probably the end of a career.

---

(1) See David Sanderson, *Modern Language Teachers in Action*, University of York, 1982, p. 87

To be successful you should, from the beginning, cultivate a voice which can be varied in *pitch*, *pace* and *volume*. For the actor such control is accepted as normal and teacher expectation must be the same. Every teacher of languages should develop the art of mimicry to represent the different characters in any anecdote he has to recount. By suggesting that the teacher can vary the voice in pitch this is not to imply that he should make a complete fool of himself by reading female parts in a high falsetto, and male roles as though he were Daddy Bear. But between these two extremes there is a whole range of voices that can be 'put on' without undue strain on either the teacher's vocal chords or the pupils' self-control and credulity.

It should not be forgotten, however, that the teacher's voice is under considerable strain and the modern language teacher's more than most. To minimize such strain he should rely as little as possible on *volume*. Shouting seldom helps to convey advice, information, emphasis and encouragement. On the other hand it does arouse animosity and it is certainly fatiguing. Moral: reserve the *fortissimo* for desperate circumstances and moments of high drama in your narration. For more mundane events it will be found that an equally good if not better effect is created by varying the *pace* of one's utterances and by *reducing volume*. If muttering begins, it pays to drop the voice rather than to yell. If what the teacher is saying has any importance at all the talking at the back will quickly subside.

Voice *projection* is an important ability to develop. Again we stress, projection does not mean shouting. It means clarity of diction achieved by taking advantage of the mouth as a natural resonance chamber. This ability to project the voice is vital for any successful teacher since it not only means that the teacher can be heard without difficulty but, in some strange way, it conveys to the listener the confidence and authority of the speaker. Whatever the reason it somehow guarantees a hearing.

Speaking in the classroom to a group audience also requires the teacher to adopt a certain formality of usage. It is important not to be casual, using 'throwaway' remarks no one beyond the front row can ever catch. If the teacher is casual the class not unnaturally adopts a casual attitude towards him. Good clear speech is not the trademark of someone seeking to dominate the situation. It is simply a mark of respect shown to the people addressed. In the case of any teacher the voice serves as a model. For a language class a good clear model is essential for the pupils to attain any kind of authentic foreign accent.

As for English usage, which every teacher of modern languages has recourse to on occasions, it is important to ensure that speech is fairly standard, not characterized by so many regionalisms that pupils from another part of the country treat his speech as a joke. Hands should be kept away from the mouth and every effort should be made to avoid the slipshod 'gerrit and gorrit' type of language frequently heard in school playgrounds. There is a school of thought which argues that the teacher increases in stature in the eyes of his pupils if he speaks in their classroom vernacular. There is little proof of this and, if anything, probably the reverse is true.

The *tone* of voice adopted for addressing the multitude, or what seems like a multitude when one meets the third form on Friday afternoon, is not appropriate for speaking to individuals. Queen Victoria, it will be remembered, disliked Gladstone because he addressed her 'like a public meeting' and he was not unique. Teachers, however, meet with more blunt critics than perhaps a nineteenth-century prime minister ever did and pupils will soon show their resentment if they are individually pinned to the wall by the teacher's every utterance.

Manner

The ideal attitude to adopt with the class is one of firmness (see the York University report) tinged with pleasantness. If the teacher is offended by any pupil's behaviour (over-familiarity, cheek or even downright abuse) the class should be left in no doubt about the effect of such behaviour. Teachers are like any other human beings and the method of 'turning a deaf ear' to offensive remarks is not one that should be frequently applied.

Equally important in the manner adopted towards pupils is one's consistency. This again was a quality mentioned in the York Report. It means simply that what is rebuked today must be rebuked tomorrow and what is praised for one pupil must merit praise for another. Pupils respect staff they can rely on. They do not cause problems for the teacher known to be 'fair' in his dealings. To be fair it is important not to get 'boxed into a corner' by making generalizations that later may be regretted. The teacher who says 'I always give double homework to anyone who forgets his homework' is riding for a fall for there are extenuating circumstances in everyone's life.

Presentation

Whilst it is well known that the teacher cannot afford a new suit each term and, perhaps, does not wish to appear ultra-smart, there is no denying that a neat clean appearance suggests efficiency and concern for personal appearance which is transmitted to pupils immediately. Any parent will confirm that their children do come home and express their opinions of the personal appearance of the teachers in the school. Dirty finger nails, dirty clothes, messy hair and general untidiness are not just noticed but criticized by pupils. The same applies to teachers' handwriting, treatment of books and writing on the blackboard. Everything matters and those teachers who leave themselves open to criticism also leave themselves open to disciplinary problems which arise naturally from lack of respect.

Credibility

Every successful teacher has this quality though precisely what it is for any individual teacher may be difficult to define. It implies that pupils have confidence in him or her, trust his opinion and accept the standards of work that are set. It is fairly easy to destroy or, at any rate, to lose this credibility by being 'caught out'. Frequent confessions of ignorance about the language taught, failure to be well prepared for the lesson, inability to cope with the various mechanical aids in the classroom, forgetfulness about homeworks and promised tests will all reduce the teacher's credibility rating in the eyes of the pupils.

Once credibility begins to disappear (or fails ever to appear) the class will almost instinctively resort to the 'try-on'. Discipline problems have begun. Inability to tell the difference between the try-on and a genuine request for information confirms the class's diagnosis. 'Please Sir, what's the French for a bra?' is undoubtedly a try-on (witness the subject matter of the question). Any doubt can be dispelled by observing the behaviour of the questioner who, having put the question loudly, looks around the room to estimate his effect on the rest of the class. If not nipped in the bud at this stage by refusing to answer irrelevant questions the problem will soon get out of hand.

Knowing your stuff

This is the positive side of credibility. For most pupils (and parents), knowing his stuff is the teacher's first virtue. Certainly among the more academic pupils this is highly respected at any level. For the less academic, a language teacher still knows his stuff if he reveals familiarity with the country he teaches about, if he talks about events he has witnessed. If, in addition, he proves in front of the class that he is fluent in the language, possibly by doing a duet with the assistant, then the problem is resolved.

Position and posture

For pedagogical and strategic reasons it is important to move frequently about the room. Even speaking from the back of the room is a positive move since:

1   it alters the voice quality — result: variety;
2   it gives the teacher a different viewpoint;
3   it gives the teacher opportunity to check the quality of
    his visuals (Is writing neat and clear? Are overhead
    projector slides properly displayed?)
4   it keeps the class on its toes;
5   it allows the teacher to hear pupils' speech more
    clearly;
6   during writing sessions it permits the teacher to have
    individual conversations.

With a full class of thirty it is hardly ever possible to sit down
at the front and to do so invites inattention and distractions.
With a smaller group, say a half class, sitting down at the
front or even perched on the edge of a desk becomes possible
but it is important to remember that the change implies a
change in atmosphere. This is not to imply that there is
hostility afoot in a room of thirty pupils but simply to accept
the fact that to make an impact on thirty people at once is no
easy task and to sit down so that half the group cannot see
the teacher is to invite trouble.

As for posture, or, to use the modern jargon, body language,
teachers need to keep in mind that the way they move, the
way they sit, the way they get up again all convey a message
to the class. If staff wipe their dirty shoes over chairs
someone else has to sit on, do they really care? If the teacher
sprawls over a desk is he really anxious to give a good
lesson? All too quickly the 'couldn't care less' attitude rubs
off onto the pupils.

Finally, in this section we should remember that it is not only
teachers who choose their places in the classroom. Pupils
also make a choice, particularly in schools which have mass
movement at the end of every lesson to permit the use of
specialist rooms. In this kind of situation the teacher will be
wise to allocate places from the start of the school year and
insist that pupils keep to the allocated places. There are
many advantages in this system and few disadvantages. In
the worst of all possible worlds non-specialist rooms are
filled up as pupils arrive. In this sort of uncontrolled

situation it will be noticed how the front row is avoided as long as possible. The class are sorting themselves out and the teacher will be wise to watch who goes where. He will be wiser still if he quickly takes a hand in helping pupils to find places!

Style

Having style means appearing to be relaxed and self-confident even when this is not so. Such self-confidence is transmitted to the class. A tense, overwrought teacher tends to have a frothy class, and a vicious circle has begun which may not necessarily be reduced by the bell at the end of the lesson.

Self-confidence also implies confidence in the pupils, which arises from knowing them well. The illusion of knowing them reasonably well can be sustained by, at the very least, knowing them all by name (hence the importance of a seating plan or name cards). Pupils immediately react much better to their names than to hit-and-miss descriptions which can easily be used for deliberate misunderstanding.

Finally good style means adopting the right tone and posture for any situation. It involves developing a tone which, although perfectly pleasant, suggests that no one will do anything other than what the teacher has asked for. Surprisingly it works, though in the early days of teaching it may just be bluff.

Humour

This is a highly rated quality in the York University report but it needs to be handled with care. Provided the humour is not barbed, provided it does not trade in sarcasm (a quality hated by pupils) it is fine. If we mean by humour simply having a sense of fun, having the capacity to create funny situations for role-playing instead of the eternal dreary station booking office, then this is indeed a desirable quality and one to be envied but not copied by those who lack it.

Patience

Like humour this is a two-edged weapon. It is the first
quality every aspirant to the teaching profession names as
an essential. In the eyes of pupils it means a teacher who
'does not go mad with you' when you get it wrong. The
teacher who 'flies off the handle' at every mistake should not
be a language teacher, and possibly should not be a teacher
at all. In language work we are so dependent on pupil
confidence and willingness to participate that anything
which inhibits such contributions is obviously counter-
productive.

Enthusiasm

This is part of the 'credibility' referred to above. If the
teacher does not convey excitement and interest in what he
or she teaches this is bound to be picked up by the class. The
enthusiast may occasionally be seen as an eccentric by some
pupils but they are still affected by him. Enthusiasm is
transmitted in so many little ways: greetings in the corridor
in French or German or Spanish, displays around the room,
invitations to foreign visitors to meet the pupils, anecdotes
about visits abroad, organization of foreign visits, obvious
delight in holding a conversation in the language, interest
and concern about pupils' own foreign contacts (letters from
pen-friends, visits).

Dealing with classroom disturbances

First be sure what the school policy is and stick to that.
Idiosyncratic punishments invented by the teacher will
almost certainly bounce back and may cause considerable
embarrassment to all concerned. Any teacher who is forced
into a position of having to withdraw and apologize has lost
his credibility and hence the respect of pupils.

If detention is a recognized school system be sure to use it
exactly as laid down. Most schools these days insist rightly
on a minimum of twenty-four hours' notice being given in

writing to parents. Such punishments should be used sparingly as they rapidly become ineffectual and can become a joke if half the class winds up in detention.

If the school policy is to set extra written work or 'lines', beware of building up resentment against languages by setting dreary exercises. Nor should the teacher set an essay in English on useless titles such as 'Why I was late to class three times'. Such methods undermine the work of colleagues — those in the English department for example, who are striving to prove that writing is exciting and creative.

If there can be such a thing as a 'best punishment' it must be one which produces something worthwhile and which does not imply a complete waste of time for the pupil. Socially useful work is the answer and in the modern languages department it means the manufacture or renewal of visual aids — posters, flashcards and reading cards. Displays on notice boards are vital to keep up interest and they have to be changed. How about letting the offender remove old displays and perhaps even help to set up a new one? These days textbooks are expensive to replace and books once thrown away as beyond repair now have to be revived. A pasting session could be very helpful. The spirit pen brought in its trail graffiti, some more obscene than others but all needing to be removed from desk tops and even walls. All such activities are preferable to doing extra work of the dullest kind.

Before deciding on the punishment it is vital to be sure that the real culprit has been apprehended. Even when sure, it pays to deal with the offender *after* the lesson because

1   it keeps everyone wondering;
2   teacher and pupil have time to cool off;
3   a ringside seat is not offered free to spectators who will delight in a confrontation;
4   the offender is denied an audience to play to and since this may be at least partly the reason for the original offence a refusal to allow him to call further attention to himself is a sound punishment.

For all these reasons the teacher's best way of putting an end to a minor disturbance is to say 'See me at the end.' He should then make sure he *does* see the offender and not allow him to slip out.

Some schools have a system which permits the less experienced staff to send a disturbance causer to a head of department. Generally it is better to try to solve difficulties oneself but this system can be useful in that it gets the offender out of the room before further trouble is caused. On the other hand, it is important to see that the senior colleague has a true account of events. Without this there is a real risk that the offender may be congratulated and sent back to the classroom.

Very occasionally a pupil can become totally disruptive and transport the teacher to the 'blackboard jungle' world of the popular press. Physical attacks do happen. When such occurrences take place, the following procedure should minimize the repercussions:

1   Do not reply in kind either by resorting to foul language or, worse still, to violence.
2   If attacked, tell the assailant he has done this in front of many witnesses and the consequences will be severe.
3   Report such an attack to the school authorities as soon as possible.
4   Either leave the classroom or get the assailant out of the room immediately.
5   Make a written report on the incident as soon after as possible. Include details of what the causes of the attack were. Indicate whether previous warnings had been issued. Describe in detail the attack and its results. Include the names of witnesses. State what action was taken to avoid a continuation of the affair. Copies of the report should go to the head or deputy head and to the union representative if he or she has been involved. Any decision to prosecute in court will have to be taken by the teacher and not by the school or even by the police.
6   When things have calmed down discuss the event with colleagues. What should have been known about the

pupil and his background? What mistakes may have been made by the teacher to cause the pupil to flare up?

In all classroom disturbances it is important to find out *why* events took the turn they did. Investigation often reveals the following causes:

- boredom;
- a dare;
- testing the teacher;
- pupil thinks he has been unfairly treated (picked on);
- sarcasm on the part of the teacher;
- things going wrong in another class or at home.

If boredom is the cause, and this is common, the teacher should look at the structure of his lesson. Any of the following may apply:

- too much of the same old thing (oral or written);
- not enough to do;
- too much to do;
- wrong sort of work either for the pupil or for the time of day.

Most minor disturbances can be dealt with before they become major confrontations. In the York University study, respondents to a questionnaire on class management indicated their belief in this. Thus one teacher stated: 'Basically I try to avoid trouble by giving satisfying work' and another commented that he avoided trouble 'by attempting to give recalcitrant pupils work with which they can succeed'.

When there has been a confrontation it is wise to try to offer the offender an opportunity to rehabilitate himself by recovering self-respect during what remains of the lesson. If, however, he or she indicates by remaining sulky that there is no wish to 'come round' it is best to leave well alone. On no account should one give the pupil the impression that there is a determined attempt to prolong the matter.

Most experienced teachers will agree that occasionally it is best *not* to see or hear something. Only if the action is prolonged or seems likely to disturb or offend others should action be taken in such cases where it is obvious that a pupil is trying it on to see what reaction he can provoke.

It is a good idea on parents' evenings to be on the look-out for the parents of any child who has caused problems. Some schools have a system which permits staff to request to see parents and this is an excellent way of nipping problems in the bud. It is certainly no confession of failure to seek to discuss a child causing disturbance in the classroom. Often the parents can reveal the cause, which may be allied to some activity in the language class which the son or daughter has taken a dislike to.

Becoming preoccupied with discipline is not unusual amongst young teachers. The York study confirmed that virtually all teachers have to pass through a transitional stage when they are vitally concerned about classroom order. Ability to manage a class does not come easily to many. One teacher is quoted as saying 'I had a lot of problems in my first year in another school; I certainly found great difficulty when I first started; in my early teaching days — very, very disrupted lessons; I think most people must go through the shouting and this having no effect.' The editorial comment goes on: 'Since all these statements come from teachers observed to have impressive control of their classes, they indicate that such problems are quite normal'.

To conclude this section on a hopeful note it may be helpful to quote from the York study what ingredients in the lesson led to ultimate control being achieved:

1   lesson pitched to enable pupils to have a high success rate;
2   teacher involves the whole group;
3   teacher is skilled with equipment;
4   teacher provides a variety of language activity;
5   teacher uses a variety of materials;

6   teacher is flexible with regard to objectives;
7   teacher builds up on pupil error.

Getting the class on your side

Following from the above we may conclude that the successful language teacher is the one who persuades the pupils that languages are worth learning and that there is a sense of achievement to be had if lessons are properly structured. To achieve this the teacher does need to feel that teacher and pupils are on the same side and the following may help to bring this about:

1   Learn names quickly (name cards or seating plan).
2   Smile at pupils whenever possible.
3   Be generous with praise: what may be a simple answer to the teacher may be a *tour de force* for the learner. The York study lists the following kinds of effective praise:

   (a)   verbal (of prime importance);
   (b)   merit cards, merit marks;
   (c)   written praise;
   (d)   house credit points;
   (e)   reports;
   (f)   prizes;
   (g)   letters to pupil or parent;
   (h)   display of work;
   (i)   positive marking;
   (j)   diploma (oral test).

In the same study, other teachers added 'the distribution of extra material', 'stretching those pupils', and the feeling of satisfaction the pupil derives from knowing he has pleased the teacher. One further interesting conclusion comes from the report, namely: 'The climate of success tended to reveal itself in a diminished need for verbal praise'.

4   Set attainable standards to guarantee success.
5   Set standards based on good work. The class should be

absolutely clear as to what the teacher thinks is good.

6 When talking to individuals use a low voice.
7 Take an interest in pupils and their welfare: ask if they are well again after illness or accident.
8 Learn to 'size up' a class quickly in order to estimate which pupils enjoy repartee, or can have a leg pulled without taking offence.
9 Be firm, fair and friendly.
10 Be consistent in class management.
11 Have ten minutes a week set aside for 'Question Time'. At this time any pupil may put any question he or she likes.
12 Talk about 'exploits' abroad occasionally. Stress the use of language learning and that the hard work is worthwhile.
13 Encourage pupils to go abroad themselves. Give help with planning.
14 Recommend relevant radio and TV programmes — good films in the language.
15 Help pupils to take part in language competitions.

And avoid the following:
1 giving the impression you don't care;
2 making threats you may not wish to carry out: 'The next person to . . .';
3 setting work which is sure to bring in large crops of errors: it demoralizes the class and proves the teacher is ineffective;
4 attempting to mimic a pupil's attempt at reading or speaking;
5 wasting time by having long debates on 'why has she got 14 and I've got 10?'
6 telling pupils you were no good at this or that (it reduces credibility);
7 making unprofessional remarks about the school, the timetable or even a colleague;
8 keeping exercise books for a long time.

7 Testing and assessing

Testing and assessing are important activities in the school and are complementary to teaching. As such, it is vital that the teacher is informed as to the devising of tests and test materials and is knowledgeable on the use and interpretation of results. There is considerable backwash from examinations and important decisions are made in the light of the results. The importance of the activity cannot be underestimated.

Aims

Assessment has several aims which may be summarized as follows:

1 *Measuring attainment.* Given that one of the main aims of the teacher is to teach a body of knowledge, then examinations and tests are used to evaluate how far this has been achieved. The care with which the test or examination is drawn up will affect the accuracy of the measure. Poorly composed tests will only confuse the interpretation of the results.

2 *Diagnosis.* It is very useful for teacher, pupil and parent to be able to see the strengths and weaknesses of individuals. The opportunity for pupils to see where they have gone wrong and for teachers to evaluate their effectiveness *and* do something about it, can be helped by the proper use and evaluation of tests. As in (1) above, the whole

process needs to be carried out with care.

3   *Motivation*. The 'stick and carrot' effect of testing should not be underestimated. Language-learning is a long-term task and pupils starting out hopefully on the long road to 'mastery' of a new language, need recognition and reward as one element in motivation. We must not overestimate the effect of examinations themselves, but it is clear that children tend to exert themselves more when clear standards of attainment have been set. It is important that the standards are within the capacity of the pupils and this is one of the important features of the Graded Test movement.

4   *Prediction*. Whether we agree with it or not, many people use the results of examinations, especially public examinations, to predict future performance in a subject. Again, the setting of the tests and the interpretation of the results obtained need care.

We are not concerned here with the setting, marking and use of external examinations such as O- and A-levels, CSE, 16+ and GCSE, but rather with the practicalities of testing and assessment within the school. Two areas are discernible — the setting of end-of-year or 'formal' tests and secondly, testing as part of short-term tactics within the classroom. We will call this latter 'informal' testing.

Informal testing, or 'quick checks'

As has been mentioned, the process of learning a language is a long-term task and thus the diagnostic and motivational functions of 'testing as you teach' are important. Any such testing should involve both the mechanical mastery of the various elements (vocabulary and verbs, etc.) as well as understanding.

It should not be that the teacher's marking burden is always increased by the frequent use of tests, for there are many occasions when quick marking in class by various means (such as 'exchanging' papers, true–false type answers, multiple choice questions, providing keys for the pupils to use, etc.) are appropriate.

What is important, however, is that the pupils take the process seriously, and see that the teacher also considers it to be worthwhile. If it is indicated that something 'will be tested', then it must be tested and not forgotten. 'Learning homeworks' in particular must be sampled or else the temptation to spend the evening watching television will overcome most pupils. Equally, tests should only be given with prior warning — surprises are counterproductive and often breed hostility and cries of 'not fair' from the pupils.

What can be tested quickly in this way? Here are a few ideas:

Vocabulary. This provides the building-blocks of the edifice, and should be sampled regularly, but not to the exclusion of using these elements in real exchanges. As each stage or unit of the course is completed, test quickly 'both ways' — English to FL, and FL to English. Pupils can mark their own or each other's work. Don't forget to review any difficulties that occur and re-test if necessary. If writing is not part of the course, then test with pictures, odd-man-out or other multiple-choice strategies.

'Grammar' or structures. This should be tested as you proceed, even in courses where 'formal' grammar is not the corner-pin as before. Tests can range from forms of tenses to use of 'si' clauses. Again, be to the point and precise. But do not think that the ability to analyse grammar will enable a pupil to become fluent — it is simply a stage on the way.

Comprehension. This can require different sorts of skills — intensive and extensive, detailed and 'gist'. Both should be sampled. It can be done orally at the beginning of the lesson after a homework or by means of written tests of varying levels of difficulty. However, make sure that the pupils know beforehand that they are to read or listen for fine details or simply to 'get the message'. The sampling at this level should be done in English, since comprehension should not be confused with composition in a test situation. (This does not mean that we never ask questions in the target language, but we are considering here the process of testing.)

Writing. Perhaps the easiest of the skills to sample, because it has the stamp of 'formality'. However, beware of the contamination of the native language when devising tests and in particular of the worrying practice of testing the written form when the teaching has been largely aural/oral.

Oral competence. This is difficult to measure in a large class when time is at a premium. There are, however, several ways of lightening the burden and yet sampling on a regular basis. Formal oral examinations do have a place in the school system, but they are time-consuming and can cause tension in the pupil, thus inhibiting performance in an unreal situation. Strategies for measuring the oral skill include:

Using the assistant. He or she must be told what to look for and what standards to expect. If possible a checklist could be devised and filled in.

'Target' lessons. During a series of lessons a group of 5-6 pupils are observed with more attention than usual. They are graded on, say, a five-point scale (A-E) and thus a whole class can be assessed over several lessons without too much interruption or extra work.

'Target' weeks. Oral work is particularly noticed and thus a picture is built up over the year of the progress of the pupils. The assessment of the pupils' oral work should take into account understanding, pronunciation, fluency, accuracy and inventiveness, but above all the ability to *communicate*.

Keeping the correct records of the tests is important and this is discussed in detail in Chapter 20.

Formal testing

All schools will have a system of formal examinations and thus the teacher as an individual or a department as a team will face the problem of devising tests that work. An understanding of the basic ideas is very important.

Devising tests

Over the past few years a lot of discussion and argument has been generated over the 'backwash' effect of examinations on the teaching of modern languages. This is particularly so at external examination level, when the syllabus and methodology of the school have been increasingly restricted by the 'need' to get pupils over the examination hurdle. The passing of examinations is seen by many — pupils, teachers and parents — as the reason for embarking on a course of study. The form and the content of the examinations, as well as the criteria used for judging 'success' thus often determine the nature of the course provided for the pupils, crowding out other worthy educational considerations. There is, however, an increasing awareness that this approach is restricting and that if we are not able to cancel out the 'backwash' from examinations, we must alter the nature of the tests so that the influence is positive. As the development of new testing instruments gathers speed, there is a growing realization that syllabus design is the first priority and that test design must follow this and not dictate it.

It is considered important therefore that tests should endeavour to simulate as closely as possible the normal language situations which have been anticipated in the course of designing the syllabus. This should increase both validity and reliability.

What do we mean by 'reliability' and 'validity'?

Reliability. A test is said to be *reliable* if it produces a consistent result from one occasion to the next for the same pupil or group, irrespective of marker.

Validity. Tests and examinations have both content and predictive validity. *Content validity* will mean that the test will sample representatively from the whole syllabus in question. *Predictive validity* will mean that the test will predict a future event, i.e. in this case the ability of the pupil to cope in 'real' language situations.

Note: It is not often possible to apply statistical measures of reliability in a single school, but by building up a file of tests of various sorts over the years, which can be gradually refined with the cumulative experience of colleagues, then reliability can be improved. Validity can be improved by careful and systematic production of the tests and by the help of a grid or checklist as seen in Figure 8, Chapter 20.

Devising tests: do's and don'ts

Do's

1   Be clear right from the beginning *when* you are going to test: *plan ahead*.
2   Draw up a list or table of what is to be tested. Draw from the syllabus and make sure that the sampling in the test covers the range of topics, situations, structures, etc., encountered in the teaching syllabus. Test only what has been taught.
3   Decide on the skills to be tested.
4   Decide on the length of the test according to the time available, the age and ability of the pupils. This judgement is one of the most difficult of all the balancing acts: too little time increases pressures and often inhibits good practice; too much time is wasteful and can increase discipline problems for idle hands.
5   Decide on a marking strategy in detail at the same time as the test is written (what are we looking for in this test?)
6   Decide on who will mark the test. Try to ensure that there is a fair distribution of the burden and consistency in

marking the test or the section. It is a good idea in internal examinations for as many of the teachers involved in teaching the particular classes, to be involved in the marking — you can learn a lot about the effectiveness of the teaching if you can go through the monotonous and tedious task of assessing the pupils' efforts.

7 Attach great importance to concise rubrics and clear instructions.

8 Devise tests which will search out what pupils *know*, rather than what they don't know.

Don'ts

1 Don't wait until the last minute to set the paper. Haste does *not* contribute to good testing;.

2 Don't draw up the paper and then fit the teaching to the test.

3 Don't present 'trick' questions.

4 Don't introduce unfamiliar routines to a class for the first time in the course of an examination.

5 Don't set the pupil against the clock. Be realistic on the length of the paper and the number of elements to be attempted.

When the paper has been set, it is a good idea to pass it to colleagues for their comments. This is particularly important if the examination is to be taken by a number of groups taught by different teachers. This 'openness' is important — secrecy should play no part in testing. When passing the draft paper round the department for consideration, the following questions should be asked:

Reviewing the test

1 Are all the questions set within the syllabus?
2 Does the test adequately sample the syllabus?
3 Is there any overlap in the material?
4 Does the test allow all the pupils to demonstrate their abilities?
5 Are the instructions clear?

6   Is the visual material clear?
7   Is any recorded material clear?
8   Is the French/German/Spanish, etc., correct?
9   If multiple choice is used, are the keys correct and properly dispersed over the range of possible answers (e.g. not all key "A")?
10 Can the paper be done in the time allowed?

What should we test?

It is reasonable to assume that we will want to test all the skills being taught to a particular class. The full range of listening, speaking, reading and writing will be discussed below but it will be up to the individual teacher to decide which of the four skills is appropriate and what weight each skill will carry in the final scoring. It will be realized that not all skills can be tested discretely. For example in the testing of the listening element of the course, there will be some reading and/or writing which will to a greater or lesser degree 'contaminate' the results. This should not worry us unduly for this is also true of 'real-life' language situations. What we must do, however, is to try to reduce the interference as far as possible so that we can measure how far the pupil can understand what he hears. Do not however attempt to be too devious so as to make the test resemble an 11+ intelligence test that bears little apparent relationship to real authentic language usage.

A second broad consideration in determining test types will be the need to reflect the general philosophy underpinning the syllabus design. If we accept, as is increasingly the case, that the main aim in our teaching syllabus is 'communicative competence', then it must follow that our tests must have realistic communication as their hallmark, and that they should be authentic and valuable beyond the classroom. Having said all this, it is to be admitted that examinations are not 'realistic', that they impose restrictions of time and type if they are to fulfil their role as measuring instruments. But the balance must be in favour of realism and in the examples below this is the assumption.

Test strategies

Listening tests

1 *Listen and do,* e.g.
   - filling in forms, filling in symbols on a weather map, completing an itinerary from an announcement;
   - following instructions: tracing route of a journey on a map, completing a picture;
   - replying to requests for information — e.g. following instructions on how to reach a destination.

2 *Listen and react,* e.g.
   - listening to a railway announcement: what do you do next?
   - listening to news headlines and choosing from suggestions as to what they are about;
   - listening to story: what happens next?

3 *Understanding a variety of registers,* e.g.
   - Identify functions/attitudes of what is expressed.
   - Identify main points: e.g. summarize telephone message.
   - Make a précis (more advanced pupils only).

There are various ways of receiving the answers:

1 answers in English;
2 multiple choice in FL/English (only where it is natural);
3 true/false answers;
4 writing down dictated messages, etc.

Reading tests

1 comprehending notices and signs;
2 extracting relevant, specific information from letters, authentic material, e.g. brochures and guides;
3 identifying important points from an extended piece of writing, for example a brief newspaper or magazine article.

These can be tested by:
- answers in English;
- true/false questions;
- multiple-choice;
- eliminating alternatives in FL.

Writing tests

1 writing postcards based on similar stimulus material in English;
2 leaving messages. e.g. to a host's family while in France;
3 writing letters, based on stimulus in FL, or on instructions in English, e.g. to a hotel.
4 describing pictures;
5 writing a description. say, as a witness.

Speaking

1 role-playing;
2 describing pictures or a route on a map, for example;
3 general conversation — directed or open-ended.

Marking

It is a good idea to mark papers and discuss a sample with a colleague in order to make sure of the standards being asked.

In order to improve the reliability of the examination. it is important to devise a scheme which will allow consistent standards to be applied over the whole range of candidates. It is therefore suggested that a member of staff be responsible for a whole paper or section of a paper.

There is often a conflict between objective marking and subjective marking. Objectivity in itself is desirable but it must not be confused with negative marking. It is easier to be 'objective' when deducting marks for errors (2 for a verb, 1 for a gender, etc.). Yet with care it is perfectly possible to reward positively, the communicative, qualitative aspects of the pupil's work. Some effort should be made to assess this aspect. Perhaps the compromise is to allow some 'negative' marks, but to place an increasing reliance on the positive. There are many attempts at this and one example will suffice. It illustrates marking a general conversation.

There could be, for example, two criteria, one judging comprehension and content, the other judging grammar and structure. Each scale would have 8 points (0–7), carefully worked out in advance; e.g. to measure grammar and structure the following could be suggested:

7. Good range of structures. Accuracy.
6. Less ambitious structure. Accurate grammar.
5. Unambitious structure. Accurate.
4. Simple structures. Some errors.
3. Simple structures. A greater number of errors.
2. Basic. Large number of errors.
1. Very basic. Gross errors.
0. Nothing of merit.

e.g. to measure content and compensation:

7. Fluent and full response.
6. Reasonably full response: ready answers.
5. Satisfactory: some hesitation.
4. Brief but still containing dialogue.
3. Uncertain and brief response.
2. Minimal and basic response.
1. Little communication.
0. Nothing of merit.

The total possible 'merit' marks would be 14, by totalling the two scales. The advantage is that pupils would be rewarded for communication and it is to be hoped that they would see this as a motivating factor.

Reporting the results

The ideal position would be for the modern language department to report on the level of attainment in each of the skills attempted. If this is not possible on the school reports as they exist, then at least ensure that appropriate comments are made in the comments section of the reports. For a full discussion on writing reports see pages 257–9.

8 The use of resources

Otto Jespersen, father of modern language teaching as we know it today, was not wrong when in 1904, in his book *How to Teach a Foreign Language*, (a book which still repays careful reading) he forecast that this new invention, the gramophone, was in future likely to play an important part in language teaching. Professor Jespersen would certainly have delighted in what Eric Hawkins has called 'recent panaceas' and he would no doubt have taken the same realistic view of such teaching aids as Professor Hawkins does when he comments, 'By the mid-1970s there were few teachers or administrators who still believed that the language laboratory was the panacea that it had been thought to be in the early 1960s.'[1]

Language teachers of the 1980s therefore find themselves in a privileged position in one sense, for they are the inheritors of a vast amount of technical development and pedagogical research which together enable teachers to deploy the technical advances in the most effective and the most realistic way. There are no panaceas but there are many useful teaching aids on the market that keen language teachers will wish to exploit to the full. But, like most aids, they are only as good as the teacher using them can make them. In other words, you can purchase the hardware, but to be effective, you have to create much of the software

(1) E. W. Hawkins, *Modern Languages in the Curriculum*, Cambridge, 1981, pp. 180.

yourself, using your own imagination.

The tape recorder

The tape recorder (the 'reel-to-reel') has been in classroom
use for more than twenty-five years now and has been
described as 'the keystone of the revolution that has taken
place in language learning . . .'[1] In recent years its more
portable descendant, the cassette player, has become
extremely popular in classrooms though it lacks the
versatility of the reel-to-reel machine. Both machines,
however, have enormous advantages over the disc and as a
result the record-player has now become almost extinct in
classrooms.

The main advantage of the tape player is that it brings to the
pupils very faithful recordings of authentic speech of all
kinds. That is to say that we do not merely have the
possibility of hearing model native speakers recorded in
studio conditions but that the techniques of recording and
playback are now so effective that the voice of the man in the
street, and indeed the other noises of the street, can be had at
a moment's notice. Even the small cassette player is
obtainable with so refined a loudspeaker that it is possible to
hear it comfortably at the back of a large room without
distortion. With all these machines, trial-and-error techniques will show how best to use volume, treble and bass
tone controls. The wise teacher makes a point of going to the
back of the room to judge the quality of output. It is
important to remember that the ear needs a minute or two to
'tune in' to a loudspeaker and it is therefore a common
remark from classes that they can understand nothing when
they first start to listen. For this reason it always makes sense
to re-run a tape for a second time. When classes are sitting
public examinations in which a listening comprehension
passage is pre-recorded it is important to use the kind of

(1) B. Hill in *Teaching Languages*, ed. Edith R. Baer, BBC, 1976, pp. 66.

machine the pupil is used to hearing and, if possible, to allow pupils to hear some familiar material on the machine before the examination proper begins.

Notes on pre-recorded material

1 Commercially produced tapes are more vulnerable to accidental wiping-out than are cassettes. The ingenious incision at the back of the plastic cassette prevents the recording head operating on the machine.
2 Some recordings are sold to schools on the understanding that a sub-master can be made for classroom use only. The label indicates when this is permissible.
3 Catalogue all tapes and store them in a central point. A borrower's book is essential and all tapes should be returned to the central store as soon after use as possible.
4 Damaged or twisted tapes must always be repaired or untwisted before being put back into store.
5 Care must be taken at the end of the lesson to wind the tape back to the beginning.
6 When a tape is indexed (a very helpful device) the box should indicate which machine the tape is indexed for and the take-up spool size.
7 On the reel-to-reel a rough-and-ready way of quickly marking a reference is to insert a slip of paper at that point on the tape and wind back. Next time wind forward till the paper drops out. With cassettes the amount of tape is so much smaller the problem of finding a place hardly arises, particularly if note is taken of the scale on the plastic case.
8 Preparation of tapes before use is vital. Time-wasting while the teacher fiddles with the tape is frustrating and the class lose confidence. 'Children can use these machines and expect you to be able to use them' (teacher quoted in the York report).
9 Always have the printed script with you. Any mishap with the machine (blown fuse or worse) can then be overcome by reading from the script.

Other uses for the tape recorder

1   Recordings made in the school to use for listening comprehension and essay stimulus material. The assistant is invaluable for this kind of work particularly in areas where assistants are spread very thinly. Schools can usefully pool material made 'at home'.

2   Recordings made abroad by pupils (street interviews), by colleagues (interviews with tradesmen, etc.).

3   Recordings made by pupils in exchange schools describing life at home and school.

4   School bulletins contributed to by many pupils. Recordings done in the mother-tongue and in the target language are an excellent beginning to pupil-to-pupil exchanges.

5   Recordings made by assistants and staff for home listening. To do this effectively cassette fast-copiers have to be acquired and the services of a technician are invaluable. Ideal for fifth and sixth form work, for essay preparation and for listening comprehension. Good for absentees.

6   When the school has no language laboratory (how many have nowadays?), it is useful for the pupils to hear their own voices, e.g. as practice for oral examinations.

7   'Off-air' recording involves copyright problems of all kinds. The BBC allows copying of schools broadcasts (indeed this is the only way to use some since they are broadcast at 2.00 a.m.). It is usually stressed that all BBC sound recordings should be erased at the end of the school year. Colleagues working in schools abroad who are often persuaded to record off-air material in their own countries for use in the UK ought to be advised to check up on regulations.

8   Transcription exercises are good in small doses: whole passages or gap-filling. The latter is good for calling attention to a particular structure or to a particular sound and a multiplicity of spellings.

9   A variety of musical activities becomes possible, such as:
    ● listening to songs in the language;

- music used to precede or accompany an activity — to give atmosphere;
- musical accompaniment pre-recorded for the class to sing to 'live';
- home-made recordings of choirs.

10 Remedial exercises with built-in self-correction for home use. These are not difficult to devise. Many traditional grammar books will supply the raw material and the value is increased if the pupil is hearing the exercises. The assistant can help with recording. A better effect is produced if two voices are used — assistant gives stimulus, teacher supplies correct response after necessary pause. Then a further pause for pupil to repeat (though not record) the correct version. Many language laboratory drills already published will go easily onto cassette for home use.

The language laboratory

The rise and fall of the language laboratory is a story yet to be related in detail. Suffice it here to note that the first

Mr Punch and the Language Laboratory: *Pick of Punch*, 1965

primitive language laboratory was in use in the States in the late 1940s and by 1961, 2,500 schools had been equipped in the USA, whereas in that same year 'Ealing Technical College was the first educational establishment in the UK to install and operate a full-scale language laboratory . . .'[1] By 1965 there were almost 200 schools equipped with laboratories. The high-water mark is probably about 1970 and the decline began (a) because of the cost of maintenance, and (b) because of the doubts raised about the efficacy of such installations except for the most highly motivated of pupils. 'The most relevant research for UK schools was the carefully controlled York study (Green, 1975). This showed that, *exploited in the most typical way*, the costly language laboratory did not improve the performance in German of 11+ beginners, when compared over three years with use of the same materials played on a single tape-recorder in the classroom.'[2]

Before dismissing the language laboratory, note the caveats: *exploited in the most typical way* and *11+* beginners. The York evidence does not belittle the use of laboratories or mini-labs for sixth-formers or in Further and Higher Education where greater maturity coupled with high motivation make the laboratory a valuable private study teaching aid.

We should finally note that many of the original drills for pronunciation and structure have now been abandoned and schools still lucky enough to have some kind of language laboratory for sixth-form use tend to use it for:
● listening comprehensions;
● transcription exercises;
● stimulus material for essays;
● dialogues and simulated telephone conversations;
● remedial pronunciation;
● creative response exercises;
● four-phase teaching and testing;
● drills for *ab initio* learners in the sixth form.

---

(1) D. H. Harding, *The New Pattern of Language Teaching*, 1967, pp 103.
(2) E.W. Hawkins, op. cit., pp 180.

The slide/filmstrip projector

This provides the other half of the duo for true audio-visual learning. Relatively inexpensive and easy to operate and maintain, the projector is vital equipment for every language department — together with a good supply of spare lamps. All staff should be warned not to attempt to move the machine while the lamp is still hot. Daylight screens or, at a pinch, whitish classroom walls can be used for projection.

When showing a filmstrip the teacher should try to cultivate some sense of showmanship. It is frustrating, even annoying, to watch a teacher laboriously winding the whole filmstrip back to the beginning, showing the class the whole programme in reverse and totally destroying any impact it may have. If it is necessary to wind back at the start of the lesson the wise teacher will at least twist the lens barrel to put the whole thing so out of focus that the newness is preserved for the proper showing. But such fiddling should not really be necessary, since extra film carriers can be purchased cheaply and films can be loaded far away from the classroom.

Many filmstrips are linked with a tape course and good teacher's instructions accompany them. The pace of the course is entirely in the hands of the teacher and we simply underline here the need for variety of activity. Every lesson should contain at least three different activities to avoid total boredom. Many filmstrips are far too long to be shown in their entirety and some teachers find that a maximum of ten frames should be presented, clarified, drilled and exploited at any one session.

Other filmstrips are ideal for imparting background knowledge of the country. Taped commentaries can accompany such programmes or the teacher himself can do the commentary incorporating into it as much question and answer work as possible. It is a great mistake to assume that once through will do. With older classes notes can be taken and one form of exploitation is to ask pupils to go over the film again explaining to the class what is depicted.

In addition to filmstrips there are, of course, hundreds of sets of slides available and a projector can be modified in seconds to project slides. Every language department should build up a set of slides from commercial sources and, perhaps more effective, from personal visits abroad to areas the school has a particular interest in. The assistant can often make great use of the projector and should be encouraged to show slides of home and to use commercial sets on contemporary life, history and geography.

The overhead projector (OHP)

For most language teachers these days the OHP is a basic tool which, in some schools has even supplanted the blackboard, since it has all the virtues of the blackboard, i.e. it can accept writing instantaneously and, in addition, slides are easily prepared and very easily transported into the classroom. Indeed much lesson preparation can be done which in earlier times could only have been done by taking the blackboard home. A further advantage lies in the colourful presentation which can easily be achieved with home-made line drawings. And the final advantage is that it is far easier to mask any possible distractors and hence present work in a logical sequence, sure of the fact that pupils can be looking only at the part the teacher wishes them to see. This is what is meant by 'progressive revelation'.

The York report, however, gives one word of warning: 'An unspoken rule . . . was to use it sparingly.'[1] In observed lessons witnesses commented favourably on the way the effective teacher switched off the OHP whenever she wanted the class to pay attention to *her*. The bright light is an attraction it is difficult to avoid looking at.

---

(1) D. Sanderson. *Modern Language Teachers in Action*. University of York, 1982. p 92.

Using the OHP

1 Use water-based fibre-tip pens to erase writing. Use spirit-based fibre-tips for permanent slides. (Cellulose thinners will sometimes clear this if needed.)

2 Any picture can be traced directly onto the acetate slide.

3 Overlaying is a good way of building up a scene or a sequence you wish to reveal in stages. Different colours can be used on each acetate sheet to give good contrast. Ideal for story-telling.

4 Always ensure the lens is correctly focussed onto the screen behind you. It pays to check from the back of the room.

5 Cut-out shapes in coloured plastic can be used to build up pictures.

6 Pupils can be invited out to superimpose or remove layers according to the teacher's instructions in the language.

7 For sentence patterns, lists of beginnings (subjects) middles (verbs or pronouns) and endings (objects) can be moved up and down to help weaker pupils compose new sentences.

8 Pupils can be invited to make visuals for future lessons, e.g. tracing from photographs or maps.

9 The actual process of writing a composition can take place in front of the class. Pupils compose the sentences and the teacher (or a pupil) writes up as the lesson progresses.

10 Acetate transparencies intended for future use need to be clearly marked in one corner with the basic details of purpose and source. A reference list should be prepared at the same time.

11 Special transparencies can be obtained onto which it is possible to type directly.

12 Very impressive permanent slides can be made by using Letraset.

13 Some photocopiers will copy straight onto acetate slides.

14 In departments where such material is used on a shared

basis it is a good idea to have a principle of 'Use one, make one.' In this way a very substantial number of transparencies is quickly built up.

15 Many good transparencies are now available commercially. They are advertised in the publishers' catalogues and are a very sound investment.

The episcope

The episcope (formerly known as the 'epidiascope') tends to be regarded as a fairly old-fashioned aid. Yet many schools have one and it is often a favourite with history, geography or science departments. Through a system of mirrors it projects printed matter (postcards, book illustrations and texts) and so enlarges print that, with good blacking out, it is possible for a class to read the printed word. It is ideal for giving close-ups of documents. The illumination is not very good and, because of the 1000 watt lamp used, much heat is generated which tends to curl up books and precious illustrations. They do recover as they reabsorb moisture from the atmosphere.

No single department needs to own its episcope but there should be one in every school. Probably the most useful function for the modern linguist is that it very simply provides excellent wall illustrations based on book illustrations. If a book illustration is projected not onto a screen but onto a sheet of white paper, it is the simplest of tasks to draw with spirit pen round the main lines of the original drawing or photograph to produce an immediately recognizable enlargement which is ideal for visual presentation and wall display. Pupils will very willingly undertake to do this kind of work and enjoy producing elaborately coloured final versions. It is certainly one way of giving the learner a vested interest in what is being taught.

The above copying technique for wall display and to create permanent pictures can, of course, also be applied to filmstrip projections. In any filmstrip there are usually four or five key pictures which can be copied directly onto one 'summary chart' for wall display. They are then ideal revision material which can be turned to at a moment's notice without the fuss of rethreading another filmstrip. (See Chapter 10.)

The spirit duplicator

This is often referred to as the 'Banda' from the well-known make. No teacher needs to be told of the existence of this invaluable tool which accepts handwriting or typing equally well, though bigger type is more successful than small. In addition to producing individual work sheets quickly and cheaply for reading, it is worth remembering the technique described above. Project onto a pinned-up master sheet with carbon behind and draw round the outline of the projected image.

Publishers have now recognized the appeal of the spirit duplicator and are offering sets of masters which the school runs off as they are needed. Users should be aware that the carbon dries up fairly quickly and the number of legible copies obtainable is then reduced.

Correcting error on masters can be a messy business. The simplest way is not to scratch off the error but to paint over it with white typing correction fluid. Allow it to dry and type over a different carbon area.

The photocopier

No machine has improved more rapidly and become more widely available than the modern photocopier. Most schools now have one, and multiple copies are produced fairly cheaply. They are so convenient that teachers must be aware of the dangers of infringing copyright law (see page 22). They are ideal for copying teachers' own work sheets, etc., though they work out dearer than the spirit duplicator.

If 'banda' masters have been kept for several years they become unusable and have to be recopied onto a new carbon. To avoid doing this it is simply necessary to photocopy the positive side of the master. If the master is lost a perfectly adequate photocopy can be obtained from a duplicated spirit copy.

Blackboard v. whiteboard

The traditional blackboard and chalk is still the standby of most teachers. Dustless chalk has made the task of erasing slightly less hazardous for clothes and lungs but, at the same time, the modern language classroom has filled up with the wonders of modern science listed above and chalk dust is ruinous to all of them.

Any teacher able to design a modern language room should therefore ban the blackboard and substitute a whiteboard which will do no harm to essential hardware. However, care must be taken to protect the whiteboard. Pupils and staff must be warned against using spirit markers which are difficult to erase. Markers left around for staff use quickly disappear and contribute to school graffiti. Erasers do need to be charged with clean water to work. Whose job is it to do this and how do you ensure the water does not get into the cassette player during a moment of horseplay?

One point against the whiteboard is that the surface offers less resistance than does the traditional wooden board and handwriting appears to be more careless. Most whiteboards look very messy at the end of a lesson and it cannot be good to set such an example to children whose books we require to be neat. Practice is needed with these boards. Care at all times. Finally the chisel-edged felt-tip gives a better style to handwriting than the pointed variety.

Better in many ways than either blackboard or whiteboard is the overhead projector (see page 100) and, given the choice, for a modern language room it is by far the best bet.

Display boards

These can be flannelgraph, teaselgraph or plastigraph. All three are inexpensive and surprisingly flexible means of displaying figurines. In the first two the figurines adhere to the nap of the flannel or nylon velvet. In the plastigraph, figurines are cut from plastic sheets and adhere to a plastic base sheet usually white or yellow.

Of the three, the flannelgraph is the most versatile. It can be a blank sheet of flannel onto which figurines are pressed by teacher or pupils. Alternatively it can be a detailed backcloth onto which individual figurines cling and can easily be moved about — into the house, outside the house, near the door, near the window, on the floor, etc. Again backcloths are simple to make by projection of a professional drawing onto a white flannel sheet serving as a screen. Pupils will enjoy elaborating the scene with spirit markers. Figurines are made by the same method. Catalogues for infant schools will often suggest excellent display materials which are easily adapted.

Flashcards

Sets of flashcards, postcard size or slightly larger, can be devised to introduce, reinforce or revise many different linguistic topics. Concrete vocabulary is an obvious area but there is no need to *draw* objects. Excellent illustrations can be cut out of magazines, colour supplements and catalogues. Pictures can be made by projection as above. Collections of cards illustrating verbs — reflexive verbs for practising the use of the Perfect Tense in French, verbs of motion, impersonal weather verbs, verbs with irregular future tenses, etc. A set of flashcards illustrating the events of a story, later to be written up by the class, is another possibility. Number work has to figure frequently in lessons to keep the language active. Flashcards with single numbers, with small sums to do, with dates and prices for items illustrated in the background. Weights and measures can similarly be illustrated. Sets of flashcards are then easily stored in clearly marked individual envelopes and, of course, catalogued.

It is a mistake to think that flashcards are only for beginners and only for staff use. Quite complex structures can be developed, essays can be prepared and many cards can be used in role-playing situations. Cards can also be distributed for very productive group work (see page 48).

Radio and TV

The following categories are of the greatest interest to teachers:

— schools programmes devised for secondary school pupils;
— language programmes for adults such as *Ensemble, Wegweise, Buongiorno Italia* and the *Get by in* . . . series;
— foreign films broadcast in entirety;
— foreign news broadcasts put out by the BBC;
— off-air recordings from foreign stations;
— cassettes of past broadcasts sold by foreign broadcasting stations;
— relevant current affairs programmes largely in English;
— local radio.

These are dealt with below under their separate headings.

For schools the advantages of using broadcast material and of recording it on a regular basis are obvious:

1   Cost is negligible apart from the outlay on tapes and, initially, a time-switch for recordings to be done after school.
2   The most up-to-date material becomes immediately available.
3   A whole new range of voices comes into the classroom.
4   New topics of immediate interest which might well have

escaped the teacher's notice are brought into the lesson.
5   For sixth-formers the more adult presentation make the programmes more appealing.

Schools programmes are put out by both the BBC and ITV. Language programmes, from beginners to sixth form, are available in French and German; Russian and Italian are also covered.

Full details of BBC programmes for schools come from:
   The Schools Broadcasting Council (Annual Programme)
   The Langham
   Portland Place
   London WIA IAA

Also obtainable from the above address is a leaflet giving details of recording conditions.

Details of ITV schools programmes come from:
   The Education Office, The IBA
   Brompton Road
   London SW3 IEY Tel. 01-584-7011

Language programmes for adults will provide very useful classroom material to listen and to watch. In addition to the basic programmes themselves there is now a vast amount of excellent support material in the form of illustrated books with exercises (often self-correcting), notes and sound cassettes of supplementary material not necessarily broad-cast, though the texts themselves will be found in the course books devised to accompany the broadcasts.

Such materials are excellent for supplementing classwork and, in addition, can be safely recommended to pupils wanting extra practice. Sixth-formers whose oral work is not good simply because they have not been abroad will benefit from listening even to the more elementary programmes for, without exception, good native speakers are heard, some of them professionals but many of them men and women 'in-the-street'. When schools do the recording themselves 'off-air', pupils can be encouraged to borrow tapes on a library basis for home use.

A third use served by these more varied further education language courses is that they provide excellent material to recommend to pupils thinking of doing a different language after leaving school. To get an idea of what the language involves, books and tapes might be borrowed from a library. In addition to Italian, Russian and Greek there are Arabic and Chinese courses.

Foreign films: happily these are appearing on TV more than they used to and they are often an excellent source of language and civilization material. However, there are drawbacks. It is very unwise to push a film you have not actually seen yourself, not only because it may contain unsuitable material but, quite simply, it may be a bad film and more harm than good is done by suggesting the wrong things. Again, films date and what may be remembered with affection from twenty-five years ago may now be so dated as to alienate sixth-formers from watching films.

Foreign news broadcasts put out by the BBC. *Télé Journal* and *Heute Direkt* have been very popular with language teachers. The timing is good at 11.00 p.m. since it allows teachers to watch and prepare in order to watch it with classes the following morning at 9.30. Programmes are slightly edited but the material put out is authentic. It is to be hoped that the BBC will continue this experiment. Teachers should write to ask for it.

Off-air recordings from foreign stations can be obtained by asking a friend and colleague abroad to do a recording in his own home from a good VHF source and to post the cassette to the UK. To be effective one needs to give a list of topics to the friend since it is difficult to know what is coming up other than news broadcasts. These, however, are worth having on almost any topic.

Alternatively, teachers who are well placed to pick up sound broadcasts direct can do their own recording. France is obviously the country in the best position to do this from. 'France Inter' on 1829 metres (164 kHZ) on the Long Wave is usually very clear. Close to it on the Long Wave (1647 m; 182 kHZ) is 'Europe I' whose signal is not quite so strong but whose programmes may appeal to teenagers rather more than 'France Inter'.

A useful source of information on French broadcasts is the London Office of *Radio France* (France Inter, France Culture, France Musique), 64/66 Great Portland Street, London W1. This office issues a list of French radio stations with brief details of forthcoming broadcasts. (See also *Quid* under 'Information' for many other details of radio stations and radio frequencies.) Sixth-formers can be encouraged to listen in their own homes to such broadcasts though, regrettably, many cheap transistor radios are not equipped to receive programmes on the Long Wave band. In advising pupils to listen it is important to remind them that they need to develop a listening habit; i.e. it is better to listen for ten minutes every day at the same time than to listen for two hours once a fortnight. They need to become familiar with voices and personalities.

Other radio wavelengths include:

Germany:
   Westdeutscher/Norddeutscher Rundfunk, 309 m. (971 kHZ)
   Deutschlandfunk, 1986 m. (151 kHZ)
   Stimme der DDR, 1621 m. (185 kHZ)

Spain:
   Radio Nacional de España, 512.8 m. (584 kHZ and 439 m, (683 kHZ)

Italy:
   RAI Programma Nazionale, 333 m. (899 kHZ) and 225 m. (1331 kHZ)
   RAI Secondo Programma, 355 m. (845 kHZ)

Russia:

Radio Moscow First Programme. 1734 m. (173 kHZ)
Radio Volga (to the DDR). 1140 m. (263 kHZ)

Cassettes of past broadcasts sold by France Inter. A catalogue of some 500 cassettes is available from:
France Inter
116 Avenue du Pt. Kennedy
75786 Paris Cedex 16
Some of these broadcasts go back to the immediate post-war period.

Current affairs programmes need no explanation. Teachers should always be on the lookout for details of future programmes of relevance to pupils. Having recommended pupils to watch. it is important to follow up the recommendation by asking for comment and opinion on the programme watched or listened to.

Local radio broadcasts. So far as we know there is no local radio station putting out a regular series of language programmes. However. a number of BBC radio stations do take a general interest in local schools programmes and are prepared to help with language programmes if asked to do so. Possibilities include:

1   interviews with foreign assistants living locally (these could be in English and in the mother-tongue);
2   broadcasts of lectures recorded at local sixth-form language days put on by language association or local college or university;
3   broadcasts with 'phone-ins' by local language teachers on examination preparation. material for a language essay. set book talks. doing a prose;
4   broadcasts with 'phone-ins' covering local exchange schemes. Programmes cover advice in English about what to do and where to go with the partner. problems. a competition. 'phone-ins' by both British and foreign partners with messages for others on the exchange.

advice about the return visit of the English. specimen conversations in the language covering situations most likely to arise abroad — introductions. mealtimes. invitations to go out. saying thank you for a trip out (Radio Leeds has many years' experience of this type of programme):

5   broadcasts of foreign carol services organized by local schools.

Teachers interested in developing this aspect of their work should get in touch with the Education Officer at their local BBC radio station to discuss ideas. It is generally found there is great support for such schemes.

One final word on all broadcast material used and that is that the programme must be watched by the teacher before it is used in class. Pupils can then have advance notice of language difficulties and sometimes receive background information which clarifies the programme. The teacher's preview also ensures that the programme is broken down into digestible proportions for use in the classroom. It is helpful to interrupt the recording for questions and discussion to take place at the end of each topic covered by the broadcast.

Many broadcasts obviously make excellent listening comprehension tests but for these to work well there has to be time between the broadcast and the lesson to allow the teacher to prepare a suitable worksheet covering both the subject matter and the language content.

Address for all BBC publications:
  BBC Publications
  PO Box 234
  London SE1 3TH

The video

There are many *advantages* to the video which teachers should be aware of.

1   they bring authentic foreign culture straight into the classroom;
2   expense is not great since the machine will be almost certainly a school machine and tapes charged to the department will not be out of the question since a 3 hour tape available for use over and over again will cost about £5;
3   sound quality is usually better on video than it is on film;
4   video is very convenient to use — no blackouts needed. It is reasonably portable for use in different rooms. It is flexible in use since it can easily be stopped, run back or run rapidly forward;
5   there is no need to disrupt the whole timetable to show a full length film since it can easily be shown in sections in successive lessons;
6   video is a modern medium and therefore appeals to teenagers with a modern outlook.

And there are certain *dangers* too:
1   watching television is such an ingrained habit pupils may quickly allow attention to wander;
2   teachers too may be tempted to use video because it is handy. To avoid this trap it is essential to ensure that pupils are watching to some purpose and not just passively viewing;
3   pupils used to slick professional TV productions may be disenchanted with less sophisticated material.

If the language teacher has any choice in the equipment used it will be wise these days to go for a **VHS** system since this is the one most producers of commercial software are now favouring. Other features to look out for are 'picture search' facility for ease of finding the place on the tape, rapid forward and back wind, clearly displayed tape counter numbers, remote control by cable preferably or by infra-red, frame freeze option which produces a 'still' for class discussion. Single frames can be photographed to make a slide or an OHP transparency can be quickly made by tracing round the outline of the picture with spirit pen.

Software materials are becoming easier to acquire. Much of

the BBC language programmes is ideal for class use and many publishers are now issuing tapes catering for beginners and for more advanced learners. Occasionally programmes in English give excellent background information. For instance the various holiday programmes have splendid shots of local scenery and customs.

Golden rules for the video   The following is a quotation from an excellent article to which we are deeply indebted. For further information on the use of the video in the classroom readers are advised to consult *Uses and abuses of video in teaching German* by Alan G. Jones in *treffpunkt*. June 1984, Vol. 16, No. 2, pp 12–18.

1   Always preview a video before showing it to a class. If necessary, select and edit the sections you wish to use.
2   Give careful thought to the purpose for which you are using the video. What language teaching purpose will it serve?
3   Even when you are using an extended piece of viewing, check from time to time to make sure that the whole class is still with you!
4   Decide in advance what additional material you will want in the way of a. handouts, b. blackboard/OHP support c. audio tape.
5   If necessary, edit onto a second copy the sections of the video which you will want to use. At the very least, make a clear note of the counter number(s) where the various sections of the video start.
6   NEVER treat the video as a soft option in language teaching. That is the surest way to wasting everyone's time.

Future developments in television will include the possibility of receiving continental broadcasts direct. This will open up exciting new possibilities. But we shall only make the most of them if we constantly bear in mind that 'video must be a means to an end and not an end in itself.'

Some useful addresses

The German Film Library, Park Hall Trading Estate, London SE21 8EL. Offers more than 500 shorts and documentaries on free loan.

Hatfield Polytechnic German Centre, PO Box 109, Hatfield, Herts AL10 9AB.

Observer Video Club, PO Box 28 Southwater, Nr Horsham, Kent.

Palace, Virgin and Gold Ltd., 69 Flempton Road, London E10 7NL.

Thames Television Ltd., 149 Tottenham Court Road, London W19 9LL.

The use of 16mm film

Any review of resources available for language teaching cannot omit the 16mm sound projector and the feature films made for the big screen. These days many films are available on video but the TV screen permits only a small audience and a great deal of impact is lost.

Teachers considering using 16mm film will usually find the modern projector is self-threading and marked by the manufacturers to trace the passage of the film through the machine. The only controls to master are on/off, back wind, lamp and focus — hardly any more than a tape-recorder. Many schools, of course, have a technician who will be happy to give instruction or show the film.

Price of hire can be prohibitive for any one school but this is an opportunity to cooperate with other schools in the district for a showing and joint discussion afterwards. Some schools show films in the evening and invite parents and friends to help defray the cost. A hundred people can comfortably watch and listen to a 16mm film using the projector's own speaker. This makes the cost per person very reasonable indeed.

Advantages of using film are, first of all, it is often possible to have 'the film of the book', i.e. a set text, and that is always a money-spinner. Secondly one or two examination boards are introducing onto the A-level syllabus such topics as 'The Cinema in France since 1945' (AEB). In this syllabus the films of Godard and Truffaut are particularly important. Away from the set book area the choice of films can be more difficult as so many continental films are given an 'X' certificate for public showing though the 'X' does not apply to private film club showings. Nonetheless one hopes that teaching staff heed the warnings and at least see the films themselves before ordering an 'X' film for the sixth form. When this does happen teachers report that sixth-formers take the film in their stride. Some schools inform parents of their intention to show an 'X' film and give them the opportunity to say if they do not wish their son or daughter to see it.

Some teachers argue against the use of the film because of their memories of scratchy film giving poor sound quality. This seems to be less of a problem these days as technical improvements have come in. The result is that pupils do undoubtedly benefit linguistically from seeing films, particularly if some kind of preparation has been possible or where, for example, in *Thérèse Desqueyroux* the film sticks closely to the dialogue of the novel.

Sources of films

Most embassies and Cultural Attachés are able to loan films free of charge, but not feature films. The specialists for feature films are:

The British Film Institute
127 Charing Cross Road
London WC2
(write for 'Films on Offer')

Contemporary Films Ltd
55 Greek Street
London W1V 6DB

Harris Films Ltd
Glenbuck Road
Surbiton KT6 6BT
(now has films held by Connoisseur Films)

Mary Glasgow Publications Ltd hire out their own excellent educational films — *Toute la Bande, Entrechaux, Dax, Fête à Coutance, Steig ein nach Oberstdorf.* All details of hire charges from the publishers.

The library

Some schools have the modern language stock in the school library in the care of the librarian while others maintain a departmental library for both pupils and staff. Yet other schools have a system which keeps a foot in both camps.

In the library, whether departmental or school, the following stock should figure:

1 Main reference books:
   dictionaries (bi-lingual and mother-tongue); grammar books; language textbooks; self-correcting exercises; up-to-date year books (e.g. *Quid*)
2 Languages and careers:
   details of language courses beyond sixth form careers books
3 Books on languages in general:
   examples of languages not taught in the school.
4 Literature texts
   set books and works by the same author.
5 Critical works
6 History   }
7 Geography }
   in the language and in English — popular illustrated books and works of scholarship (if not stored in modern languages then reference blocks on shelves should refer to location.)
9 Social sciences
   books in the language relevant to the different countries.

Popular introductions.
10 Graded readers
   ideally one or two copies of every reader currently available in the catalogues.
14 *Bandes dessinées*
12 Pedagogy:
   latest publications on modern language method;
   full and up-to-date set of all language publishers' catalogues; film catalogues; CILT catalogue;
   details of in-service courses.
13 Journals:
   good weekly picture magazine;
   weekly news magazine;
   a newspaper;
   language teaching journals.
14 Cassettes (for library listening with headphones)
   serious programmes, recordings or all material used in sixth form. Also light music, songs and poems.
   Readings from set books, performances of set plays.
15 Travel brochures
16 Applied language texts:
   science books, business and commercial material.

Computers

The new technology so often talked about by colleagues in other disciplines is just beginning to make its presence felt amongst the modern linguists. We hear of machine translation, automatic dictionaries, word processing and speech synthesis. As linguists many of us have kept well away when we should perhaps have been taking a close interest in the new language growing up before our eyes: bits, bytes, bootstraps and bugs, the use of floppy discs and fuzzy matching have invaded the classroom whether we like it or not, and if we fail to bring language learning into this field, our pupils will opt even more positively for those subjects which use the learning techniques they are familiar with.

Fortunately there have been some pioneers who have

investigated CAL (Computer Assisted Learning) and in
particular CALL (Computer Assisted Language Learning)
and a role for the computer is being developed. Very early
experiments began in the 1960s on mainframe computers
(i.e. a large computer serving many terminals at the same
time) but the coming of the microcomputer has brought real
possibilities into home and school. CILT is building up a
research register detailing what sort of individual work is
going on to develop software for use on the micro.

At the moment the microcomputer can be of considerable
assistance with teaching reading, writing and aural skills. It
cannot help with oral work because the voice synthesizer is
not part of the micro. Exercises such as the following are
now possible:

- question and answer dialogues
- gap-filling exercises
- multiple-choice tests
- vocabulary tests
- grammatical drills
- jumbled words and sentences
- games
- mazes

The next stage in the development will involve the use of the
videodisc, which is an entirely new idea in microcomputing
in which, as the name suggests, the disc stores data and TV
pictures at the same time; i.e. a normal TV programme can
be shown and the language learner can choose to see or not
to see the dialogue in subtitles as he listens. Translations can
be called up if needed. Any section can be re-run as often as
the learner needs it in order to grasp the sense. This could
then be followed by a set of tests to enable the learner to
check all that he has learnt. When this becomes available in
the classroom, before very long, language teachers will no
longer be able to dismiss the computer as no more than
'mechanized Whitmarsh'.

The purpose of this section is not to give instruction in the
art of making computer programs but simply to alert

language teachers to the fact that we are dangerously near the back of the list in taking up the computer seriously. Not entirely our fault perhaps, since we have had to wait for the machines themselves to become capable of doing what the linguist reasonably wants them to do. The danger is, however, that we may lag behind too long. To avoid this, linguists will be wise to begin now to explore possibilities, to learn BASIC (Beginners' All-purpose Symbolic Instruction Code) and to seize opportunity to examine available software: *Apfeldeutsch, Atari Conversational French,* German, Spanish and Italian, etc.

In addition there are some excellent introductions to the topic, in particular CILT Information Guide No. 22, *Computers, Language and Language Learning.* See bibliography for further reading and Part 4 for computer acronyms.

Courses, course books and materials

Any work purporting to give an overview of resources for the classroom must refer to the wealth of materials produced regularly for and by teachers to enable them to do the job most effectively and with the most suitable equipment for the courses as they are conceived at any particular time. As philosophies of language learning evolve so the teaching materials must respond to new classroom needs. Anyone looking at a language course book published twenty-five years ago will immediately see the truth of this. Indeed even ten years ago many books were in common use which have now almost totally disappeared from classrooms as pupils' needs have changed.

The rate at which new materials are coming out and old favourites are gradually dropped means in fact that any publication which tries to include everything will be out of date in less than a year. For this reason we have chosen not to attempt to produce any complete lists.

There is also a second reason which dissuades us from

attempting a huge and fruitless task: namely that the work has already been done and is continually being revised and brought up to date by CILT. Consequently any teacher seeking a comprehensive review of teaching materials available including recorded and visual courses, supplementary material, textbooks and grammars, general readers, background readers and vocabularies need only turn to the following books:

Teaching Materials for French
New Teaching Materials for French 1981–82
New Teaching Materials for French 1982–83
New Teaching Materials for French 1983–84
Teaching Materials for German
Teaching Materials for Italian
Teaching Materials for Russian
Teaching Materials for Spanish

These guides are extremely comprehensive and well annotated, giving, in addition to author, title, publisher and date, a simple classification by levels, Level I being for beginners going up to Level 5 — 'for learners working beyond A-level'. In cases where published works have been reviewed in the professional journals, a bibliographical reference is also included.

Finally it should go without saying that every conscientious teacher must keep up with the publishers' catalogues which appear annually. An even more effective method of being fully up-to-date is to attend the annual conference of the language associations which usually takes place in March. At this conference the educational publishers put together the most comprehensive exhibition of the latest teaching materials that can be seen anywhere in the country and probably in Europe. Details of the conference are put out by all the associations and schools are, in addition, circulated directly. See you there!

Human resources: the foreign assistant (FLA)

In the seventies, schools in the UK received annually about 4,500 language assistants. Cuts made in local authority spending have reduced this number to approximately 2,000. The effect has been that many LEAs no longer employ any assistants and most have reduced their numbers considerably. All the more reason, therefore, for using the assistant to the best advantage when we have one. The notes which follow are intended to suggest how to derive maximum benefit from an extremely valuable resource. Details of how to prepare for the assistant's arrival and settling in the school are given in Chapter 16. In this Part we are concerned with his work in the classroom.

Preparation. The assistant must understand from the start the need to prepare beforehand and keep records of what has been done.

Levels. Initially the main difficulty for the assistant is to get a clear idea of what level of French, German or Spanish or Italian he can expect from the pupils. Observation will guide him, but we should also ensure that he has the chance to listen to recordings of oral examinations if possible.

Progress. The assistant should be warned that pupils learning *English* as a foreign language make much more rapid progress in the early days, because of the analytical nature of English and because of the relatively simple basic English grammar — no genders and little agreement.

Wide ability variations need to be talked about as do personality differences. Is the reticent speaker to be left to listen? Should he or she be pushed or ignored? Home difficulties need to be pointed out occasionally.

Correction of error. The assistant should be warned against over-correction, which tends to inhibit contributions. On the other hand, ignoring basic errors does no good whatsoever.

Speed of delivery. It is wise to warn the assistant not to speak at the speed he would use with a similar group of native speakers. This certainly applies down the school and even in the sixth form for many pupils. The assistant should understand that speed is not the most essential acquisition. All foreign speakers have at some time to ask a native speaker to slow down until they reach near-native speed themselves. Much more important than speed is the acquisition of a range of expression — vocabulary, idiom and established forms of speech (*Ils sont sages comme des images*), which one only learns from the native speaker.

Problems to be encountered. It is a great help to the assistant if the language teacher goes over the problems he is likely to meet in the classroom. The following headings may be helpful to guide a staffroom chat:

1 Behaviour — what to do if it is not good.
2 Lateness to classes — report to the class teacher.
3 Failure to prepare — report to class teacher.
4 Failure to attend — report to class teacher.
5 Learning difficulties. Each assistant should understand that his language presents particular problems to an English speaker:

   (a) *Pronunciation* the 'u' in French and the 'ü' in German, for example. Each language has its own pitfalls and these may never have occurred to the native speaker. The assistant should be encouraged to give a few minutes' practice at the start of the lesson to a particular pronunciation problem, e.g. the nasals in French. In Spanish, *b*, *d* and *v* will repay some attention.

   (b) *Gender* practice will help. So will the giving of rules, e.g. 'All words ending in "ment" are masculine except "la jument"'. But warn against too much practice, as it will inhibit fluency.

   (c) *Numerals* are a real source of problems for foreign speakers. Do encourage regular doses of arithmetic, multiplication, addition, etc., as well as dates and telephone numbers.

   (d) *Questions.* Remind the assistant that the foreigner abroad needs to *ask* questions more often than he

answers them. The assistant therefore should
ensure that every lesson affords the opportunity for
pupils to put questions either to the assistant *or* to
his fellow pupils. It is helpful for the assistant to do
exercises in putting questions, particularly collo-
quial forms which are widely used orally but not so
common in the written form. For example the
assistant says: 'A quelle heure est-ce que tu
partiras?' and the pupil replies 'Tu partiras quand?'
(e) *Tenses.* Practice with tenses is essential and fortunately such practice can take the form of games.
For example, the assistant says what *he* is doing.
Pupil A has to say what he did yesterday, and pupil
B what he will do tomorrow.

Authentic materials. Reference will have been made to the
need to ask assistants to bring authentic materials with
them, but guidance will be needed on what to do with such
materials. The following points will be helpful:

1 *Postcards.* Show the postcard to the class, explain what it
is, but always insist on a reply from the pupils in return:
say what the picture represents then question the group:
'Where do you think it is?', 'How far is it from Vienna?'
Then hand the card to a pupil to do a presentation to the
class. Any type of picture will serve for this.
2 *Mail-order catalogues.* These are not just to look at. They
can be used for imaginary shopping expeditions for
example involving comparisons: 'This is bigger than,
more expensive than . . .' It can involve number work.
Each pupil has 33 Deutschmark to spend and they can
choose and explain their purchases.
3 *Telephone directories.* Pupils look up telephone numbers
and say them to each other. They read and discuss the
introductory pages on emergency calls, etc.
4 *The Highway Code.* Pupils look at the details and say
what they *would* do (use of Conditional) at all the various
signs. The subject can lead on to driving, how to drive,
road safety, accidents, what to do in case of accidents
abroad, being a witness and answering questions.

5   *Newspapers, journals, comics.* All to be looked at, but more important to be talked about. For example pupils could 'interview' the main character in a story. In the sixth form a comparison of several versions of the same story would be instructive.

6   *Official forms.* If the assistant will plunder local post offices, etc., a large number of useful forms will provide excellent role-play material.

7   *Maps.* Town-plans from the local tourist office provide extensive work for pupils at all levels — direction-finding is just one way to exploit the material. The use of geographical maps of the country is very important, firstly because pupils need to be familiar with the location of the main regions and cities, and secondly because practice with the names of places can be important to the traveller.

Songs. It is important to warn the assistant against becoming known as the one who does nothing but play records. Songs are learnt in schools for sound pedagogical reasons as well as for pleasure. The song should be chosen carefully for its language content, the clarity of the singer's voice, and possibly the subject matter. The class should listen to the song and the assistant ask simple questions about it. Then work begins. The assistant does a vocabulary/grammar study of the song, commenting on detail and whenever possible asking pupils to supply synonyms for the actual words used. To round off this part of the work the pupils receive a printed copy of the words (NB not first). The assistant then reads the words and the class follow. The record/tape can then be heard again and pupils may even join in. Finally the pupils may learn a verse or two and exercises may be brought in (e.g. 'fill the gap' exercises). This sort of activity may well be tried in the 'language club'.

Help with composition. The assistant may often be asked to help with essay planning in the sixth form. To do this most effectively, he must encourage the group to talk around the subject, to pass ideas from one person to another, possibly based upon a text or texts used in class. Equally important is his role as provider of appropriate language. In any discussion on 'Atomwaffen' the sixth former is not short of opinion to express but he *is* short of the language whch will permit him to express these ideas. Here the assistant is very useful.

Below the sixth form the assistant can also help, with an equally valuable contribution to fourth and fifth year work in this field, confining attention to simple details, e.g. tenses. (From the study of horoscopes future tenses can be used and practised; from the 'Courrier du Coeur' the conditional can be exploited — 'What would you do if...?') Very important is the idea of structure in an essay, and most assistants are well versed in this. They bring the ideal antidote to 'splurge-type' essay writing which so many sixth-formers mistake for composition.

Finally, it is worth remembering that the assistant will have a better idea of the problems of pupils and what he needs to do, if he is involved in the correction of essays. (See page 127).

Spelling and the alphabet
1   The assistant should be asked to make sure that every class he teaches knows the alphabet in his language.
2   Spelling 'bees' should be frequent and can fill in the last few minutes of the lesson.
3   Every pupil should be able to spell his name in the language without hesitation.
4   Making up other words from one long one such as *prestidigitateur* or *anticonstitutionellement* involves calling out letters.
5   Crosswords are good group activities. Plenty of collections are available. Alternatively, a crossword can be devised on the blackboard, then copied and circulated for another group to attempt.

Sixth-form literature. The assistant may help with this in several ways, but teachers will be wise to ensure first that there is a real willingness to help in this task. A negative approach from a less than enthusiastic exponent is likely to counteract the teacher's approach. If the assistant is agreeable it is a good thing to give him time to read the book carefully, and, if possible, discuss it with the teacher. The main thing is to avoid a duplication of the literature class. Examples of activities:

1   Class reading of key scenes from a play — assistant corrects pronunciation and asks for comments on character, motivation, etc.
2   Class discussion on certain roles — the parts to be taken by the class, i.e. character defends his/her action in the first person.
3   Class reads and discusses other works by the same author.
4   Discussion of topics from past examination papers.
5   Quiz of the 'Who said . . .?' kind or 'What did X do to Y?' or after reading a silent extract, 'Tell me what happens next.'
6   *Narration*. After reading an extract the class retells the events in the first person.
7   The class listens to a recording of an extract and discusses the interpretation offered by the actors.

Having said this, we recognize that many teachers have perfectly valid reasons for not involving the assistant in teaching literature.

Civilization topics. As the A-level syllabuses change and greater importance is assumed by 'civilization' elements, the assistant will play an increasingly important role in updating vital information. The following suggestions are intended not just for use in the sixth form, though they are all possible there. It is hoped, however, that skilful treatment of these and similar topics will provide a stimulus which may encourage some pupils to want to continue their language(s) in the sixth form.

1   *Assistant's home and home town* as a microcosm of the nation. The assistant talks and presents illustrations of all kinds and insists that the class gives back all they learn. Some individuals write to the Tourist Bureau of

the town being studied. Other places to write to include the local newspaper (follow up promising adverts), the town hall, *mairie*, *Rathaus*, Chamber of Commerce, town twinning bureau.

2   *Schools.* Not a talk on 'Education in West Germany' or 'Educational Policy in Barcelona' but 'The school I went to and what I did'. Assistant shows books, primary readers, marked exercises, etc. Class asks questions as well as replying.

3   *Major industries.* Cars, 'haute couture', wine, electronics, etc. Assistant collects examples of publicity, etc. Some class members could write for information.

4   *The capital city.* History, geography and growth. Involves slide show with commentary.

5   *Youth activities. Colonies de vacances, classes de neige,* scouting, religious and political movements.

6   *The role of women* in X. Some talk from the assistant but this will stimulate class response.

7   *Language varieties* within the community. This leads to a discussion on whether schools should standardize speech.

8   *Food*: regional specialities. Pictures and recipes. Some class members asked to bring recipes. For the end of term why not sample a delicacy by courtesy of Home Economics colleagues.

Involving the assistant in school. As stated earlier, we should do our best to make the assistant feel he or she is fully a part of the school community. The following suggestions will, it is hoped, contribute to that aim:

1   *Marking.* Here we distinguish between marking and assessing. All parties benefit if the teacher and the assistant read the pupils' work together. The teacher updates his knowledge, the pupil gains from the authentic suggestions made to him by the assistant, and finally the assistant himself gains by acquiring a firsthand knowledge of what his pupils are capable of. The *evaluation* of the work is, however, entirely the teacher's responsibility.

2 *Preparation for visits abroad.* Exchange visits should be a
   high priority on the department's list of activities.
   Preparation is vital and the help of the assistant should
   be sought.
3 *Preparation of teaching materials.* All good teachers
   concoct new material for teaching or testing and the
   assistant will be ideal as consultant.
4 *Modern Language Days.* Assistants can make a valuable
   contribution to these activities.
5 *Language evening for parents.* If the assistant is invited,
   real authenticity is guaranteed. Such meetings can also
   result in invitations for assistants to visit homes.
6 *The choir.* A carol service puts the modern language
   department in good light if there are one or two foreign
   carols and even bible readings in other languages. The
   assistant can help to train performers.

Don'ts for the assistant

It may be helpful to the assistant if the regular class teacher
says at the beginning what he or she should *not* do if the class
is to have good, effective and worthwhile lessons.

1 Don't lecture on any subject, i.e. ensure that the class
   contributes.
2 Don't give the impression that you don't care if pupils
   come or pay little attention.
3 Don't allow pupils to cause major distractions which
   demand lengthy use of English.
4 Don't allow time-wasting.
5 Don't ask pupils to do things that are way beyond
   them.
6 Don't ask pupils to speak at length on subjects without
   preparation.
7 Don't mimic a pupil's attempts.
8 Don't over-correct a pupil as this may inhibit.
9 Don't play records/tapes every lesson.
10 Don't expect pupils to be very knowledgeable about
   institutions in your country.
11 Don't be disappointed if pupils don't seem very interested

in politics or film as an art-form.

Do's

While the class teacher lists the above points, it is essential to be positive as well. It will be worth stressing the following:

1 Cultivate a good attitude — pleasant with a serious attitude to work in general and the language in particular.
2 Develop a good voice and manner for public speaking — one which expresses confidence and which is not monotonous. If the class seems lost, *slow down*.
3 Prepare material carefully.
4 Present material effectively. Don't use all the best material in the first few minutes.
5 Learn names as quickly as possible — use labels or name-cards.
7 Conclude the lesson by telling the class what will happen next time. If a topic is to be prepared, give some guidance and help.

Outside the language class

Finally it is worth underlining the fact that many assistants may be able to make valuable contributions to the classes of other colleagues outside languages. History, geography and European Studies are three obvious examples, but there may be others such as home economics who would welcome the occasional contribution. The best way to bring this about is to encourage other colleagues to invite the assistants to their lessons, in the first instance mainly as a way of improving their English. From this, spontaneous offers can come from the assistants.

Miscellaneous resources (Things to make, do and collect.)

Visual aids can be made which illustrate those things and

actions not available and not demonstrable in the classroom. It is a waste of time and resources to draw hands, faces, figures, walking, etc.

When abroad make an effort to collect: old telephone directories (they are excellent for number practice and also ensure all pupils know how to use one); post office forms; car showroom literature; tourist leaflets; food packets (useful for role-playing); posters from cinemas, supermarkets; timetables from railway and bus stations (good for number and role-playing); shop window dressing — pictures of foods, plastic fruits; pictures from photographers' shops and, especially, those life-size Kodak cardboard girls (much better than a vocabulary list for teaching parts of the body!).

Calendars and diaries are useful for many purposes. Out-of-date ones can be bought very cheaply after June each year. Look in the supermarkets in early August. The language room must have a current calendar too. Old calendars can be collected from sympathetic or bemused friends abroad and the illustrations are often excellent for regional studies.

Catalogues of all kinds are worth hoarding. Mail-order catalogues are particularly good for number work, everyday vocabulary, role-playing and general arousal of interest in things from across the Channel. Seed catalogues, furniture catalogues are also excellent classroom material.

Old magazines preferably well illustrated ones are invaluable. They provide cut-outs to make figurines and flashcards and they are ideal five-minute fillers. Magazines specializing in television programmes (*Télé 7 Jours* in France) arouse a great deal of interest and amusement amongst keen TV viewers here.

Children's indoor games no longer wanted by the French or German family who bought them will have an extended useful life if brought into the classroom. In France there is a jigsaw puzzle in which each piece is a *department*. All the well-known English games are available but a hotel in the rue de Rivoli sounds different.

School stationery purchased abroad has a special appeal. If all department notices are put up on French squared paper they will always be recognized. Some pupils like to use it too. It is worth encouraging them to do so and makes a cheap and different present to be brought back by those able to go abroad.

Maps, town plans and out-dated red Michelin guides are all ideal material for group work/role-playing. Finding your way around, following directions, interpreting the Michelin symbols, booking a hotel room are all essential tasks pupils must learn to perform.

Stamps do not seem to have the appeal they once had but a subscription to the Philatelic Bureau of the country whose language you teach will provide advance information on new issues which makes excellent wall display material.

Car number plates. To arouse the interest of the car fanatics a collection of these from abroad is fairly easy to assemble. French and German friends are happy (though puzzled) to hand on old plates and they can be removed quite easily from derelict wrecks. With a column of *plaques minéralogiques* to refer to, France's local government comes to life. Belgian plates are impossible to obtain legally but the characteristic red figures on a white plate can be bought very cheaply in any car supermarket and anybody's number copied.

Food is of primary interest and a wonderful collection of pictures of food, menus from restaurants, recipes, etc., can quickly be assembled. Again magazines are an excellent source of pictures.

Pupils' hobbies can be reflected in collections made. The crazes for CB radio and computers have produced as much specialist literature abroad as in the UK. Interest in fashion is easily catered for, especially by importing the teenage magazines. Sports in general are well covered by the press — football especially. Why not ask two or three pupils to maintain an up-to-date chart of First Division football results in France? Results on *France Inter* every Sunday evening. The programme can be recorded and the cassette passed on for the pupils to decode.

Animals are a frequent source of interest. Guide books to zoos. Books on horses and dogs are common. Magazines about animals are popular with younger children.

The aim of building up collections of the kind outlined above is pedagogic in that some useful teaching material is made available at no financial cost, though friends abroad may well occasionally question one's sanity. At the same time the interest value is very high when material is put on display. With display material the actual language content may be minimal but the insight it gives our pupils into the everyday ways of our European neighbours makes all the effort worthwhile.

The psychological impact of all this should not be overlooked. Pupils should be invited to help with displays. Often contributions are volunteered when it is realized what the teacher wants and it is certainly worth asking for help.

It sometimes works well if pupils are given advance notice of a display, or of a need for particular pictures. 'Next week I shall need a poster with ten photos of differently coloured cars. Who can make one?' 'Who can bring me pictures of people brushing their teeth, washing their hair, putting on make-up, scratching their chins, getting sun-burnt?' Even a 'banda'd' list of pictures sought would be a good idea to get class cooperation, class involvement and, hence, class interest.

Finally when it comes to taking down the old display and putting up the new one, who better to help than the pupils who have contributed? The important thing is that wall space should be well used with eye-catching display that is frequently changed. Encourage pupils to get into the habit of actually looking at what is on show. A weekly competition is a good way of arousing interest. If it is well displayed. Newspaper cuttings on topics of interest are another. For a development of this theme readers will find *Using Authentic Resources*, edited by Barry Jones, CILT 1984, gives many imaginative suggestions.

9 The sixth form

It is in the sixth form that so many problems concerned with modern language teaching come together and in this chapter we shall consider the most important of these and note the solutions already available or those proposed for the future.

The students

It has become the fashion in recent years to speak of 'the new sixth', meaning by this the much broader intellectual range the sixth-form teacher is required to provide for as post-16 education becomes increasingly necessary.

As a result we have sixth-formers who fall into the following categories:

1 the traditional student doing two, three or more A-levels, having come into the sixth with a respectable number of O-levels;
2 students doing mixtures of O-levels plus one A-level;
3 students intending to leave at the end of the lower sixth;
4 students starting an *ab initio* language;
5 students preparing for examinations conducted by examining bodies other than the GCE boards;
6 adult students 'dropping-in' to do say, one A-level.

Whatever their background the language teacher has to
beware of thinking of them as sixth-formers from the word
'go'. Usually they are fifth-formers of two months ago and
some, if not all, are none too sure of themselves. They will
need an 'induction course' to initiate them into the mysteries
of sixth-form work. (See below.)

Organization

Not only has the number and type of sixth-formers
increased over recent years, but also the type of establishment in which they are taught may have changed. This will
depend largely on the pattern of sixth-form work chosen by
the LEA:

1   a conventional sixth in the same building as lower
    forms;
2   a conventional sixth serving as a consortium for a group
    of schools;
3   a sixth-form or tertiary college;
4   an FE college.

The induction course

Methods may vary according to the kind of establishment in
which the teacher works but nevertheless the wise sixth-
form teacher will ensure that whatever the background and
past experience of the students it will be very helpful to
initiate them into methods of working in the sixth.

Study skills

The ultimate goal is to produce students who are capable of
working by themselves effectively so that they are ready for
the next stage in their development whether it is in higher
education or in the world of work. For the language student
we suggest the following study skills need to be fostered:

1   Reading to some purpose: for this a programme of guided reading needs to be evolved which will require the student to find and evaluate information.

2   To achieve success in (1) the student has to acquire the skill of questioning what he reads and reaching his own conclusions. This will come about only if we avoid 'feeding answers' such as were often provided by the old literary histories.

3   Dictionary use is a vital skill for sixth-form studies, and useful exercises can be set which will require the student to read carefully before selecting a word, e.g. looking for synonyms and antonyms, taking an English word such as *what* to find out how many different translations are possible. Work with bi-lingual dictionaries and FL dictionaries with definitions in the language is essential.

4   Specialist dictionaries and reference grammars should also be properly introduced, e.g. dictionaries of proverbs, dictionaries of difficulties, with tasks assigned, will ensure that students become familiar with these works.

5   Reference books such as *Quid* should quickly become friends and this is best done by setting assignments such as comparing basic details about towns or countries, or by requiring the student to find out the meaning of acronyms well established in the foreign language.

Study habits

In addition to the process of familiarization with the tools of the trade there are habits of work which the students should be encouraged to develop:

1   Listening habits. Encourage students to have a regular listening time to the foreign radio. If this is too remote or if the material is unsuitable for any reason, the provision of cassettes for home listening is equally effective and probably easier to control.

2   Reading habits. Unless we take magazines and news-papers into the classroom and show students what is in these publications they are unlikely to be read. It is worthwhile spending fifteen minutes a week going

through the papers and handing out papers with requests for brief summaries to be presented orally in class.

3   School library. Students will not be confident in the library unless they are shown what is available. Half an hour in the library at the start of the course is time well spent.

5   Local resources — a visit to public libraries, to the local reference library will pay off later. If there is a good working relationship with a local college or university it may be possible for sixth-formers to work in the library even if they are unable to borrow books.

5   Habits of study should already be well fixed but they may not be. It is therefore our duty to foster habits of regular study by setting and marking work on a regular basis.

6   Coupled with (5) is the need to teach students how to take criticism constructively. To do this there does have to be a regular discussion with individuals about standards of work.

7   Revision skills should not be neglected. In the present A-level where separate set texts are taught it is wise to require students to return to work already covered to revise it for a test.

General attitude

All the above might well be labelled the bread and butter of all sixth-form instruction, but without it the average student will not get far and this is why we advocate some kind of induction course at the start of the sixth form. Perhaps more difficult to inculcate are the right attitudes to language study. Here it is not so much a matter of *precept* as of *manner*. Right attitudes are contagious and the keen sixth-form language teacher can pass on almost imperceptibly his or her enthusiasm for the subject:

1   creating opportunity to hear, better still, to speak the foreign language;

2   setting oneself translation problems when one suddenly

hears an English phrase: it may be silly (His candyfloss
is next to the fire hydrant!) or it may be a grammatical
teaser;
3   taking a general interest in the happenings in the foreign
country — political, social, artistic, etc.

Examination syllabuses

To cater for the much wider range of needs of sixth-formers
we can now offer a wide range of courses, which we
summarize here to remind ourselves of the possibilities
open to us. The important thing of course is that not only
should the language teachers be aware of the existence of
such variety but also pupils and parents need to be well
informed long before the pupils enter the sixth form. This is
why a department booklet listing courses available is so
essential. Good advertising down the school will produce
viable groups.

Advanced Level. There is no need to describe a syllabus which
in its broad lines has existed since 1918, for despite the
coming of taped comprehension and one or two other
variants there is no denying that prose composition,
translation and set texts going back to the seventeenth
century have been the sixth-form staple diet for almost
seventy years. Nevertheless things are changing and before
long it is likely that we shall see a new A-level which
emphasizes different skills, which relies on authentic
materials in a wide range of registers and which, therefore,
builds on the skills effectively taught for the examinations at
16+. New syllabuses will soon appear and while literary
studies will probably not disappear totally, the type of
exercise which requires long discussion in English, almost
certainly will. New content areas from other than literary
spheres will provide the substance of much discussion and
enquiry. To operate such an ambitious and imaginative
scheme will of course entail much new work for us and
perhaps more than a few in-service courses.

Institute of Linguists: Grade II: this examination is often said to be of roughly the same standard as A-level and a number of colleges will accept a Grade II pass in a language as equivalent to A-level for entry on a language course. For some, the attraction has been that there is little or no compulsory literature but there are other subjects for which a considerable depth of knowledge is required to pass. Until recently the examination has been a bigger favourite with FE colleges than it has with schools but things are now changing. Syllabus details are available from the Institute of Linguists (see Addresses).

The Royal Society of Arts organizes vocational and non-vocational language examinations. There is now a new series of examinations 'designed to reflect the recent emphasis on communicative language learning and testing'. Stage II is 'rather above O-level' and Stage III is defined as 'rather above A-level'. There are translation, essay and oral tests. In addition there are Languages for Business. Examinations are offered in French, German, Italian and Spanish.

The Business and Technician Education Council (BTEC) validates language courses proposed by institutions. As the name clearly indicates, courses will be of a vocational nature: 'The emphasis is on realistic *use* of authentic material through asignments and tasks for communicative purposes, rather than on conventional language exercises.' Examinations are criterion-referenced, e.g. 'Make a telephone call to leave a message on behalf of a third party,' or 'Take a telephone message on behalf of a third party and report in writing in English.'

Foreign Languages at Work (FLAW) The London Chamber of Commerce and Industry runs FLIC (Foreign Languages for Industry and Commerce) and roughly 2,000 people a year do the examination. From this has grown the new proposal suggested jointly by the LCCI and the British Overseas Trade Board (BOTB), the Foreign Languages at Work Scheme (FLAW). Here again teachers propose syllabuses for adoption and aims are defined as skills to be acquired. The most exciting aspect of this scheme is that it is specifically aimed at pupils who would otherwise drop their language in the sixth form. Full details are obtainable from the London Chamber of Commerce and Industry (see Addresses).

GCE: AO As the FLAW Examination above, AO examinations are conceived for those who have elected to do other A-level subjects but wish to keep up a language. Syllabuses can be devised by individual establishments and proposed for validation. Many such proposals make very economical use of time, allowing students to join with some A-level classes and requiring them to work on their own with minimum staff time involved.

Intermediate Level Examinations or I-level. The MLA has published proposals in view of the immense number of sixth-formers 'who have no real opportunity to pursue their foreign language studies'. The aim would be not to produce a watered-down version of an A-level but to offer a different opportunity for placing 'a clear emphasis on the skills of reading, listening and speaking... and on a systematic study of one or more aspects of the foreign civilisation concerned'.

General Studies Some General Studies syllabuses require students to do reading comprehension tested by multiple choice questions. Though very limited in scope it is a gesture to modern languages. We would, however, much prefer to see the development of such schemes as those outlined above.

O-level repeats Every sixth form has the problem of coping with pupils who wish to resit a failed O-level language. Timetabling is a headache and often the only possible solution is to fit the candidates into as many fifth-form lessons as possible and to require extra written practice to be regularly submitted.

Links with other subjects

An important attitude to foster is one which ceases to see

modern languages as a subject apart from other school activities. Instead we would hope that more and more of our pupils and our colleagues would come to see languages as a skill which can enhance other subjects. To this end we consider it important to seek to involve other colleagues in sixth-form classes which have direct links with other areas on the curriculum — history and geography are obvious links and so too are the various literary movements that are reflected in the different languages.

Preparing for beyond the sixth form

All sixth-form teachers should have in mind what the aims and ambitions of their students are. For those who have none we should try to provide some! The following are possible ways of arousing interest beyond the sixth:

- talks on languages other than those taught in school;
- careers talks done by modern language staff and others;
- visiting speakers (former pupils, college lecturers, industrialists, etc.);
- organized visits to universities and polytechnics to hear about languages.

Visits abroad

The sixth-former has almost certainly outgrown the school party unless one or two go as escorts. Generally it is far better to get them to go abroad under their own steam. The following ways are possibilities:

- exchanges;
- au pair posts;
- visit to reside in a school for a week or two;
- working holidays offering unskilled labour, though grape-picking is too late.

See *Volunteer Work Abroad* Central Bureau for Educational Visits and Exchanges (CBEVE).

Useful contacts

The assistant can become a real friend to the more mature sixth-form members. This is well worth encouraging as both parties can benefit from such a contact.

Students should be encouraged to seek out every opportunity to attend conferences, study days, plays and films in the foreign language. Many excellent sixth-form days are organized by local universities and colleges.

Some sixth-formers benefit from being asked to help with pupils lower down the school. They effectively consolidate their own sometimes shaky grammar and benefit also from additional self-confidence acquired from teaching someone else how to do something. In some schools, this practice has been developed as a major teaching technique and it is capable of extensive application.

10 Five-minute fillers and end of term treats

Every lesson probably has a five-minute 'corner' into which the discerning teacher can tuck a language activity which will

- provide a bridge between one main activity and another;
- provide a well needed change of activity;
- relax the class or permit more noise when noisy activities are going on in adjacent rooms;
- get over a difficult patch (e.g. after a 'ticking-off');
- provide very necessary extra practice in an area which needs constant revision (e.g. numbers, counting);
- introduce pupils to an activity well worth doing in itself but unrelated to the tightly structured course in use.

In addition such activities can be very welcome when, for unforeseen reasons, the planned lesson has to be abandoned (unexpected room change, timetable rearrangement, tape recorder or projector breaks down). Or again substitutions for absent colleagues are a daily problem. Here is something to do which does not interfere with the normal course of the lessons planned by the absent colleague. Finally we have all occasionally got through our material more quickly than we thought possible and switched on this kind of activity at a moment's notice.

This last point is the main characteristic of the true 'five-minute filler'. It can be turned to quickly and little or no special material is required to make the thing go.

Games

1 *Jacques a dit* (using imperatives but the command is only to be obeyed when preceded by 'Jacques a dit . . .').
2 *I spy* . . . .
3 *I am thinking of* . . . (description can be simple or complex).
4 *Where is the* . . .? (a Hunt the Thimble game).
5 Spelling games:
   Spelling Bee (easy word but names of letters in foreign alphabet to be used.)
   Word chain: choose a letter, go round the class giving other words beginning with the same letter.
   Anagrams: teacher puts anagrams on OHP or pupils each have to make an anagram.
   Word formation: how may words from one long word?
   Hangman: do not allow letters to be called out at random — pupils take it in turns.
6 Counting games:
   Bingo (does need equipment)
   Counting round the class (backwards and forwards)
   Cocorico: every 3 or multiple of 3 is dropped and 'Cocorico' substituted. Wrong number and the pupil is 'out'; an elimination game for staggered departures.
   Arithmetic: little sums to do mentally: answer in the language.
   Number recognition: fill the board with random numbers. Pupil has to give the number pointed to.
7 Memory games:
   Grandma went to market: and there she bought . . . Good for vocabulary revision.
   What do you see in the picture? or *on the tray?* Two minutes to look then class calls out (Kim's Game).
8 Question games:
   Twenty Questions
   What's my Line?
   Yes, No (the two words which must never be used). Pupils question one individual about anything. Must not reply 'Yes' or 'No'. Must survive one minute.

Whispers —passing a sentence down a line. Sentence becomes distorted. 'What we want is efficient ships' becomes 'What we want is fish and chips.'

Matchsticks (for groups) Pupil arranges matchsticks into a pattern. Stands a book up to conceal it. Pupils who can't see have to make the same pattern based on information obtained by questioning. (With cuisenaire rods colours can be involved too.)

Crosswords — blank diagram put on board or OHP. Pupils add the words (and the clues).

9 Talking games:

Tongue-twisters

Counting out rhymes

Opposites — teacher says a word, pupil says the opposite.

Animal noises — hear the noise say the animal.

Riddles

A Quiz — on the country and the language.

10 Drawing games:

What is it? Pupil thinks of an object and gives one fact about it (e.g. 'C'est un animal.'). He then draws one line to begin a picture of it and asks 'What is it?' Any pupil who can tell (or guesses) scores 10 points for his team. If no one guesses, pupil says 'I add...' and again asks 'What is it?'. Correct guess scores 9. Game continues down to one.

What's the difference? Banda'd pictures almost the same.

11 Commercial games:

Monopoly is available in all main languages. Good for a long session at the end of term.

Cluedo: as Monopoly. Certainly not a five-minute game.

Départements jigsaw. Learn where every department in France is. (For up to four pupils.)

Card Games — Happy Families and similar. Again for the end of term.

Class discussions

For the odd five minutes, every now and again, teachers will find it very useful to invite a general discussion in English on topics concerned with languages and language learning. The following are simply a few suggestions and teachers will easily add many others:

1 Why do you think we learn languages?
2 What can you do with languages? Careers.
3 How can we make language classes interesting?
4 What have you learnt from this week's lessons? Today's lesson?
5 How can the teacher best help you to improve?
6 What do you like least/most about German?
7 Who has been to France/Germany? Tell us about it.
    Why do we have different attitudes to different nations? The traditional view of the French, the Germans, etc. Are they fair descriptions?
9 How do other nations see the British?
10 Books to look for in the library.
11 What is a foreign accent? Does it matter?
12 What are the qualities of a good linguist?

Professor Hawkins' book *Awareness of Language: An Introduction* makes many more similar suggestions.

Songs

It may be that songs appeal mainly to younger pupils though if a good tradition of singing is built up in the lower school it is possible to continue, possibly with a choir or in cooperation with a music colleague. If we fail to provide our pupils with this rich traditional background of culture then, to that extent, we are selling them short.

Songs should be taught properly. They are not a means of passing an easy twenty minutes. They must justify their place on the timetable and this they can do easily on clear pedagogic grounds:

— pupils are helped to improve accent and intonation;
— some vocabulary is acquired painlessly;
— pupils have an insight into tradition and/or popular culture;
— those not particularly gifted linguistically may have the opportunity to shine because of musical talents.

A serious attempt to teach a song does not admit the mere playing of pop records. This is probably always fatal anyway, for the sophisticated pop experts of today will have nothing but scorn for what they may think is your taste or, worse, what all French, Germans or Spaniards like.

For the above reason it is far better to choose a traditional song with an 'everlasting' tune and words which are not too complicated nor too contaminated with Anglo-American. Some modern *chansonniers* also fall into this category (e.g. Guy Béart, Brassens). Such traditional songs have often survived for centuries and must have something which makes people like them.

There are many collections of traditional songs which teachers can buy in the UK, and an even richer choice is to be found in the bookshops abroad. There are, in addition, plenty of records and tapes which colleagues in schools abroad could be persuaded to send in exchange for English equivalents.

As Christmas approaches, teach carols. The MLA Carol Book (available from Central Office) contains the words to about sixty carols in all the main languages. Music is obtainable separately.

Teach rounds, drinking songs, story songs and traditional nursery songs, which often sound particularly attractive when presented on record with a modern orchestration. Some student songs may also be usable with older classes, though obviously common sense has to reign here.

Method

First listen to the song once or twice. Explain briefly (in the

language) what the song is about. For musical accompaniment either enlist the aid of a talented pupil or persuade a
colleague to play or, play a recording on disc or tape or, play
the guitar yourself. Then say the words and look at them on
OHP transparency or banda'd sheet. Choral repetition is
needed and it is essential to keep the rhythm of the song by
pronouncing in French the normally mute 'e'. Clarify any
problems of comprehension and once satisfied that the
pronunciation is acceptable encourage the class to join in.
Good results will be obtained only if the teacher shows
energy and concern. The song needs to be conducted, not
mildly tolerated. Once fixed, songs become part of classroom
life and ideal 'five-minute fillers' — but they are not so to
start with! Two useful collections are: *Jeunesse qui chante* and
1000 chants which give songs from many countries. (See
bibliography.)

11 Emergency Lessons

Emergency lessons fall into three categories:
- cover for the languge teacher's absence;
- cover for a colleague's absence;
- cover to deal with the unexpected.

1   When a teacher knows he is going to be absent for any reason it is normal to leave appropriate work for a class to do. This is not strictly speaking an emergency lesson. Nevertheless some of the suggestions below may be of use at such times.

The first advice we would give is that it is always possible to be prepared for an emergency by holding a stock of material which can be brought out at short notice which will prevent pupils wasting their time. The following are possibilities:

(a) sets of readers stored according to year: magazines are also possible;
(b) sets of worksheets on specific topics for vocabulary or grammar revision; word searches are especially useful;
(c) sets of comprehension passages with questions for reading comprehension;
(d) sets of past examination papers stored according to year;
(e) tapes or cassettes for a substitute to put on;
(f) recordings for sixth-formers to listen to on their own from Exeter Tapes and similar on set texts.

(g) recordings made of speakers at sixth-form days on prose techniques, exam techniques and set books.

Any of the above can take place *in the absence* of a language teacher.

2   If a language teacher is able to cover for a fellow linguist all the above are possible and, in addition, the following apply:

(a) All the five-minute fillers referred to in Chapter 10 are capable of being extended if necessary.
(b) A set of OHP slides for essay work provides immediate work.
(c) A set of colour slides on the towns of . . . make an excellent talk.
(d) A unit of appropriate standard from a disused audio-visual course makes a refreshing change.
(e) A talk on language — how languages change, why words change their meaning and form. Comparison with English.

3   The unexpected is usually due to mechanical failure or sudden changes in the timetable.

(a) OHP breaks down — go back to chalk and talk.
(b) Tape recorder breaks down — read from the script.
(c) Change of timetable means pupils have no books. Use OHP/tapes and issue scrap paper to write on.
(d) Vital notes left at home: quick test of yesterday's work with assurance afterwards marks will not be taken in. Finish lesson by using five-minute fillers. And don't do it again.

12 Answering the difficult questions

Every teacher has to face questions from time to time about his subject, its rationale, aims and objectives, methods and results. Such questions may come formally from the governing body and in the years to come, as governors become more influential, this will grow. On other occasions parents will quite rightly put the same sort of questions, perhaps at a parents' evening. Finally, and not infrequently, pupils will themselves question the teacher on why they have to learn languages at all, why this particular one and what will they get out of it.

The wise teacher will have answers ready when this sort of questioning occurs not only because he will have conscientiously thought deeply about such issues but also because he knows that part of his professional duty is to be able to speak up for his subject and defend his actions. The following ideas should be seen as suggestions which may well come in useful at a time when the teacher is already under heavy pressure and he needs to draw up quickly a response to a request from on high or else he faces a class which suddenly feels they have to challenge the assumption that French is good for everybody.

Formal requests for statements

These will usually come to a head of department from the

head teacher or from the governing body via the head. Questions cover any of the following topics:

Why is French the first foreign language?
Tradition and teacher supply are the two strongest reasons. 'A routine of French teaching has been set up.' Proximity to France and close cultural ties together with the origin of much English vocabulary are further strong reasons.

Could a good case be made for making another language first language?
Spanish is a strong contender. The proximity argument applies almost as well as it does to France. Spanish is generally regarded as an easier language for English beginners because of its pronunciation and phonetic spelling. The same arguments apply for Italian. German, with admittedly more complex grammar, gets beginners off to a good start.

Could the school staff another first language?
Many teachers of French have a second language they could turn to. Even more important those with first languages other than French have to teach French to get a job. To ensure fair coverage the best plan is to allow the languages to alternate year by year or, introduce two first foreign languages in parallel. Practicalities such as resources and finance may be prohibitive.

Which pupils should do a language?
Every pupil should have the opportunity to develop whatever potential he may have. Languages offer opportunity for the development of skills which might otherwise be unused. Once started every pupil should continue for as long as he continues to benefit in any way from such study.

Should a slow learner do a language?
While we admit it is unlikely that he will use the language at work there is a good chance of him deriving personal satisfaction from what he does achieve. He will become aware of the nature of language and, at the same time, he is

learning how to learn a language and that may well serve him well later. Ability to take part in a bi-lingual dialogue is a real possibility. A language has a positive effect on other subjects. The slow learner needs to do a language to ensure he is of equal status within his year group.

Who should do a second foreign language?
More pupils than at present. The ability band is too narrow and produces a particular kind of teaching. With a broader ability band teaching methods would be adapted and a greater proportion would succeed. If the groups we start with are small we shall never provide a viable sixth-form group.

"Excusez-moi, Madame—est ce qu'on parle Anglais ici?"

Punch. 11 August 1948

Why do girls do better than boys in languages?
The question is not so simple. True, more girls pass O-levels and A-levels but this is because there are more candidates since many boys of high ability (even in languages) are attracted to (masculine?) science subjects. The social pressures work in the opposite way for girls. We do not favour this. (See HMI report *Boys and Modern Languages* 1985, and work of Bob Powell at Bath University.)

Parents' evenings

Some parents may come with the intention of seeking advice and guidance, others may casually put a question in the course of a discussion about Tracy's chances of passing the 16+.

Were your exam results as good as St Thomas' School?
Comparison with one school is meaningless and a comparison over one year even more meaningless. The important statistics are the city/national ones. The average pass rate in ... is ... per cent and we had x per cent and given that Mrs Y was away for a month we are pleased with German and checking on the French.

My neighbour's daughter does three languages. Why can't Karen?
In this school we try to ensure every pupil has a balanced curriculum which suits each child's ability. The language policy in another school is not what we can discuss here.

If she does French and German in the sixth form, what job can she do?
The Careers Teacher is well briefed with all the possibilities open to linguists and there is a display outside his room listing these. The list can be based on careers referred to in Chapter 25.

What sort of books should I buy to help with languages?
Not necessarily books in the language. They may be far too hard. Books about languages. Books about the countries whose languages are studied.

Three years Spanish and in Tarragona last year he wouldn't say a dickybird. Why?
Lots of children don't like performing in front of parents. Are you sure the waiters all spoke Spanish and not Catalan? Did all the hotel staff speak good English? Were they nearly all English at the hotel? Any of these reasons will put a shy person off. If he had had to sort himself out he would have done.

Two years in the sixth and she still can't translate a letter I've had from France about some spare parts I've ordered. Why?
Up to now we have not been able to offer business studies French and it's a specialist field. The A-level syllabus is so full it would be wrong to take up time doing things untested in the exam. Things are changing.

We have two children doing the same language yet they never speak it. Why?
It's slightly unnatural for two people who know each other well in one language to use another. Language is a very basic reflection of the personality.

In my day we learnt verbs and knew them well. Now they don't.
Verbs are learnt nowadays as well but they are learnt by using them in real conversation. When you recited 'Je suis, tu es . . .', could you say anything worth saying?

She hates French. What can we do? Can she drop it?
Mary has shown that she has the ability to do French to O-level and that is why she is doing it. It would be wrong to drop it and we need to find out why French is unpopular with her. Is there an activity she is frightened of? A test she hates doing? This needs investigating further.

My son is getting very bored with French. What can you do to arouse his interest?
Will he come to our language club? We are having a day-trip to Boulogne just before Christmas. Could he come? We take magazines from various sources. Could he subscribe? We have an exchange scheme with France. Would he be interested in taking part?

Why can't my son do Latin? He might need it later.
A lot of teachers regret that Latin has had to disappear but
the curriculum has to change to make room for new areas of
knowledge such as computer studies. It is not likely it will be
a compulsory requirement for any subject when he goes into
higher education.

*Fiona has always wanted to do Russian at university but how can
she when you don't offer it in school?*
There's a whole range of languages which can be started *ab
initio* in universities and polytechnics, these days. They are
normally four-year courses and the prospectuses make this
clear.

Questions from pupils: 'Do we have to, Miss?'

Teachers are frequently asked to justify to their pupils why
so much time is spent learning a modern language, and it is
right that they should ask and vital that teachers should be
able to give answers which satisfy.

Nonetheless the question is not always put because of a
burning desire to argue the philosophy of education. The
time chosen to put the question and the manner in which it
is asked indicate clearly enough whether the question is
seriously intentioned. If the teacher suspects it is a 'try-on' he
should offer to deal with the enquiry after school.

The question 'Do we have to do French?' is a fair one.
Equally fair when applied to any other language, or indeed
to any other school subject, and it is one we have to be
prepared for and anticipate. In other words the teacher
should remind the class periodically why we do this. When
introducing something new, the class can be told why they
need to know it. Revising number, the teacher can remind
the class how important number is. 'You might need a
telephone number in an emergency. You want to know how
much things cost.' Verbs of motion? 'You're always needing
to say where you've been and where you're going.' Before a
repetition session it pays to remind children how much
repetition practice a baby puts in learning its mother-
tongue. Think of small children's stories in which the same

rigmarole is repeated and children love to join in. 'I'll huff and I'll puff till I blow your house down', or 'Chicken Licken and Hen Len'; of the French 'Anne ma soeur Anne ne vois-tu rien venir? Je ne vois que le soleil qui poudroie et l'herbe qui verdoie.'

Anticipating the question 'Do we have to, Miss?' is a sensible way of preventing the question arising as a distractor. Children soon spot the airy-fairy answer and have respect for the concrete and the practical. Consequently in some areas it may be wrong to overplay the line 'You will need it when you go to X,' although it is fair enough to recall how easily people do move around Europe these days on package tours.

To start the ball rolling we give below a selection of possible reasons which might be put in class to the question 'Are you forced to, Sir?' Some will suit certain situations and certain types of class: others may be regarded as totally inappropriate. Any experienced teacher will have his or her own stock of answers to add to these. If so, all the better.

1 When you leave school you will often find that a pass in a foreign language is regarded by an employer as a good sign that the applicant is intelligent and hard-working — even if the job itself does not require a language.
2 Later on in life you may need to learn another language quickly for your job or perhaps just for a holiday. When you've learnt one language you take to another more easily.
3 Think of the wide range of jobs for which a knowledge of a language is very helpful if not essential — the hotel trade and tourism, long-distance lorry-driving, coach-driving, journalism where an ability to skim through the foreign press easily may lead the journalist to pick up 'a good story' for his paper.
4 Foreign travel gets easier and relatively cheaper every year. You will almost certainly go abroad for a holiday and perhaps even to work within the next few years.
5 You never know when you may meet a Frenchman or a German in your own town and not *all* of them speak English.

6 We are Europeans now. Other Common Market countries teach English in their schools but not every pupil is good at English. It is only fair that we in England should make a similar effort.

7 Everybody should be given a chance to find out whether they are good linguists just as everybody should have opportunity to try football or tennis. We aren't all star footballers but many people get satisfaction from it. In the same way we don't expect every language learner to become a fluent speaker.

8 Even if you feel unable to express yourself fluently in the foreign language you will find you can often *understand* what people say to you. You can, in addition, *read* and understand many notices and signs in the street.

9 Using a foreign language is fun and you feel a real sense of achievement when you come out of a shop with exactly what you went in for.

10 You will make many new friends that you would never have got to know if you had been unable to communicate in a foreign language. There is no knowing what such friendships can lead to.

11 The coming of many more TV channels within the next few years will give us a greater opportunity to see foreign plays and films and even news programmes.

12 Learning a foreign language certainly helps you to understand and use English more effectively. Explain by referring to words directly derived from French and German cognates.

13 It's interesting to look through foreign magazines and even mail-order catalogues. (Build up a collection of foreign comics, women's magazines, car and sports mags and catalogues to use as five-minute fillers.)

14 Many pop records are made in Europe. Isn't it better to be able to understand some of them? It is possible even now to listen to European pop music programmes on Long and Medium Wave.

15 Finally note there is an excellent summary of reasons advanced by pupils for choosing particular languages in *The Second Foreign Language* by Phillips and Stencel (see bibliography).

13 How to avoid fatigue

All jobs conscientiously carried out make heavy demands on the worker. This we recognize, of course, but the burden placed on the teacher is a particularly heavy one as a result of the constant need to provide for thirty or so individuals. Within the teaching profession it is often said by language teachers that the constant demand to provide material for oral work makes the linguists the most hard pressed of all.

True or false, such a statement requires us to pause and think for a moment about ways and means of easing the burden, even for a short time, to allow the teacher to gather strength for the next major contribution.

The following suggestions are to be taken in the spirit they are intended and are in no way dodges to avoid work. They are included here to make more efficient, more effective teachers.

Voice

1 No one will deny that the modern linguist has to talk — a lot! But need he shout? To emphasize a point, slow down and even reduce volume slightly. Less strain, more effect.
2 Make plenty of use of others' voices. Use tape recordings instead of always reading aloud. Use teacher substitutes for questions — an essential part of pupil practice. In group work some of the talking will be done by group

leaders. With shadow reading do not try to be heard over the top of thirty pupils all the time.

3   There is a legitimate place within the modern language lesson for silent periods. A fifteen-minute reading session once a week can, if properly planned, make an excellent contribution to a week's overall programme. At such times the teacher moves quietly from pupil to pupil having a word or two about the reading — numbers of readers covered, extent of comprehension, etc.

Marking   A very heavy burden since every letter written must be checked.

1   Keep up to date with marking. Have regular marking sessions.
2   If pupils write in class the teacher can mark in class by going round from desk to desk.
3   To avoid major misunderstandings about homework let pupils begin in class and check the well-known muddlers — and a few others.
4   Class tests can be marked by changing papers but the teacher needs to take a few in as a sample to check closely.
5   Good presentation eases the strain of marking. Insist on this at all times. Pupils can only benefit from high standards set by the teacher.

Preparation   Fatigue often stems from strain and strain is caused by anxiety. Anxiety comes from lack of preparedness. Be prepared as follows:

1   An academic year diary is an essential. Ensure all dates and deadlines are put in immediately — exam dates, dates for exam paper completion, parents' evenings, reports to be completed by ... number of weeks in the term so you know exactly where you are. Important dates in red.
2   Good preparation is based on good record keeping. Twice a day jot down exactly what was done in each class.

3 Have hand-outs ready to distribute as you need them.
4 Prepare OHP transparencies before the lesson — far better and less wearing than scribbling on the blackboard — and you don't have your back to the class.

Discipline Fatigue is often caused by wear and tear on the nerves caused by poor discipline. See Chapter 6, 'Discipline in the Classroom'. Very often disciplinary problems can be seen in embryo by the experienced teacher. Two pupils starting to talk, perhaps even argue, can be distracted and brought back into the lesson by asking one of them a question or by requesting one to give a hand with a piece of apparatus. Result: problem goes away. It is always vital to step in early, before there is a real problem. Finally, don't allow known disturbance causers to sit together.

Some disciplinary problems stem from the fact that the class don't know where they are or what they are supposed to be doing. See next point:

Routine Everyone is more relaxed when they are following a regular routine. Get classes quickly used to particular ways of doing things and habituated to certain standards.

1 Have a reputation for always starting promptly.
2 Always take and mark written homeworks.
3 Return homeworks promptly.
4 Insist on quiet before the lesson starts but avoid, at all costs, making tempting offers such as 'I won't start till you are all quiet.'
5 Be consistent from day to day. If there is a seating plan, stick to it except during flu epidemics.
6 Do as much class administration in the language as possible.

All the above will help to ensure smooth running of classes, with a consequent reduction in fatigue.

PART TWO

Running a Modern Language Department

14 Managing the department

The quality of leadership

While we may reasonably start from the proposition that the members of the department ought to work together as a *team*, sharing a common interest in a particular part of a child's education, we must also acknowledge that it is the quality of leadership shown by the head of department which is a prime factor in creating a happy and above all efficient team of teachers.

The HMIs have recognized this:

> The vital importance of the role of Head of Department is that it lies at the very heart of the educational process; it is directly related to teaching and learning; whether a pupil achieves or underachieves is largely dependent on the quality of planning, execution and evaluation that takes place within individual departments.[1]

All schools are different: structures and management styles vary. Some departments *appear* to run themselves, others seem to need cajoling and pushing. Whatever the case, those responsible for reporting on teaching in schools and colleges in this country are quite clear on the need for firm but enlightened leadership:

> HM Inspectors are more than ever convinced that the Head

---

(1) *Departmental Organisation in Secondary Schools*, Occasional Paper from the Education Department of the Welsh Office, 1984.

of Department is a key figure. the most important single factor governing the quality of language work in the school. His effectiveness is seen above all in the help and guidance he gives to colleagues.[2]

There would appear to be two extremes of style in running a department. The first is authoritarian and dictatorial: schemes of work and suchlike are handed down from on high and all other teachers are expected to follow blindly a pattern of teaching which they have had no part in devising. The other extreme is simply a collection of individuals who go off in various directions to meet occasionally at the end of term. Both extremes are less than satisfactory from the point of view of the pupil, and the frustrations caused by having to work as a slave to someone else's ideas, or cut off from any real help. thrown back entirely on one's own resources, are not good for staff morale.

We are sure that the department will be most efficient, coherent and happy when decisions are taken by the group as a whole. The head of department should be seen as a first among equals. an organizer and leader, and certainly not the only source of wisdom and ideas.

> **The two principal aspects of the head of department**
> He or she will be a first-class practitioner in the classroom.
> He or she will be a manager of resources, human and material.

Our concern in this part of the book is therefore with management and the strategies to be employed. It is not to be an exploration of the *theory* of management, but rather a guide through the complexities of the job. It will be descriptive rather than prescriptive. seeking to lead rather than direct.

---

(2) *Modern Languages in Comprehensive Schools*. HMI Matters for Discussion. 1977.

What will leading mean?

1 *Sharing by example.* There can be no effective management and leadership if the head of department does not take his full share of all aspects of the departmental work. It will mean taking a fair share of all types of classes; the situation in which the head of department has contact with the sixth form and top-band classes only, to the exclusion of all else, is not an ideal to be encouraged.

2 *Delegation.* Leading does *not* mean doing everything oneself. There are only twenty-four hours in the day and shouldering all the burdens is the surest way to a breakdown and the quickest way to lose colleagues.

3 *Being responsible and responsive.* Being responsible means listening to the wishes, ideas and aspirations of others; it means being constantly available to colleagues and pupils; it means having foresight. It does *not* mean trying to be a superman.

4 *Efficiency.* Good leadership means being efficient, paying attention to detail in order that members of the departmental team may work to their highest standards. It does *not* mean making efficiency the aim of the department — it is a means to an end.

5 *Broad view.* Leadership means being outward-looking — to other parts of the school and to the world outside. It will mean having a sense of proportion, and an eye for public relations.

Perhaps the best image is that of the conductor of an orchestra!

15 The image of the department

Relationship with the head

The school will not flourish effectively unless there is cooperation between all members of the teaching staff and others. Under the leadership of the head, the heads of department have a vital role to play, and for the benefit of all members of the school community, the relationships between the head and the heads of department must be based on trust and confidence, on both sides. It is to be hoped that in appointing a head of department, the head will lay out the duties and the responsibilities of the post in order to provide an agreed framework of operation. In return the head of department must agree to carry out conscientiously the duties *delegated* to him. At the same time there should be some freedom within which to operate, with room for initiative in a climate of open discussion.

A wise head will see to it that the head of department is a member of the school management team. At this level he must:

1 Represent his subject area within the whole curriculum.
2 Be clear as to the contribution modern languages can make to the education of the pupils in the school.
3 Be able to take a broad look at the whole perspective of the school and to take part in a 'whole-school' debate on important issues.

How can these ideas be put into action?

First of all the head of department will see himself as a specialist adviser to the head on a whole variety of matters. These will arise from the particular subject area and will demand a broad knowledge and appreciation of the aims of the school and the special needs of the subject in question. He must be a specialist on the latest methodology and technology, on syllabuses and curriculum developments, on external examinations and the demands of the world beyond the school. In interpreting such issues to the head, the departmental leader must be able to translate all such ideas and theory into action, being conscious of the demands of the department in order to carry out any such policy as may be collectively determined.

In keeping the head briefed, the head of department must be able to discuss openly the ideals of his own departmental team and the constraints of the available resources.

Tools for the job

1   *Time.* Discussion and negotiations will centre on the allocation of teaching-time for the subject at various levels in the school: the balance with other departments; the balance across the age and ability range.
2   *Money.* Discussion of 'capitation' allowances and 'capital' money to service the department in the framework of provision for the school as a whole.
3   *Staff.* Negotiation with the head and the LEA to allocate sufficient staff with the appropriate specializations to carry out the departmental programme.
4   *Space.* Planning for sufficient classroom space and a departmental base for efficient operation.

The head of department will also be seen as a link between the head and the departmental team. He must keep them informed on school policy, and also, just as importantly, keep the head informed on ideas and perspectives from the department. This role as 'link-man' will involve fighting for the subject, defence of its position but also compromise and statesmanship.

Perhaps the best way to review the importance of the job and position of head of department is in the 'job description' itemizing the various areas of responsibility devolved by the head.

The role of the head of department

The staff
— to see that staff work effectively;
— to advise the head on the level of staffing required;
— to assist in the appointing of new staff;
— to devise appropriate help and support for new staff as well as continuing to care for all the team;
— to ensure all staff are informed as to school policy and are able to carry it out;
— to allocate responsibilities within the department and to ensure that such duties are carried out;
— to organize effective departmental meetings;
— to ensure that the school administrative procedures as they affect the department are carried out;
— to oversee staff development and to assist in the writing of references.

The subject
— to devise and keep under review an agreed scheme of work;
— to be informed on all aspects of curriculum development.

The pupils
— to oversee the work, development and behaviour of pupils within the department;
— to arrange teaching groups;
— to maintain appropriate pupil records;
— to advise in matters of option choices and careers.

The timetable
— to liaise with the school timetabler to ensure correct allocation of timetable space.

Parents
— to inform parents of departmental aims and objectives;
— to oversee the writing of reports and other communications with parents.

Resources
— to ensure that equipment of all kinds is provided, maintained, and kept secure;
— to determine, in consultation with colleagues, the priorities for allocating the departmental capitation allowance;
— to liaise with the school librarian and resources officer;
— to advise the head on the need for equipment;
— to ensure that staff are informed on and can use available resources.

Students
— to plan student timetables and programmes of work;
— to liaise with training establishments and to provide supervision;
— to prepare reports and references.

Examinations
— to ensure that all internal examinations are set, marked and evaluated;
— to ensure that for all external examinations, the correct syllabus is studied, and that pupils are entered appropriately;
— to see that all information from the examination boards is distributed to all who need to know and in particular that examiners' reports are noted.

Records
— to keep appropriate records of all pupils (information

from previous schools, internal assessments and external
examination results);
— to keep staff records to assist in writing references,
etc.;
— to minute staff meetings and circulate as agreed.

Extra-curricular activities
— to oversee activities such as visits, exchanges, pen-friend
provision, etc.;
— to maintain links with other bodies such as LEA
advisers, HMIs, FE and HE establishments, the subject-
teaching associations, etc.:

You will find, as head of department, that it is well
worthwhile to join a professional language association.

Finally, *keep a sense of humour and a sense of proportion!*

Relationships with other departments

It is extremely important for both pupil and teacher to feel
that the work carried on within the language department is
not isolated from the work of other departments, remote in
aim and character from the activities which engage the
attention of the pupil groups during the kaleidoscope of the
rest of the school day. Of course there are differences
because of the very nature of the subject we teach, but there
are many areas where there can be fruitful cooperation. It
follows that the head of department and his colleagues must
be willing to establish points of contact with other subject
areas and the benefits will be mutual. Other colleagues will
have a better understanding of the aims and objectives of the
language staff and, more importantly, they will come to
appreciate the challenges and difficulties of teaching a
modern language in today's schools. The language staff
should also be able to see how their work fits into and
complements the work in other areas, particularly in respect
of the language policy of the school.

The head of department is the key figure in this respect,

initiating and maintaining contacts with other sections of the school, both as a matter of routine and on 'special occasions'.

Ideally, the language department, in common with other groups in the school, will feel part of the total team of the school and, in offering its specialization it can also contribute to a whole-school approach on matters of policy, ideals and thinking about the education on offer to the community

First steps towards informing and cooperating with colleagues

— Circulate departmental syllabuses and guidelines to other colleagues — or perhaps a 'digest' of the main documents.
— At the heads of department committee, arrange a special time (or incorporate it over several ordinary meetings) when departments in turn talk about their aims, objectives, new developments and ideas. Be ready at such times to answer questions and defend your stance. It is surprising how informative and well-received are such sessions.
— Arrange for departmental 'at homes'. When possible, make opportunities for colleagues to see and examine rooms, equipment, texts and other aids 'in situ'. When we are all teaching a full timetable it is not always easy to see the latest additions to the computer workshop or the new ideas in CDT.

Equally, colleagues may not know how we use the foreign language in the classroom as a medium for teaching, or how we use that scarce resource — the assistant. Such 'at homes' could very well be in the lunch hour, when pupils may be on hand to make the visit more 'real'.

As linguists, we must pay special attention to the work of colleagues in the English department and any policy they (and others) develop in respect of 'language across the curriculum'. Such topics can very properly lead to discussion about real classroom issues rather than filling the staff meeting with 'administration'. Such matters, once thought the private concern of the English staff, must actively be taken on board in the language department. Incidentally — but very importantly — teachers of foreign languages can also learn a great deal from TEFL (English as a foreign language) colleagues. In many schools, especially in inner-city areas, with a multi-cultural intake, there may very well be a TEFL specialist and such a teacher can most positively contribute ideas and methodology to many departments. Active, communicative lessons are often the hallmark of such teachers who do not have the heritage of traditional grammar methods behind them.

In our search for communicative competence in the foreign language, we must look to more flexible methods and shift the focus away from the 'teacher-centered' lesson to the classroom with 'multi-centered' activities with pupils inter-acting among themselves and not simply with the teacher.

It will pay to investigate how the English department
— organizes small-group talk;
— encourages independent reading;
— involves personal experience in pupil work;
— encourages creative personal contributions from pupils.

It may be possible to cooperate with other departments as well — geography, history, music and art come to mind. Cooperation can simply be a matter of timing. For example, if dealing with the 'Dreyfus Affair' in the sixth-form literature course, mention of it may coincide with the study of the relevant period in the history department. The textbook chapter set in the 'Pays Basque' or in Berlin, can coincide with some project work in geography.

On the other hand, cooperation may be at a deeper level, with all departments adopting a flexible teaching strategy, child-centered rather than teacher-centered, as a result of discussion amongst staff. An interesting discussion on such an approach can be found in Douglas Barnes' book *From Communication to Curriculum*[1] and from his distinction between 'Transmission' and 'Interpretation' styles of teaching and learning.

Cooperation will also be called for in other areas of the school. For example on timetable planning and in the sharing out of the timetable space in the school week. This will be looked at in the section on timetabling. However, it can be mentioned here as one aspect of cooperation — namely that of seeking a correct balance of subject choices for various age groups, ability groups and between the sexes. It is an unfortunate fact that at fourth-year option time, we see far more girls choosing a foreign language than boys. There may very well be a good case for positive discrimination and bias in the way the options are timetabled. When the choice is between German and chemistry or between French and physics, we discourage boys from including a language in their range of subjects. The language department needs to discuss and present its case to the senior staff in the school, so that doors are not closed at an early age to any member of the school. Tact and diplomacy are called for, especially when lesson allocation is at a premium and rivalries tend to come to the surface.

Putting the department on show

Putting the department on show in the broadest sense of the term is an important part of the work of the departmental team. It will always be important to bring languages out of the routine of the classroom and to seize every opportunity to bring languages to life throughout the school. The public in general has yet to appreciate the need for language competence in a wide variety of situations and so in schools, the language department must try to create the feeling that languages are to be used in 'real' situations, that they are not just a funny game to be played in the classroom, with no relevance to the world outside. It is therefore vital to exploit every opportunity to 'show off' the department to the school, to parents and to the community outside.

---

(1) D. Barnes. *From Communication to Curriculum*. Penguin Books. 1976.

Contacts with parents vary from school to school, but a
readiness to meet parents will always be much appreciated
and a good, encouraging 'image' can do much to foster a
positive atmosphere in the classroom.

Possible activities — ideas to exploit

Use the foreign language
Encourage all staff to talk in the foreign language as much
as possible and in the most natural way possible. If a visitor
arrives in the middle of the lesson, talk to him in the foreign
language. It does work even when the head comes in. It will
soon get about that it is considered natural to use French,
German, etc., without embarrassment and such a reputation
will rub off to the pupils. When meeting pupils in the
corridor or the dining room greet them with a cheery
'Bonjour Marie', etc. With practice it will seem the most
natural thing in the world and not at all eccentric. Being a
showman brings satisfaction and can be contagious.

Help others with language problems
Be willing to help staff with their language queries — for
example by translating letters or writing for the holiday 'gîte'
in Normandy. Helping people in this way to go to the
continent can pay you back in surprising ways — by the
bottle of brandy from the cross-channel boat or the
unexpected poster to display in the classroom.

Do the same if requested by pupils or parents. Any such help
may very well be the spark to set off a lasting interest.

A news blackboard
Arrange to have a departmental blackboard in a permanent
prominent position in the school. It can easily be made out
of plywood and painted with special matt 'blackboard' paint
available from many DIY shops. Put it on a wall in the
language area corridor for all to see. Head it in white paint
'Les Nouvelles' and divide it into sections entitled 'A
L'Ecole', 'A L'Etranger', 'En Grande-Bretagne', 'Les Sports',
'La Météo'. Daily news items can then be chalked up by staff

or pupils for all to see. It creates interest and can be done in a variety of languages. A good source of information is the foreign newspaper or radio broadcast. French and German broadcasts can be received quite easily in many parts of the United Kingdom. (See page 109.)

A foreign dining corner
It is often easy to create a French, German or Spanish corner in the dining room. Tables are designated where only the target language is spoken — it can bring life to the role-playing scenes acted out in the classroom.

A foreign tuck-shop
Why not have a 'special' day in the school tuck-shop? In the local area there may well be a baker who produces *croissants* or other continental delicacies. A stall at break-time can be set up to sell them to pupils and staff using the foreign language as the medium of communication.

Languages at the school concert
On the occasion of the annual school concert or carol evening, an item in the foreign language can be offered. It could take the form of a song, reading, carol, playlet, etc., and is invariably well received. Some schools even run a French, German or Spanish choir. This will depend on the talent of the staff but can be seen as a fruitful avenue of cooperation. The MLA has published a book of foreign carols and is well worth consulting.[1]

Helping other departments
Always be ready to meet the requests of other departments. For example you may have, from your travels abroad, a collection of slides which could help the geography or history departments or simply help a pupil engaged in a project. The PE department may also ask for help. They may have an interest in dance for example. This could form part

---

(1) *Carols* published by the MLA. Available from Head Office — see Part 4 for address.

of a 'Breton' evening after the school holiday to Brittany.

A language 'club'
Many activities can be tried out especially with the help of
the assistant, depending on the age of the pupils. The main
aim of such a club will be to do just those things that might
be squeezed out of the normal classroom because of the
pressure of time.

Suggestions for activities:

1 *Showing films.* Many can be hired free from various
  commercial bodies such as tourist offices and foreign
  railway companies, and even commercial firms. Commercial distributors should not be forgotten; if the fee
  they charge is high, then it may be possible to join up
  with other local schools to share the cost. Local MLA
  branches often show foreign films and may help put the
  school in touch with those who can help. (See 'Resources'
  page 117.)
2 *Showing slides.* These can come from teachers, pupils,
  local teachers' centres, etc.
3 *Making cassette recordings* to send to the twin school as a
  sort of *correspondance sonore.*   ·
4 *Food.* By 'borrowing' the housecraft department, it is
  possible to prepare simple dishes for the pupils. It is a
  good idea to print out a recipe in advance in the target
  language and hand them out to pupils at the beginning.
  Making a *salade* or even snail butter can be great fun and
  will certainly be remembered by the pupils and provides
  a lively activity. 'Bought-in' food can also be used,
  especially if there is a baker or delicatessen in the
  vicinity to provide croissants or salamis.
5 *Playing games.* Depending on the age of the pupils it is
  possible to play games, do foreign crosswords, use
  French, German or other versions of, for example,
  'Monopoly'. On trips abroad, it is possible to pick up the
  latest 'box' games popular across the Channel very
  cheaply.

Open days
These events can be very time-consuming, but if properly planned and thought-out they can play a very useful part in promoting the cause of the modern language department. It doesn't always seem easy to compete with the more 'spectacular' displays that attract spectators to science and computer departments. But here is an opportunity to show to visitors, parents and prospective pupils that language-learning can be *fun*. Some ideas for open days are given below.

Arrange a French/German/Spanish café. Buy in croissants, cakes, etc., and coffee for sale in the café, arranged around the *terrasse* created from the garden parasol, tables and chairs. In the background will be playing a cassette recording of French, German or Spanish 'pop' music to create the atmosphere. In the course of the language lessons the pupils can be trained as waiters and waitresses and the 'script' for the customers to act out the other half of the role-play should be printed on the back of the menu and price-list. It will soon be evident just how much the visitors will enjoy playing the game to the benefit of the pupils. With careful budgeting it is easy to make a 'profit' for the departmental funds to buy the extra cassette recorder badly needed and at the same time provide real motivation for the pupils.

Slide-show. It is a good idea to have a slide-show on open day of the recent school visits abroad. These not only help those who participated, but are a good recruiting aid for the next planned trips. Make sure that the exhibits include a substantial contribution from the pupils themselves, such as 'diaries', etc.

The 'twin school'. If the school is lucky enough to have a twin school in Europe, then it is a first-class idea to arrange a display of material which may include timetables, posters, slides, letters, projects and so on. This can be part of an ongoing contact with the partner establishment.

Demonstration lessons. Depending on the aims of the open day, much can be gained from putting on demonstration lessons. If the aim is to reveal what pupils can do, then the opportunity for visitors to see 'real' lessons in progress can be invaluable. It may be possible, for instance, to arrange an afternoon sequence of lessons to take place in the evening and so allow parents and others to witness classes in action. On the other hand, the aim of demonstrations may be to allow parents to have a 'taster' lesson of a language that they know little about, in order to better appreciate what it is to be in the position of the young learner, as their children are in their everyday school life.

Displays. It is usually to be preferred that work on display is 'normal' — that is work that arises naturally from the work of everyday teaching.

Don't forget the language laboratory if it exists. Visitors can usefully be shown how the hardware of the school contributes to the work of the department.

Open days are single events in the year. However, there is much to be said for keeping parents and other interested people very much in the picture throughout the school year. Many researchers have found that one of the most important factors to help pupils in successful language learning is a positive attitude held by parents, and a supportive family. Therefore always be ready to answer questions about methods, aims and objectives, both in writing, as for example, in the school prospectus referred to below, and via any other form of communication that might be appropriate.

In some schools the writing of reports on individual pupils may be the only form of communication the department may have with parents, but this is not enough on its own.

Parents do have a right to be well-informed about the school and the progress of their children (or the lack of it, before it is too late!). It is not always appreciated by staff, how reluctant some parents can be when it comes to asking and finding out about school matters and so anything we can do will be beneficial.

The school information booklets

A large number of schools produce, in addition to the statutory prospectus for prospective pupils and parents, a series of other publications, booklets and handouts at certain critical times in the life of the pupil — at 'option-time' and before entry to the sixth form, for example. These are very important documents and the modern language department must be properly represented. The head of department should consult with colleagues to determine the kind of image it is desirable to present. It is advisable to write the contribution in language which is 'non-technical' and easy to understand, avoiding jargon, which the professional may appreciate but which can so often confuse others.

A suggested format for a new pupil booklet 'chapter' might be as follows:

MIDSHIRE EDUCATION COMMITTEE
GREENWAY HIGH SCHOOL
MIDTOWN

The Modern Language Department

Introduction
The modern language department in this school teaches French, German and Spanish. We have six full-time staff, together with the help of the deputy head and two foreign-language assistants.

The staff are as follows:

Mr K. Jones *Head of Department,*	French and German
Mrs S. Brown *Second in Department,*	French and Spanish
Mrs G. Smith	French
Mrs M. Lewis	French and Spanish
Mr E. Rigby	French
Miss J. McCall	French and German
Mr H. Forest *Deputy Head*	French

Our assistants this year will be Mlle Denoyelle from France and Herr Strauss from Germany. They will take conversation classes with all age groups.

Over the last few years, we have enjoyed good success, with many of our pupils going on to study at university or polytechnic. However, we also aim to give a good grounding and lasting interest to all our pupils at all levels of ability.

General aims

We try to develop the various language skills with all our pupils. For all, the skills of listening, reading and speaking are important, and for many we would also add the skill of writing. As a nation, it is vital that we increase our knowledge of foreign languages, especially as we are in the Common Market, and because of the needs of the world of work and leisure beyond the school. We believe that the apprenticeship of language-learning at school will lay good foundations for the future, in order that our pupils will be adaptable in their future lives.

We do not forget that learning and using a language can be fun, and can help you to enjoy a holiday abroad even more.

Examination aims

We encourage as many of our pupils as possible to enter for public examinations. Most pupils enter for the 16+ examinations or a CSE (Mode 3). These terms are explained in the section "Examinations made easy!" In the sixth form, the aim is the A-level, or alternatively, for non-specialists, the A/O-level. The latter qualification is particularly important for those students who do not wish to specialize in language studies, but who wish to keep their language alive as an extra skill, which will add a further dimension to their chosen course of study.

All our pupils are encouraged to enter for the various levels of the Graded Examination Scheme (a series of stepped examinations rather like the various grades of the music examinations). A decision as to which examination your child will enter will be delayed for as long as possible in order to allow for individual development.

Classes

Along with other subjects in our school, French as a first foreign language is taught in mixed-ability groups for one year, and in the second year in broad bands. In year three and above, ability sets are introduced. German and Spanish may be chosen by third-year pupils as a second language *in addition* to French if they so wish. Please note that this option is *not* restricted to the more able pupils. Sixth-form students may begin a new language from scratch.

The option-choice scheme in our fourth form allows languages to be studied in combination with almost any other subject on offer to the pupils, and we are pleased to say that almost 70 per cent of our pupils in year four continue with their language studies.

Methods
We try to develop skills that will be of real use in the foreign country and so we put a lot of emphasis on listening, reading and speaking. Writing is a skill which is less important for some pupils, but it is not neglected.

Resources
We have a language laboratory for our use and in our language-teaching rooms there are tape recorders, projectors and a library of tapes and cassettes to help us.

Visits and exchanges
Each year we arrange trips abroad to various countries, usually for periods of a week or ten days. A one-day "taster" trip on a "Boulogne Flyer" is a regular feature of our school year. We always encourage other forms of contact (e.g. via pen-friends and an exchange of cassettes with our "twin" schools in France, Germany and Spain).

At our school Open Day in October, why not pay us a visit and see us at work? Come to our French café and demonstration lesson. You will be very welcome.

16 Making the most of the staff

It is a basic assumption in this section that the modern languages department will function most effectively when the members of the department are cooperating as a team. However, it would be naive to assume that in the hurried life we find in schools, such a spirit is found everywhere. But such cooperation will bring personal and professional satisfaction and thus the head of department will be wise to do everything possible to foster such a cooperative spirit. Nothing is worse than major decisions being taken in isolation, without debate amongst colleagues who will have to work in the light of such policies.

The bringing together of such a team is partly in the hands of the head of department and it begins with the process of appointing staff.

Making appointments

Appointing a new member of the departmental team is not a task to be taken lightly. On the contrary, it is a process which demands great thought and tact in order to foster the well-being of the department as a whole. Very careful consideration must be given to all the stages of the process. It is inexcusable that the head of department be excluded from any part of the procedure. He should make every effort to act on behalf of the whole department throughout, and his opinions should weigh heavily with the team making the final decision.

Ideally the head of department should be involved in all the stages outlined below:

- deciding on the needs of the department;
- outlining a post description, and advertisement;
- shortlisting;
- meeting the candidates;
- interviewing.

Each of these stages will now be dealt with in detail.

Deciding on the needs of the department

As part of the consultative process, the head of department will have informed the head in good time of the need to make a new appointment. In a well-regulated team, the 'surprise' resignation shouldn't normally happen, because the head of department will have his ear close enough to the ground to know the intentions of the staff well in advance. The head of department should take careful stock of the staff resources required to carry out the policy of the school, and in so doing he should try to maintain a balance between experience and inexperience, full-time and part-time appointments, language-balance where more than one language is taught, etc. As well as the present situation, one must look to the future, where flexibility will be vital, involving an ability to teach for example two languages or even another subject.

All this preliminary planning should be done in good time, if at all possible, in order to avoid last-minute panics, which often lead to hasty appointments from a reduced field.

Drawing up the advertisement

It is unlikely that the head of department will draw up the final version of the press notice giving details of the vacancy, but nevertheless he should have a clear idea of the image it seeks to project.

**Midshire Education Committee,
Greenway High School, Midtown High Street, Midtown, MD2 6QQ.
Tel: 123456 (STD 0345)**
(An 11 – 18 mixed comprehensive school – 1,400 on roll.)

Modern Language Department – Scale 1 Post
· Required for September 19–, an enthusiastic teacher of *French* and *German* up to A-level.

Greenway High School is situated on the northern edge of the market town, with a socially mixed intake. The campus is self-contained within its own playing fields and purpose-built accommodation.

French is taught to all pupils in years 1 – 3 (including the remedial classes) and in mixed-ability groups for the first year. In years four and five, it is an optional subject where some 60 per cent of the year group maintain their language study. The more able linguists may begin German as a second foreign language in year three.

The fifth-year courses lead to the 16 + examinations of the Mid-England Examinations Board. The department has also developed a Mode 3 examination for the less able pupils. All the department's syllabuses are based on "communicative" lines and we enter pupils for the Midtown Graded Examinations Scheme.

In the sixth form, there are courses to A-level in French and German (up to ten students per year in each language) and the department is also responsible for the sixth-form O-level Latin course.

The Language Department has a well-equipped suite of rooms, each with audio-visual aids and has also a twenty-place language laboratory. There is usually a French and German assistant and the shared use of a technician.

There is a thriving link with the Lycée Courvoisier in Cognac and the Gymnasium Michelsberg in Trier. Pupil exchanges are seen as a vital part of the departmental programme and help of any kind in this area will be appreciated.

In the coming year it is hoped to introduce into the sixth form, French and German for non-specialists as part of a pattern of diversification, and candidates should indicate what contribution they could make to this work.

The successful candidate will be expected to teach the full ability range and to make a positive contribution to the life of this busy school.

Application should be made by letter to the headmaster enclosing full *curriculum vitae* and the names and addresses of two referees.

Applications to be received by 30 April 19–. Please enclose a stamped addressed envelope for acknowledgement.

This is the first contact the school has with potential candidates, and as such it is worthwhile giving some thought to the wording. If at all possible there should be a short job description together with some information about the department. After all, you are trying to tempt as wide a selection of possible colleagues as circumstances allow in order to have a good field to choose from.

In most cases a brief description of the school and the department is sent to enquirers, and the head of department should help draw up such a document, maximum A4 size, giving an honest account of the post available. Information will vary from school to school but the first part should contain factual information as follows:

- school name, address (including post-code) and tele-phone number;
- geographical/social location;
- number on roll, age-range, and whether boys, girls or mixed;
- language(s) and qualifications required;
- level of teaching required: 16+, A-level, etc.

Information about the department will contain information such as:

- external examination aims;
- composition of classes;
- resources available;
- special projects, etc.

And finally the advertisement should include the date by which applications should be received.

Shortlisting

The sifting of the pile of applications is often a tedious and frequently unscientific job. It is best done therefore by two or three people whose combined opinions should produce an acceptable shortlist. Each application form deserves careful consideration from several points of view:

- the needs of the departmental timetable;

- the present composition and strengths of the department;
- the future needs of the department;
- the expertise any new teacher could offer;
- possible contribution to the general life of the school.

When reading the applications and the references, take note of what is said as well as what is left out. However, it is important to avoid being too cunning a reader and imputing qualities or failings which are not really there. Try to ask positive questions about the applicant as well as looking for such things as gaps in the sequence of experience and career. Discuss your choice and reasons for deciding, with the head, or the deputy concerned with staffing.

When concerned with appointments to modern language teams, as well as these general considerations, there are particular items to look for: qualifications in the languages in question, residence abroad, continued contact with the target country, etc. These should also form a major part of the points which lead to an interview.

Meeting the candidates

Before the formal interview, there is an equally important stage in the selection process which should not be ignored or treated lightly. It is essential to invite the candidates on the shortlist to visit the school before the formal interview, so that this informal, more relaxed scrutiny will allow the head of department to assess the potential strengths of the applicants *and* equally important allow the candidates to make *their* assessment of the school and the department, prior to entering into any sort of commitment.

The 'informal' visit

As the candidates arrive, introduce them to the other teachers in the department and show them around the whole school as well as the departmental area. If possible this is best done on a 'normal' working day, when it is possible to glean some idea of the atmosphere of the school.

Try to arrange visits to a couple of lessons, with the consent of willing colleagues. It will be important to allow the opportunity to look at the departmental resources, to get at least a glimpse of pupils and to see something of the departmental 'style'. In order to give a balanced view of the work of the department, make a point of letting other colleagues have the chance to talk to the candidates — after all, the new teacher will be working with a group of staff and not just with the head of department!

Talk with the visitors over a cup of coffee and give them a chance to ask questions and air their views. Throughout this 'informal' half-day or so you will be able to judge the reactions of the potential colleagues in a way which should complement the impression gained at the formal interview. Such insights will enable more pertinent and probing questions to be asked at the interview.

Interviewing

It may be the policy of the school *not* to invite the head of department to participate in the formal interview. We take the view that this is to be regretted, but if this is the case, it is essential that the head of department makes known his point of view on the candidates and that the interests of the department are represented. It can be argued that the work of sifting the potential candidates during the earlier stages outlined above is the proper concern of the head of department, and that his views, carefully considered, should, in the final stage, be but one aspect of the choosing of a new colleague to fit into the overall staff team. On the other hand, the presence of the head of department can be seen as valuable in offering a special point of view on the proceedings.

If he *is* included on the interviewing panel he is just one of a team and *not* the star in the limelight. The aim of the panel is to allow each candidate to be seen at his or her best and to allow a proper judgement to take place in the interest of all concerned. Since one doesn't sit on interviewing panels all that often, it is essential to think out the strategy very carefully beforehand if opportunities in the all too brief 15–20 minutes are not to be wasted.

Interviewing techniques

1 It is essential to have *a clear idea of the kind of person needed in the team.* Only candidates who have the essential requirements should be invited for interview.
2 When the shortlist has been compiled, all members of the interviewing panel should study the documentation very carefully, noting the strengths and weaknesses of the candidates in the light of the job specification.
3 Interviews should be carefully planned, both individually and collectively.
4 All candidates should be given the opportunity to settle down and feel at ease at what is often a stressful time. They must be allowed to present themselves in their best light.
5 The chairman will welcome each candidate in a friendly manner, making sure that the various members of the panel are introduced in turn. Some basic questions should be asked of *all* the candidates so that comparisons can be made, followed by other questions to individuals which will suit the circumstances. Questions should be prepared beforehand, on the reading of the *curriculum vitae,* in order to be able to pose follow-up questions in the light of the candidate's answers.
6 All questions should be clear and precise. 'Trick' questions and those designed to convey the questioner's own position and views are best put aside. Avoid asking such questions as 'Wouldn't you agree that . . .?'
7 Give all interviewees ample time to answer.
8 Allow them all the chance to ask their own questions.
9 Don't 'hog' the questioning: allow all members of the panel to put their questions.
10 When interviewing modern linguists, opinions are divided on whether part of the interview should be in the target language. Those against suggest that this is best done during the 'informal' part of the day. Others

maintain, however, that an adequate command of the spoken language must be publicly demonstrated. Whatever method is used, it is a good idea to use a simple factual question such as 'Tell us about your year abroad as an assistant.' Remember that at some time during the day's proceedings each candidate should have been heard speaking his or her language.

11 At the end of the interview, each candidate must feel that he or she has been given a fair interview and has been able to do his best.

Samples of questions that can be used at interviews

— Why did you choose to teach?
— Have you any experience in other jobs?
— Why do you want this post?
— Where else have you taught *or* where did you do your teaching practice?
— How do you keep up to date with your language?
— How often do you go to (France)?
— What in your opinion makes a good teacher?
— What does a modern language contribute to the education of children?
— How do you relax?
— Do you see any special problems in a large school?
— Where do you see yourself in the profession in five years time?
— How do you foster a good atmosphere in the classroom?
— Should you teach *in* the language?
— How do you cope with the high-flyer in the class — or the weak pupil?
— What else can you offer to the school in general?
— What is the role of the form-teacher and pastoral staff?
— What are the aims of teaching a foreign language?
— What, in your opinion, makes a 'good' lesson?

And don't forget:
— Have you any questions that you would like to ask?

The new colleague

The process begun at the interview is but the beginning. The important work of integration starts as the selection of the new colleague ends. It is all too easy to forget what it is to be a new teacher, especially if it is the first appointment. Once we are established in a school, all the familiar routines are taken for granted, simply because we have trodden the path many times over. However, the wise head of department will take every care to ensure that the integration is as smooth as possible.

Ideally there will be a coordinated policy in the school for welcoming new teachers and, if that is the case, then the head of modern languages should be part of the overall policy. If the school does not have such a policy, why not suggest it to the head? What is totally unacceptable is that a new member of staff (and especially a probationer) should arrive on the first day of term without the benefit of both formal and informal meetings with colleagues beforehand.

A welcoming letter

As soon as the new appointment is confirmed, the head of department should write an informal letter of congratulations and also confirm the dates of visits to the school before the beginning of the new term.

Arranging visits

The informal visit should be arranged in term time, if at all possible, when the school is in action and colleagues are around in order to allow for full consultation including, if appropriate, a chat with the 'outgoing' teacher whose classes are to be taken over. Much valuable information about individuals, methods and the like can be passed on at this time.

The staff file

In order to help the new teacher it is a good idea to present a staff file containing the whole range of material that has to be assimilated before the rush of the first few days in school. Knowing the mechanics of the school, the departmental routine, the room numbers and the times of the lesson change-overs — all this can be a boost to self-confidence in the presence of pupils *and* a help towards efficiency.

The departmental staff file should be in a looseleaf folder that can be added to (or taken from) as circumstances change. It should contain at least the following information:

The modern language department staff file

- A copy of the departmental policy file.
- A detailed scheme of work for each language/year group.
- A plan of the school.
- A full staff-list and the codes used to designate them on the timetable.
- The teacher's personal timetable, annotated to make sense!
- A copy of the school rules and other papers affecting the daily routine, e.g. fire orders, detention duty rota, etc.
- A copy of 'set' lists as appropriate.
- A calendar of the major events of the school year.

In addition, if the new colleague is new to the district, possible contacts in the area for flats and accommodation may be helpful. The LEA often has a service, via the 'Weekly Bulletin' giving such information.

The probationary teacher

Some authorities have special policies for the induction of new teachers, involving a variety of strategies — lighter timetables, day or half-day release, proper supervision, etc. It is very difficult for the individual head of department to 'go it alone' when such a policy is lacking, but in such a situation when there is no LEA or school-wide policy, it is more imperative that the head of department should take

some initiative — and not just at the start of the school year.
It is just as vital that there be continuing support, for
although very few probationers fail their probationary year,
it is surprising how quickly the initial stock of good ideas,
enthusiasm and inventiveness can be used up in the rush of
term.

How can one arrange for continuing care over the year?
Several strategies are possible:

1   Arrange to be 'free' at the same time as the new colleague
    and thus fix a regular meeting.
2   If the probationer isn't given a 'form' to register, use the
    registration time once a week.
3   If the school is allocated a student for practice, it may be
    possible to arrange 'tutorial' help in conjunction with
    the probationer.
4   'Pair' off another colleague (it needn't be a senior
    teacher) who is sympathetic and who can help the
    newcomer overcome the inevitable early problems.
5   Above all, be 'available'.

It should be obvious that the new teacher does not come into
the school as a featureless blank, waiting to be fashioned in
the school mould. The head of department should quickly
assess the interests and strengths of the new colleague and
establish mutual confidence as soon as possible.

The timetable

Perhaps the single most important factor in the life of the
new teacher is the sort of timetable he or she is faced with in
the first year. It is clearly unacceptable to give out a
succession of 'bottom' classes. It is the surest way of bringing
on a breakdown, or at least total demoralization. You
should offer the probationer an appropriate balance of
classes, bearing in mind the sometimes conflicting demands
of pupils and the question of continuity. If the school allows
a policy of a lightened timetable load for the beginner, all
well and good. If not, discuss it with the head.

Observation — a two-way process

When we are students we have ample opportunity to observe teachers in action in the classroom. But the need to see examples of good practice does not stop when we take up our first appointment. On the contrary, it is when we have taught for some time, that we can arguably benefit most from seeing others in action, for we are then more able to observe to good effect — we are more likely to know what to look for. There is a clear need to allow teachers to see each other in action with a variety of classes in terms of age and ability. Equally important is the need for the head of department to see the probationer in action and this must be done in a climate of mutual confidence and not with the atmosphere of student and assessor, with all the stress that such a situation entails. Without doubt, you will be called upon to write a report on the probationary year — how can this be done without proper monitoring? If we wish the newcomer to get the most benefit from such visits, it will be important to discuss the classes seen openly with proper analysis and advice. To this end it will be useful to keep a file of notes — preferably that the teacher concerned may have access to.

The problem of discipline

This can be an area of worry for the new teacher. The problem of discipline in general in the language classroom is discussed in chapter 6 but the head of department will have a very important supportive role to play during the induction period of the beginner. The discipline problem can be eased if it is discussed openly and with the realization that even teachers of long experience still have difficulties and cannot solve all problems. You will have to be seen taking a lead, for example by receiving the awkward pupil into your class to take the pressure from a colleague's class. Above all, do not pretend that behaviour problems are a disease, not to be brought out into the open, for in so doing one will isolate the probationer who is still finding out those tricks of the trade, the personal wizardry and the dashes of good humour which can often extricate the teacher from the difficult situation.

Anticipating the problems and deadlines

Real help can be given by the experienced teacher in other ways: by giving a sympathetic ear in the staffroom and on the corridor and in particular by always being one step ahead of deadlines and important dates, such as report writing, assessment dates, etc. For example we should look ahead to report time, give advice on obtaining report blanks, completing them in the school 'style'. When the first parents' consultation evening comes round, anticipate the understandable nervousness of the new colleague who is facing parents for the first time. Give advice beforehand on the school system and the individual's approach — for example how to get parents on your side by knowing the pupils well.

Patterns will vary from school to school and any attempt to prescribe a programme of induction in exact detail would be out of place. However the 'in at the deep end' theory should have no place in a well-run department. What we suggest below is a list of topics which should be covered by the head of department or a designated colleague at some time during the year. If an organized training session — say one lesson per week — is envisaged, then the order of the various topics will to some extent be dictated by the progress of the school calendar.

Topics in a school-based or departmentally-based training programme

The school day: Lesson change times, assemblies, etc.

Audio-visual aids: Tapes, slides, films, cassettes, records, OHP, etc. Duplication and reprographic facilities: when, where and how. TV and radio facilities. Copyright laws.

Departmental stock: Whereabouts, age-range, availability, suitability.

Departmental systems: For record-keeping, pupils' assessment. issuing and collecting of textbooks, etc. Recording damage, loss, etc.

School policy: As it affects the department; e.g. how pupils are selected for various courses. School policy on detentions, pastoral care, etc.

Examinations: Where are past papers stored? Where is the set-book list? Who sets internal examinations? Who decides on external examination entries?

Homework and marking policy

Overseas links: School, class and individual links; policy on visits and exchanges.

Sanctions: School and departmental policy; helping with troublesome pupils.

Parents: School policy for contacting and informing.

Library: Facilities for staff and pupils.

The form tutor: How to carry out the administrative duties.

Other staff: Information relating to other staff: ancillary help, caretakers, etc.

Outside agencies: Role, function and usefulness of LEA advisers, teachers' centres, etc.

Working with the assistant

In latter years, the presence of a foreign assistant has become something of a luxury in many areas, and so if the school is fortunate enough to be a host to an assistant it is the responsibility of the head of department to make the best use of this valuable resource.

In order to maximize the contribution of the assistant, it is wise to bear in mind the following major points, especially at the beginning of the school year:

1 The assistant is *not* a trained teacher (and may not intend to teach). As an unqualified teacher, with probably the barest of instruction in the skills of teaching, he will certainly need very detailed advice and guidance, especially in the first few weeks. Simply sending out a group of pupils to 'do conversation' is unrealistic and will certainly be counter-productive.

2 It may very well be the first lengthy visit of the assistant to this country, and he will need help, patience and sympathy in order to settle in.

What to do before *the arrival of the assistant*

Together with the 'official' letter sent by the head, it is helpful if an informal letter is also sent, setting out the following details:

1 Name and full address of the school (type or print it to avoid confusion, as handwriting styles can lead to error).

2 Type of school (comprehensive, junior high, etc. — explain).

3 Numbers and age-range of pupils.

4 Dates of start and end of terms.

5 Possibilities and/or offers of accommodation.

6 Address of previous assistant who will be able to pass on advice.

7 Your name and address for contact before the start of term.

8 Requests for material.

9 Precise intentions for arrival in order to arrange reception.

10 The school prospectus.

11 The timetable (if known.)

12 The appropriate MLA Assistants' Handbook. (See Bibliography.)

During the first few weeks of term, schools are always busy and the assistant may be 'forgotten'. If there is such a risk, delegate a member of staff to look after the new arrival. It is often a good idea to ask a younger member of the department to do this since such a teacher will quite possibly be nearer the age of the assistant and may only recently have served as an assistant in a foreign school.

Things to do as the assistant arrives or in the first few days

In order to help the new assistant to settle in quickly, there is much to be done, both inside and outside the school. It is to be hoped, however, that if the groundwork has been covered before the start of term, and if sufficient information has been sent out, then the assistant will already know quite a lot about the framework in which he will be working.

1 Arrange for someone to meet the assistant at the local station or airport.
2 If at all possible, introduce the assistant to the host family. If a flat has been arranged, what about a 'starter kit' — a supply of bread, milk, etc., for the first few days? Or better still, even if a flat has been rented, why not arrange for the first few days to be spent as a guest in a family? The first steps are often awkward and strange.
3 Introduce the assistant personally to the head, the deputies, etc. Included in the list of 'important' people will be the office staff as well as anyone on the staff who has shown a particular interest in previous assistants. It is to be hoped that all the language staff will make a special point of the arrival. At the first full staff meeting, make sure that the rest of the staff know who the assistant is — staff of all subjects will probably take an interest.
4 Arrange for the assistant to open a bank account at a branch nearby so that documentation may be ready in order to receive salary payments on time. Explain and demonstrate how to write a cheque, pay in funds, etc.
5 Pass on full details to the school office so that the LEA is informed about arrangements for paying into bank accounts.
6 Explain about National Insurance and tax liability. (Tax is normally waived for assistants under a reciprocal agreement for certain countries (*not* at the moment for Algeria or Spain — though please check)). Assistants

must keep an eye on this, because tax is often deducted
in the early months under 'emergency coding'.

7 Give the address of a doctor and explain how to register.
Explain 'sick leave' notification arrangements and the
necessity to inform the school.

8 Local 'geography' and transport. Provide a map and a
bus timetable. If possible take them on a 'tour' of the
local area pointing out landmarks of interest.

9 Explain the facilities which are available for study and
recreation, and which are provided for example, by the
local university or college, assistants' committees,
language centres, evening classes, sports centres, MLA
branches, libraries, etc.

10 Make a special point of introducing the assistant to the
sixth form. These students will very often invite the
assistant to tennis clubs, parties, discos and even the
local pub.

11 Unravel the mysteries of initials: HOD, LEA, DES,
HMI, CSE, GCE, 16+, O- and A-level, U6, L6, etc.

12 If you have to share the assistant with another school,
introduce him to the staff there.

13 Make sure the assistant gives the school information —
for example if he is to be away to sit examinations, the
dates in advance.

Finally it should not be assumed that if this has all been
done at the start of the term, that is the end of the task. The
year can pass very quickly, but it can also drag despairingly,
if the assistant is put to one side during a busy term.

Using the assistant in the classroom

In the first weeks insist the assistant begins classroom
observation, in order to ascertain the school's methods of
teaching languages, and to learn a standard (how good are
the pupils?). Alongside this period of observation, the
assistant should study the main textbooks used in the school
as well as looking at some external examination papers and
procedures for oral examinations. Colleagues should also
be closely involved and it is a good idea to discuss before and

after, the contents of lessons observed. Pay particular attention to question and answer techniques as well as to ideas for *involving* pupils, the correction of faults, use of audio-visual aids, etc.

It is a mistake, however, to restrict the period of observation to the first week or so — it is in everyone's interest to allow observation throughout the school year.

It is equally important to allow staff to see the assistant at work, in order to give sound advice. (See Chapter 8.)

Preliminary tactics

1 Make sure the timetable is understood.
2 Ensure that the assistant has appropriate rooms to work in — it is simply not acceptable to relegate the group to the hall, cloakroom or the back of the stage. The assistant deserves a classroom just as any other teacher.
3 See that the assistant is given lists of the teaching groups. Why not also issue a 'mark book' as to other staff?
4 Keep the assistant groups to a reasonable size — ten or twelve at the maximum.
5 Show the assistant how to use the basic audio-visual aids.
6 Give clear and precise instructions as to what to do if problems of discipline arise. Pupils must also clearly understand what is expected of them.
7 Vary the lesson format. Sometimes work with a group for the whole lesson in another room. Sometimes work with a group in the same room — this can be noisy and needs planning. Sometimes work *with* the normal teacher in the same room in a form of team-teaching (two 'native' speakers can be most useful).
8 Encourage *enjoyment* of the lesson. Pupils are much more likely to want to go to the assistant's lessons if they are enjoyable.
9 It would be foolish to confine the assistant's work to the regularly timetabled classes. With only twelve hours per week allowed, priority will probably be given to the older

pupils facing examinations. However, groups should not be disadvantaged by being missed out. During the year, other classes, even 'low-ability' groups can benefit from 'guest appearances'. It may be that such lessons involve the assistant talking in English about their own country — but these contacts can be valuable.

Non-specialists

So often it is the case that schools are forced to employ non-specialists to teach a particular subject. Various pressures force this upon us: falling rolls, redefined catchment areas, changing status of schools, etc. Such a non-specialist may be a part-timer, working for several half-days scattered about the week. In this case the problem is often to provide a coherent timetable from the point of view of the pupils and the teacher. On the other hand, the part-time commitment may be because of commitments to other departments or to the management team of the school. Thus, non-specialists may have loyalties to other areas in the school which prevent them from a full teaching timetable in the language department.

Being drafted into a second department may be a cause of resentment from various points of view. For example they may have developed a style of teaching which is not in keeping with the general style of the department or the modern language classroom. Many non-specialists may be hesitant over new developments and their views may be out of date. If they are members of the management team, they may be called out of the classroom for other business.

What can and should the head of department do in such cases? In the first instance the head of department should have a say as to who teaches in his team in a part-time capacity, in the same way as he should have a say in the selection of full-time staff.

When a part-timer or a non-specialist is part of the departmental staff what help should the head of department give? It would be reasonable to expect the non-specialist to do some preliminary reading about teaching modern languages. A selection in the departmental library would be appropriate.

The non-specialist should be encouraged to attend all relevent departmental meetings and to contribute beyond the classroom. Involvement in a particular area of responsibility is a good way of increasing expertise.

It is very important that the non-specialist be made aware of the materials, books, audio-visual aids, etc., that are available for general use. A simple catalogue is of limited use: an effort should be made to put on show and demonstrate new ideas and materials.

The non-specialist has the same right to expect support as does the new entrant to the profession. It is a mistake to expect that just because part-timers have twenty years teaching behind them that they will be at home in the new teaching situation.

Ideas worth exploring in order to increase confidence include:

— invitations to observe other experienced colleagues at work in the classroom;
— pairing the new colleague with a full-time specialist as a 'shadow';
— attendance at in-service courses (contact the LEA adviser or other training agencies);
— including the non-specialist in any training work undertaken on behalf of students in school, etc. (tricky to arrange, but it can be done tactfully).

Lastly, encourage the newcomer to feel he *is* an expert in the field.

Helping students in the department

The possibility of working closely with the local teacher-training institution should be welcomed, not only to enable staff to participate in this vital work of training the next generation of teachers, but also because of the undoubted spin-off effect of having contact with new and, one hopes, inventive minds, when the students are present. As the proposals for restructuring initial and in-service training take shape it is clear that the schools will have a bigger role to play. If properly organized, the mutual stimulation and interaction between school and training department can only do good. It is clearly part of the job of the head of department to so arrange matters that the pupils will benefit from the experience.

There will be conflicting pressures — chief of which will be to marry the demands of the pupils in school and their welfare and the needs of the visiting students allocated to the school for a short time in a crowded academic year.

At best, the practice period can be refreshing and stimulating, at worst an excuse for the regular teacher to gain a few extra 'free periods'. The head of department needs to plan well ahead with the opportunities and challenges. Early contact must be established with the training department and certain information gathered.

1   What is the overall shape of the training year(s)?
2   What are the main components of the students' year?
3   What level of subject competency can be expected from the student?
4   What is the shape of the school-based practice? If there are several sessions of work in schools, clearly we expect different things from the student at different stages.
5   What will be the pattern of supervision provided?
6   What weight is attached to the report sent from the school?
7   When is the assessment wanted?

You should see to it that the student in training is considered as a 'junior' member of the department, enjoying the 'rights' and *some* of the responsibilities of the regular staff. Ideally, as soon as the student has been allocated, you should make contact in the same way as when a full-time permanent appointment is made.

If possible, arrange for the student to come in beforehand, to meet the staff, whose classes he will be sharing for a time. It may even be possible to sit in with some classes at this first visit in order to sample the atmosphere of the working environment.

What sort of timetable should be arranged? It is very important to take careful note of any information given by the training institution, and in particular of the *curriculum vitae* of the student. What combination of subjects is on offer? Will it mean cooperation with another department? Try always to give as balanced an experience as possible over the age range and ability range of the school. It is best to avoid 'notorious' classes, yet it would be wrong to shelter the student from the realities of school life by going to the opposite extreme.

Where possible, allocate to the student the full subject time of a class. This does not imply that the student will always take every lesson alone. On the contrary, the inventive teacher will be able to fit in observation, small-group teaching, team-teaching as a variation over a period of time. Pupils will welcome a carefully planned change in routine. Within the classroom there are diverging views. Some staff favour the 'in-at-the-deep-end' approach, others the 'toe-in-first-to-test-the-temperature' idea. Experience would suggest the latter strategy, but it should be flexible. After an initial, but not too long, period of observation, the student must be allowed to establish his or her own working relationships with the pupils. This does *not* mean that there is no more observation. It will be important throughout the practice. It is only as experience increases that the real job of observation begins — as the student learns what to look out for in the performance of the regular teacher.

Careful planning of the lessons is essential. At first this should be under the direct supervision of the regular teacher. It is invaluable if members of staff discuss the student's lessons both before and after the event, but gradually the independence must be increased.

Appropriate evaluation is needed of course. You should keep a file of notes and it is ideal to use a carbon-copy system, giving a copy to the student as one discusses the lesson with him. Never offer criticism of any sort in front of the class — save all comments for the relative privacy of the staffroom.

Finally, it is essential to see that the student gets a broad view of the work of a teacher. If at all possible attach him to a 'form tutor', and allow him to see the work of other departments and see some of the work of, for example, a year tutor.

Supervising must not be seen as simply the work of the head of department but should be seen as part of the collective effort of the departmental team

Staff development

The head of department will have an important role to play in the career development of many staff. If the department is to be healthy and forward-looking in its approach, it is vital that innovations be considered and that staff horizons are widened.

Inevitably, monitoring the work of colleagues will be important, and at the same time it is that part of the professional duty which calls for the greatest tact and care. Assessing the work of teachers must not be approached with the attitude of an inquisitor, but rather with the aim to foster good practice and individual and corporate development. It will mean treading carefully through a minefield of personal relationships, but having such a skill was one of the reasons for being appointed to run a department.

Why assess departmental staff?

1   to allocate our staff resources to give the most beneficial outcome to the pupils in our care;
2   to decide if new teaching strategies are possible (e.g.

Have we the appropriate expertise to set up a new 'mode three' course?);

3   to contribute to the writing of references;
4   to recommend to the head those teachers who should be promoted internally;
5   to assess the needs of, and best method of, in-service training.

What should we assess?

1   *Administration.* Are mark-lists, minutes, etc., appropriately completed according to previously agreed and circulated deadlines?
2   *Lesson planning and review.* Is the teacher's record book up to date, realistic and meaningful?
3   *Homework.* Is it set, marked and commented on in an appropriate manner?
4   *Examination results.* Are they reasonable given the level of the class and in the light of experience?
5   *General contribution.* Is there an extra dimension beyond the classroom to the teacher's work?
6   *The work in the classroom.* This is the most important aspect of the review.

This is the most delicate of all tasks and the way it is carried out will depend to a large extent on the maturity of the relationships within the department. It cannot and must not be done in an underhand way, such as 'dropping in' to look in a cupboard (though such interruptions can reveal a lot). Ideally the criteria for assessment should be discussed openly with colleagues before and after the event.

Figure 1 is a suggested checklist to be used as an aid to assessment, using a five-point scale from positive to negative and based on observation within the classroom.

Knowing the qualities of the departmental staff is one step in producing an appropriate scheme for in-service training. Teachers are individuals and to some extent they must take

CLASSROOM OBSERVATION CHECKLIST					
Negative → Positive	1	2	3	4	5
Relationships with pupils					
1 Cooperation with pupils					
2 Pupil cooperation with teacher					
3 Reactions to pupils as individuals and their problems					
4 Class control: ability to anticipate problems					
Ability to create learning environment					
Ability to be consistent and fair					
Organization					
5 Suitability of material used					
6 Arrangement of materials					
7 Appropriate use of aids					
8 Knowledge of subject material					
Communication					
9 Clarity of voice					
10 Ability to receive pupil contribution and to react					
11 Ability to arouse and keep interest					
12 Progress during the lesson					
13 Initiative					

Figure 1

the responsibility for their own development, but neverthe-less the head of department must also initiate and be in a position to help staff to seize opportunities.

Identifying needs

As a regular item on the departmental agenda, identifying needs is a preliminary to initiating a programme of self-help and in-service work.

Questions to be asked include:

— Where is the department heading?
— What expertise does it need to implement its policy and the school's policy?
— What is the departmental view on the latest developments in the subject area?

Where can one enlist help?

It is important to realize that there is help both within and beyond the school:

— Staff within the school and the department may have particular expertise which they can share.
— The LEA adviser, the local college, the university in the area may help.
— Subject teaching associations such as the Modern Language Association and the local branches can be a valuable source of information and shared experience.

It is a good idea to use part of the departmental meeting for in-service work. After routine matters such as who is setting the third-year examination papers, why not discuss new ideas? The head of department (or someone else) could be asked to prepare and introduce a topic for discussion. Very often the invitation to an outside speaker (outside the department or outside the school) will act as a good focus. It will need careful planning, for it will be of little benefit to invite a speaker on a wide topic such as 'oral work' — that is far too vague. On the contrary, only with careful planning around a specific brief will such a venture be worthwhile.

A much more positive approach would be to invite someone to conduct a seminar on for example 'Communicative strategies in the oral lesson' — where staff are briefed beforehand and are prepared to participate in discussion.

Invite the LEA adviser in, and think also of the contacts that may be available at the local college or university. The Department of Education in the local institution will often be willing to help by providing a speaker or, if demands seem to warrant it, by putting on a course for local schools.

Other local and regional agencies provide courses and facilities at various levels and it is important to keep colleagues properly informed of meetings and events.

LEA Courses. Make sure that all information about local courses is circulated in the department. If kept centrally, read them and make sure all colleagues are informed. It is often a good idea to delegate a particular teacher for a course if the head of department can see real benefit to the individual as well as to the department.

DES courses. Two publications should be seen regularly by staff — 'Long Courses' and 'Short Courses'. These booklets are sent to all schools.

Visits abroad. Staff should be encouraged to maintain and improve the quality of their language and their knowledge of the country. Various bodies run courses, visits and exchanges. The local town may be 'twinned' and such arrangements can be of great help. Finance can be a problem, but it is sometimes possible to get help from various sources and it is useful to contact the adviser who may have sources of information, if not finance.

Post-to-post exchanges. These can be very useful to the linguist and, if properly planned, to the receiving school by bringing a trained teacher and native speaker to the 'host' school. For full information, contact *The Central Bureau for*

Educational Visits and Exchanges. The address will be found in Part 4, Chapter 30.

Professional reading and the staff library. Members of staff should be encouraged to keep up to date in their reading. In the busy term at school, it is surprising how much this is neglected. If at all possible the school librarian and the various departments should cooperate to provide a basic range of books on curriculum development, methodology, the latest research, etc. In addition the ideal library would have copies of the various journals and publications of the subject teaching associations.

Reporting back. This is essential. In order that the widest possible audience may share experiences, it is vital that' anyone who has been on a course or any form of in-service training should report back to colleagues. This form of self-help is often overlooked.

Career development. The head of department is one of the members of staff responsible for helping teachers to think about their career development. This is not always easy at a time of falling rolls, but it is very important to urge teachers to think ahead and try to avoid professional staleness.

Senior colleagues should be kept informed about the work of staff — and above all the good work. It is not always easy for the head in a large establishment to know everything that is going on.

Try to see that the individual timetables of the staff facilitate development. The timetable should ideally have an eye on staff development as well as the immediate demands of the term or the year.

Keep an ear to the ground. A good head of department will know beforehand of the various aspirations of his colleagues and will do what he can to help them in a *realistic* way.

Suggestions for topics for 'in-service' work within the department
The following, not exhaustive, list of ideas could well form a

basis for short-term and long-term discussions within the framework of the language department:

- setting of examination questions;
- testing the various skills;
- marking pupils' work;
- assessment for internal and external examinations;
- continuous assessment;
- making worksheets and other audio-visual aids;
- using the hardware of the department and the school;
- the oral component of the lesson;
- exploiting the particular courses in use in the school;
- using the assistant;
- writing reports;
- using the library;
- using authentic materials.

17 The organization of resources

Whatever grand ideas we may have, whatever master plan we elaborate to transform language teaching in the school, sooner or later any such plan has to be worked out within the framework of the available resources, the timetable space, the staff expertise, the accommodation, and the capitation allowance.

The drawing up of the timetable, agreed by colleagues and acceptable to the timetabler, the head and other departments, is discussed fully in Chapter 18. Likewise the appointing of the departmental staff, their induction, further training and deployment have been discussed in detail. This section is concerned with the narrower (but equally important) idea of resources — the rooms, equipment and books.

Rooms

Ideally every teacher in the department will have his or her own room, for in such circumstances they are more easily maintained. Alas, this ideal is not always possible, so that the minimum to be asked for is a suite of rooms for the almost exclusive use of the department. The physical conditions in which we teach have a great bearing on the morale of both teachers and pupils. If the department can create a tradition of tidy, well-cared-for rooms, so much the better.

The minimum to be bargained for would seem to be:

1   Exclusive (or major) use of a number of classrooms,
    depending on the size of the staff. These should be
    equipped so as to allow teaching to take place in the
    departmental 'style' with the minimum of carrying and
    transferring of equipment.
2   Appropriate stockrooms/cupboards, conveniently sited
    so as to encourage maximum use of resources.
3   Limited rights over other rooms of various sizes so as to
    allow assistants and other small groups to function
    effectively.

The advantage of fixed accommodation of this type is
enormous and will enrich the possibilities of teaching and
collaboration in so many ways.

1   Heavy, expensive equipment will not have to be moved
    long distances (if at all) and this will save wear and tear
    on both machines and staff. It will also reduce the
    temptation for staff to reject the use of equipment
    because it is not to hand.
2   Staff cooperation will be all the greater if they are
    grouped together in adjacent rooms.
3   Support for new staff, probationers and students is much
    easier in a compact area.
4   Displays are easier to manage.
5   Borrowing and returning of stock is easier to control.

There are disadvantages in the 'suite' arrangement, the main
one being that pupils are forced to move for each lesson to
different areas of the building. With careful timetabling this
can be minimized, even in a busy school, and should not be
allowed to tip the balance against such cooperative arrangements.

Equipment

Basic requirements

● a tape recorder/cassette recorder;

- external, fixed speakers to increase sound reproduction quality;
- a projector/OHP;
- a blackout system, screen;
- use (shared?) of VTR/TV/radio;
- electric sockets, in sufficient quantity and in strategic positions;
- cupboard and display space;
- pin-boards.

This may appear to be an extravagant shopping-list, but it isn't, if it is compared to the amount of money spent on the science and craft, design and technology departments. Of course the case for spending money on capital equipment will be greatly enhanced if the equipment is regularly used, and seen to be so.

It is not our intention to discuss detailed plans for each room — size, layout, etc., for conditions will vary so much from school to school. However, staff must be aware that the way the room is laid out — desks in rows or other forms of grouping, will affect the style of teaching that will take place in the classroom. Desks in rows may very well favour 'teacher-orientated' styles, whereas group-work and 'communicative' activities may be better in a room with more informal arrangements of the furniture. Discuss it with the departmental staff and work out what suits the team of teachers.

Maintaining the equipment

Equipment will be of no use unless it works efficiently and is available. Whatever method is used for storing, retrieving, returning and monitoring the use of equipment *the system must be understandable and easy to use* or it will be abused.

The gold-rush, or how not to use resources

It is bad planning to use this method, whereby the

departmental stock-cupboard is opened at the start of the term and the various members of the department (or at least those in the know!) take away for their own use all that they need — or think that they might need. This is the surest way of building up the 'staffroom window-sill' method of storing and not using efficiently all that valuable material. It will encourage an individual and not a collective approach to the departmental work. Once this initial rush is over, then there is little you can do about it until the time to collect in all the goodies in July.

On the contrary, proper pre-planning before the beginning of the school year and preferably at the same time as decisions about the scheme of work are made, will go a long way to easing frustrations about stock and equipment.

Maintaining the hardware

It is essential to have regular (weekly or even daily) checks on the valuable equipment in the department, together with a proper system for reporting and correcting faults. Unless malfunctions are reported *and* acted upon quickly they tend to be forgotten. It will then almost certainly be the case that

MODERN LANGUAGE DEPARTMENT. A/V AIDS FAULTS BOOK. 19 .... — 19						
Date	Machine	No.	Location	Fault description	Staff	Action
19/10	Tape recorder	4	Room 6	No Fast Winding	DM	To Teachers' Centre 20/10

Figure 2

the tape recorder will fail to work at the most crucial time in the school year — just as the O-level orals are about to begin! Maintenance will be easier if a 'faults book' is used and is kept in a suitable place. Each page should be ruled out appropriately and space left to record the action taken as in Figure 2.

It is usually possible, via the LEA, to negotiate a regular maintenance schedule — it is well worthwhile in order to avoid frustration. Minor matters can be speedily dealt with from within the department. The changing of projector bulbs, cleaning of tape heads, etc., should be part of the training programme offered to the staff.

The departmental tool-kit

It is a good idea to have a collection of 'odds and ends' in the departmental area in order to effect minor repairs, etc., as quickly as possible. Such a tool-kit will have at least the following items:

- spare bulbs of the right sizes;
- spare plugs and fuses of the correct type — be sure to read the instructions carefully on all equipment;
- spare leads, jack plugs, audio connectors, etc. (labelled);
- a tape editor;
- a tape eraser (very useful for recycling tapes and ensuring clean recordings);
- screwdrivers, insulating tape, etc.
- the operating manuals of the various pieces of equipment.

What each teacher should know about the departmental resources

Each member of staff should have an up-to-date list of available equipment and should include the following:

- available 'hardware' — recorders, cassettes, projectors, OHPs, etc.

- available 'software' — tapes, slides, cassettes, videos, etc.
- worksheets;
- flashcards;
- books and other printed material beyond the basic texts;
- past examination papers;
- duplicating and other reprographic facilities in the school;
- loan facilities operated by the school advisory service and other agencies;
- school library facilities.

Such a list could very well be annotated in order to give some idea as to the age/ability range of the materials.

Ordering books and equipment

Much will depend on the policy of the school, but it is usual to allow the head of department discretion in using the funds allocated to the department. It is important to ascertain at the outset what is covered by the departmental capitation allowance. Does it include exercise books, audio-visual aids, etc., or are such items covered elsewhere? What items of expenditure are in the sphere of the department — it is important to know at the beginning because, as always, planning is vital. One must view the process of 'requisitions' as a year-long process and not a matter to be dealt with hastily at the start of the financial year. It is wise therefore to establish a departmental policy in consultation with colleagues. When drawing up such a strategy, it would be reasonable to discuss openly with the staff and the head in order to establish a budget and target for the year.

How should this be done? What factors need to be taken into account? Read on.

The departmental budget

1   Establish a departmental 'teaching load'. The more pupils you teach as a department, and the more frequently you see them in a week, the more expensive it will be to equip them properly. To calculate the teaching load, calculate for each year, the number of groups, multiplied by the number of pupils in each group and then by the number of periods taught to the group. For example:

1st year:
6 groups – 30 pupils per group – 4 lessons per week
= 6 × 30 × 4 = 720.

Add together all the year totals for all languages to find the departmental total. The figure itself is quite meaningless — but it will be interesting when compared to other departments, and can be used as a bargaining counter for a proper share of resources.

2   Consider the needs of the different languages within the department.

3   What are the needs of examination classes — e.g. for 'set books'?

4   What are the needs of special groups — e.g. low-ability classes?

5   What will have to be spent to make up depleted stock? Depleted sets of books will always be there, even in a well-run department.

6   What proportion needs to be spent on expendable items such as card for flash cards, glue, files, etc.?

7   Does the department need to contribute anything towards capital items such as a new cassette recorder?

8   Is there a 'contingency fund' for unexpected needs during the year?

And perhaps the overriding consideration:

9   What are the long-term aims of the department, which may involve expenditure over a number of years? Will a change of syllabus or the introduction of a new series of

course books be feasible, given other ongoing items of expense?

Buying materials — reviewing the range and making a selection

Having established the long-term strategy and general policy, the next thing to do is to build up a bank of information on what is available.

1   First of all, try to build up an annotated collection of publishers' brochures (not forgetting to discard last year's out-of-date version). A 'concertina file' with lettered sections is a useful cataloguing method. Be a magpie in collecting, but be sure to keep any material up to date.

2   If possible go to exhibitions where material will be on display.

3   At the annual JCLA conference there is always the most comprehensive publishers' exhibition and display, including workshop sessions, which are most informative. (The local branch of the MLA will supply details.)

4   Whenever possible, you will find it useful to talk to teachers in other schools to ascertain opinions on books and materials which you may be thinking of adopting.

5   The approval and inspection copy service is a most useful device to see and examine new publications.

6   If new books are received, it is a good idea to keep a systematic record of opinions.

7   The journals of the teaching associations are an excellent source of information in their editorial and review sections.

When reviewing inspection copies, it is best done systematically, with an index-card system that can be referred to later, as in Figure 3. Keep these cards for requisition-time and include your colleagues' opinions.

Title	Author	
Publisher	Date	Price
Age range	ISBN	
Components		
Tapes	Illustrations	
Comments		
Action		

Figure 3

Ordering stock

It is important to order sufficient stock of each title to allow for some wastage. In addition it is a good idea to order for staff a selection of other titles which may stimulate new ideas. Even if a course book is not quite suitable for your school, there will still be many good ideas to pick up. So in addition to class sets of major courses, five or six copies of a variety of other material for the staff library will prove to be valuable. These can be stored in the departmental library together with books on methodology, the MLA handbooks, reports from the examination boards, the CILT catalogues, etc.

Keeping track of stock

This is most important and can help in the smooth running of the department. In an effort to keep wastage to a minimum, try to keep to a routine, whenever new material arrives.

Title French For You (Book 1)			ISBN 0 09 146641 5	
Date	Additions	Deleted	In stock	Initials
1/9	40		40	DM

Figure 4

1   As soon as an order arrives in school, log it on an index-card as in Figure 4. Use one card per item and above all endeavour to keep it up to date. It is also possible now to use the school computer to keep track of materials. It will be time-consuming to put the inventory into the data-file in the first instance, but thereafter it will be quick to obtain a printout, up-date the figures and thus keep an accurate record of departmental resources.

2   As soon as the stock has been recorded, all material should be stamped with the official school/departmental stamp in order to identify it.

3   It is essential to have a fixed time every year to take stock. A physical check is essential — and it also allows the staff to check for damage and perhaps enlist pupils to do remedial work.

4   It is also essential to keep a record of stock issued (date, class, staff).

5   Number books with a system that is consistent: e.g. 85/21 is book 21 of that title bought in 1985.

6   If the school allows it, operate an approved system of

monitoring damage and loss — charging, issuing receipts, etc., in accordance with school policy.

7   Try as far as possible to avoid the staffroom window-sill syndrome. It is frustrating to see the odd copies missing from complete sets of books lying around gathering dust. Be ruthless, and have regular 'round-up' sessions from all the nooks and crannies in the school buildings. It is also well worthwhile having a large box in the staffroom, labelled *Modern Language Department Depot* for people to use as an 'amnesty' box.

Keeping track of audio-visual software

Looking after tapes, cassettes and other such material is important. A properly thought-out system is vital, not only to minimize loss, but also to allow staff to take full advantage of the material available.

1   Every cassette, tape, etc., should be clearly marked with a sticker to identify the contents.
2   The tape/cassette box could carry a self adhesive coloured marker to indicate the code (e.g. red for French, green for German, blue for A-level, etc.). This will enable material to be returned more easily to the correct shelf.
3   Try to allot a space on the shelf for each tape/cassette, so that it will be easy to see if one is missing.
4   If pupils have access to tapes, etc., *never* lend out the master copy. Have a loan copy and operate a loans/ returns book which is checked regularly.
5   Make sure that all those concerned know the system.

18 Drawing up the timetable

The production of the school timetable brings to life the decisions made at many levels about school priorites and concerns. It is a complicated task, but not one so shrouded in mystery that it is impossible to understand. The head of department must seek close liaison with the timetabler, and the attempt to exert some control over his part of the pupil-day will mean understanding the process. Of course it will mean understanding the logic of the task but it will also involve persistence in order to make the appropriate intervention at the right time.

This understanding falls into two parts: the school dimension and the departmental point of view. Issues to be taken into account include:

The school dimension

the contribution modern languages make to the general education of pupils;
— the specialist needs of pupils;
— the overall time allocation to the various interests in the school;
— cooperation with other departments, e.g. in respect of language policy;
— the number and qualifications of the staff.

The departmental demands

Points to be considered are:

The needs of pupils
— the size of class groups, taking into account the age, ability and aims of each group;
— the experience of particular pupils with a member of staff in the previous year — was it fruitful or not?
— the need for continuity in teaching especially with examination classes;
— the desirability of a change of teacher to give a contrast or a change of emphasis.

The needs of staff
— the necessity to give, so far as is possible, a fair timetable to each member of staff (the view that the 'established' members of staff automatically get first choice is not acceptable in a team situation);
— the need for a policy on staff development — for example a point of view that makes it possible for each member of staff to have experience of the whole variety of classes available in the school;
— the individual wishes of the staff;
— other responsibilities within the school which may demand a time-allocation — for example, being a year tutor or head of house — not forgetting those extra, time-consuming jobs that go with leading a department;
— new colleagues and their particular needs.

The process

It is a mistake to think that the timetable can be produced in a week or two. The whole process must be seen as a long-term operation which begins several months prior to committing decisions to paper. The making of a timetable usually has an optimistic beginning ('We'll get it right this year!'), but compromise and reality frequently temper this optimism.

The initial steps to be taken

1   Review the working of the existing arrangements: have
    they produced the desired effects in terms of pupils'
    performance? If not, what are the obstacles from the
    points of view of the pupils, the staff and the use of
    resources?

2   Talk with the curriculum coordinator about new ideas
    coming from the department.

3   Discuss in the heads of department committee the
    overall curriculum pattern being proposed.

4   Calculate the staffing requirements in the department in
    terms of the total class-periods to be taught as against the
    staff periods available. If these do not tally, discuss the
    problem in good time with the head so that appropriate
    appointments can be made. Try to avoid last-minute
    decisions which may produce less than satisfactory
    results.

5   Discuss proposed arrangements with the departmental
    staff. Topics which need airing include:
    (a) 'blocking' the timetable allocation, i.e. teaching a
        group of classes at similar times to allow for
        flexibility of grouping and cooperation between
        staff;
    (b) the desirability of 'single' or 'double' periods for
        pupils of different age/ability groups;
    (c) the spread over the week of the lesson allocation.
        Here we may take account of Professor Hawkins'
        recommendation that there should be 'a policy on
        timetabling subjects which takes sensitive account of
        the unique needs of teachers who have to plant their
        seedlings in a gale of English';
    (d) the optimum use of departmental rooms.

The intricacies of the proposed timetable in a large school
will demand compromises. It is here that the judgement of
the head of department will come into play. This overview of
the total situation and of the competing demands of the
various interests within the school will demand a wide
vision and a measure of statesmanship.

Committing the ideas to paper

At this stage it is patience and cups of strong coffee that win through. Try to do everything on paper and not simply in your head. Prepare beforehand the blanks which can be ruled out to suit the particular pattern of the school week, and to show classes to be taught as well as staff availability. Ascertain beforehand from the timetabler any restrictions that are likely to affect the allocation — for example it may be that a particular teacher is not available on Mondays as he is only part-time, or another colleague may also be involved in boys' games on a Wednesday morning. At whatever stage the head of department is called in, it is useful to employ a 'visual-planner' technique to plot the proposed individual allocations (initially in pencil, to allow easy alterations). This could be done as in Figure 5.

While it may not be possible for the individual head of department to affect the total layout of the periods for a particular colleague, it is useful to have a further visual check to try to ensure for example that the total allocation of 'free' periods doesn't fall on one day with none for the rest of the week. Such a chart will also help to see the distribution of lessons from the point of view of an individual group of pupils. (See Figure 6.) Always keep a copy of all your decisions and allocations as they are handed in to the timetabler. You may be asked to 'juggle' with proposed allocations, so be sure to receive and return any changes promptly and *in writing*.

Above all:
Try to the *reasonable* in all things.

- Be *diplomatic* in suggestions.
- Be *alert* and *ingenious* in trying to solve the 'impossible'.
- Have *alternative ideas* ready.
- Try to *predict* and *anticipate* any problems that may arise because of the demands of the department.

GREENWAY HIGH SCHOOL

Timetable   19 .... − 19 ....   Department MOD LANGS

Staff	DM	AS	JC	SS	CM	SB	VO
Subject	F-G	F-S	F	F-S	G	F-G	F
Class U6 A	4^F	4^S	4^F	4^S	4^G	4^G	
L6 A	4^F	4^S		4^S	4^G	4^G	
L6 O	−	−					4^F
5 option 1	4^F set 4	−	4^F set 3	4^F set 2			4^F set 1
5 option 4	−	4^S	4^F set 1		4^G	4^F set 2	
4 option 1	4^F set 1	4^F set 2				4^F set 3	
4 option 4	−	4^S					
3	4^G set 1	−	4^F				
2	4^F set 3	4^F set 4		Allocate staff to classes to enable visual check to be made			
1	4^F M/A	4^F M/A	4^F M/A				
OTHER DUTIES	H.O.D			TUTOR			CAREERS

Notes

Indicate staff by initials
Indicate subject by letter

In each box indicate periods allocated,
followed by class title (eg. set 1, set 2
or mixed stability = M/A)

Figure 5

| | | GREENWAY HIGH SCHOOL | | | | | |

Dept. ....   Timetable 19 ...... – 19 ....

Staff / Period	DM	AS	JC	SS	CM	SB	VO
MON 1	U6^F	4/4 s					
MON 2	5/1^4 F		5/1^3 F	5/1^2 F		U6 G	5/1^4 F
MON 3	2/3 F	2/4 F	2/1 F	U6 S	U6 G	2/2 F	
MON 4	4/1^1 F	4/1^2 F				4/1^3 F	
TUES 1	3/1^1 G	U6 S					L6 F
TUES 2	L6^F		U6 F				
TUES 3		5/4 s	5/4^1 F		5/4 G	5/4^2 F	
TUES 4		L6 S				L6 G	
WED 1	1M/A F	1M/A F		L6 S	L6		
WED 2		U6 S				U6 G	L6 F
WED 3	2/3 ^{F}	2/4 ^{F}					
WED 4	U6 F	4/4 ^{S}					
THURS 1		5/4 s		U6			
THURS 2	5/1^4 F						
THURS 3		L6 S					
THURS 4	3/1 G						
FRI 1	L6 F		U6 F				
FRI 2	4/1^1 F	4/1^2 F					
FRI 3	1M/A F	1M/A F					
FRI 4							

> Assuming 20 period/week
> enter class taught in box
> to check allocation
>
> Class indicated by
> year/option/set
> e.g. 4/1^1 = 4th year
> option 1, set 1
>
> Language by letter

Figure 6

19 Designing
     the syllabus

Schools cannot work in isolation, as an island with no contact with the world outside. The pressures felt by all departments are considerable, and come from a variety of agencies and sections within the community. To design the syllabus for the department means taking account of all these demands — from parents, industry, other schools and educational institutions, the pupils, staff and, not least, the demands imposed by the nature of the subject itself. It is not possible to lay down watertight rules applicable to all schools and it must be assumed that the head of department will take into account the local circumstances.

The concern of this section will be liaison with feeder schools and the drawing up of the departmental scheme of work. Contacts with parents, other outside agencies, careers, etc., are dealt with elsewhere.

Liaison with feeder schools

When the study of the foreign language is begun in the secondary school at the age of eleven, liaison with feeder schools is less crucial than when there is foreign language teaching in the primary or middle school.

It is a mistake to think, however, even when there is a break at the age of eleven and the pupils then embark upon the secondary stage, that contact is of no use. Pupils as they arrive, are not blank moulds, devoid of individuality. Liaison should be seen as one positive way to build up a picture of the new entrant to the school.

However, the most important type of liaison is called for when the pupil arrives having studied a language for two, three or even four years in the previous school, and such experience must not be discounted or even ignored if a healthy attitude to foreign language learning is to be fostered. One of the major lessons acquired from the Burstall Report in Primary French[1] was that good liaison between the different sections in our education system was of prime importance.

All sectors of the school system must work together and be regarded as interdependent in the interests of the pupils and their progress. Teachers in secondary schools, and in particular, the head of department, should work very closely with the neighbouring schools whose pupils will be arriving at the start of term. In the ideal situation such contacts will be both formal and informal.

Making formal contact with schools

The vital reason for such formal contact is an *exchange* of information:

- information *into* the receiving schools about pupil progress; and
- information *from* the receiving schools about past pupils now passing through their care.

Over the course of the school year it is a good idea to arrange for the *mutual* exchange of the following material:

- Syllabus and schemes of work
- Examples of main textbooks
- Examples of pupil work

(1) Clare Burstall *et al.*, 'Primary French in the Balance', NFER 1974.

At the time of transfer, the head of department or his delegate should seek information on the following areas:

The achievement of pupils about to transfer
Grades/marks with an explanation as to how these were obtained: e.g. by end-of-year examination, cumulative testing, etc. If possible a copy of the test instruments should be seen to fill out the picture. It is useful if such information can reveal attainment in the various skill areas.

Background comment about the pupils
Individual remarks about the pupils that are *relevant*. For example has the pupil been abroad? Is he or she shy in oral work? Are there any brothers or sisters that you already know?
Are there any special problems such as dyslexia or speech defects?

A possible 'transfer' form is seen in Figure 7. It is comprehensive in scope if properly completed. The years of French section will show just that, but could also indicate the type of class-groupings used. Thus an entry over the 'middle school' years M1, M2, M3, M4, could read thus: MA, MA, 2/4, 1/4, indicating that the pupil was in a mixed-ability group for two years, then was in set 2 out of 4, and in the final year was in set 1 out of 4.

The assessment of performance section should record marks or grades in as objective a way as possible, and should refer to the assessment immediately prior to transfer. Such assessment will refer to the group in which the pupil was taught. It may be that a pupil in a low-ability group has higher 'marks' than a high ability pupil, particularly where the groups have differentiated objectives. However, the section headed 'overall rating in the year group' will provide some sort of ranking.

This latter will be best expressed according to the curve of normal distribution — that is we could expect more or less the top 10 per cent to be 'A' grade, the next 20 per cent 'B', approximately 40 per cent 'C', the next 20 per cent 'D' and the final 10 per cent 'E'. Finally the 'effort' grade will be an

FRENCH TRANSFER REPORT

Transfer from: .... Middle School to: .... High School (date: ....)

Name	Years of French studied				Assessment of performance				Overall rating in year group (A – E)	Effort grade (A – E)	Comments
	M1	M2	M3	M4	Listg	Spkg	Rdg	Wrtg			

Figure 7

independent grade, and not related to attainment. Remember an 'E' in attainment may be the result of Herculean efforts!

In other words we seek as complete a picture as possible. And it is fruitful to try and obtain this information by means of a visit to the feeder school rather than by an exchange of letters. Talking to a colleague can reveal much that is difficult to describe in a brief report.

The two-way process

All such consultation must be seen as a two-way movement. It is immensely helpful and a sign of good relations to feed information *back* into the middle or primary schools, not least because staff in such schools can feel isolated if they are the only specialists in the school, running a one-man department and also because the public 'reward' of external examinations never comes to pupils in their immediate care.

It is particularly important for example that the syllabus and examination requirements for such public examinations are known. This topic could well form part of the agenda for a meeting of teachers from 'linked' schools.

The need for such meetings will vary according to the circumstances. If well planned and relevant to the needs of the area, they will fill a vital need. This type of meeting could be arranged on local initiative or could be part of the provisions made by the local adviser.

At the beginning of the school year, take back the following information:

The examination results for past pupils. It is surprising how well such pupils will be remembered, even though they left some time before.

The record of progress of the previous year's cohort — what they did in the first year of their new school; did they take up another foreign language? Did they continue with language study at all?

All this exchange of information will help to increase mutual confidence and experience so that the grading will be all the more effective. It is surprising how often feeder schools ask if their grading policy is on a level with that in neighbouring schools. It is also important that the welcoming school does its best to see what the relative marks and grades really mean. If school A is more lenient in its assessment than school B, or more erratic, then the only professional way to resolve problems is by open discussion based on mutual confidence and respect.

Making informal contact with feeder schools

Visits, exchanging timetables, pupil contact, etc.
The most convenient time for personal visits to the feeder schools would seem to be in the relatively relaxed summer post-exam period.

Mutual visits to schools During such a visit, ask if it is possible to see some classes in action. It is also a good idea to see, wherever possible, samples of pupil work, textbooks and other materials.

The visits must not be 'one-way', but it is sometimes difficult to release the primary or middle school teacher who only rarely has 'free periods'. One interesting idea is to use the possibly more flexible secondary timetable to 'free' the secondary colleague in June or July to spend a morning or a day getting to know the pupils 'in situ', while the opposite number is able to visit and possibly teach in the secondary school. It can be very refreshing teaching pupils outside the normal age range!

Arranging assistant contact

Other ways of helping establish contact is via the pupils themselves and even the assistant.

At certain times of the year, particularly in exam and post-exam periods, the timetable of the foreign assistant shrinks.

It is useful at such times to use him or her with classes in the school that don't normally benefit because this valuable resource has been restricted to examination classes during the school year. The same principle may be extended to the local primary or middle school, where the assistant could spend an afternoon during the week in June or July. Thus not only do the younger pupils (and their teachers) benefit but it will open another window for the younger learners as they meet a native speaker. It is always important to seek the agreement of all parties — but the initiative is rarely refused.

Involving pupils

Pupils can help as well. They often relish a return to the 'old' school! One way is to arrange a 'presentation' of short playlets, role-plays, songs, etc. These need not be elaborate and may be a compilation of work done in the classroom, at the open day and so on.

Most secondary schools invite new pupils to come on a preliminary visit before the September term begins. It is perfectly possible to arrange part of the visit in the foreign language: those 'sophisticated' pupils, now a year older, act as guides in French around the language teaching area. Inviting the new pupils to see a presentation about the school can be useful and break the ice before they move from the familiarity of the smaller school to the overwhelming size of the secondary school.

Continuity is the aim

Whatever arrangements are made, both formal and informal, the ultimate aim is to ensure as far as possible that the transition from the children's point of view is as smooth as possible. Mutual acquaintance is but one aspect of this. Equally important is the need to ensure that the aims, objectives, methodology and approach, in each sector of the system are compatible. And so the careful drawing up of a scheme of work is essential.

The scheme of work

Assuming that the head of department has done his or her homework and is fully aware of the contribution the feeder schools make to the total process of learning a foreign language and that the aims beyond the school are recognized, then the drawing up of a scheme of work is a difficult task that we put to one side at our peril.

In the decentralized system of education which operates in the United Kingdom, the decisions as to *what* to teach, *when* and to *whom* are largely left to the individual school, and *within* the school, by delegation from the head, to the head of department in discussion with colleagues.

The leadership of the head of department is perhaps most easily seen in the way in which an agreed scheme of work is drawn up.

Every department is supposed to have such a document:
● The visiting student wants to consult it.
● The new colleague wants sight of it.
● The head uses it as a yardstick.
● The adviser asks for it.
● The HMI may ask for it at short notice.
But often it is gathering dust in the head of department's cupboard!

A working document

Such a scheme, if it is to be of use (otherwise why bother?) should set out the *why* and the *what*, the *when* and the *how*:
● It should be an agreed document, reflecting the views and the experience of all the members of the departmental team.
● It should be up-to-date and not like last year's Michelin Guide gathering dust and useful only for its nostalgic value.
● It should be precise and pointed, rather than general and vague.

• It should be practical and rooted in the realm of the *possible*.

Drawing up such a document can be an arduous business especially in a crowded term; it will not be done in the course of a few lunchtime meetings and, if it is to be of real value, the finished document will never really be definitive and will always need revising.

The HMIs are very specific in their belief that such a document is needed. A few years ago, in their discussion document *Modern Languages in Comprehensive Schools*, they stated:

> The ideal Head of Department, would have formulated, in consultation with colleagues, a programme of work which spelt out realistic objectives and indicated how these might be achieved within the limitations imposed by the ability of the pupils, by school organization and by the availability of equipment.[1]

But even putting aside these outside pressures, why bother? Could not the head of department put the paper together in the last few days of the holidays and so save a lot of time? What are the benefits of compiling together an *agreed* document?

There are five good reasons for writing the scheme of work collectively.

Security. It should provide a framework within which both staff and pupils can feel secure. No department is stable; staff come and go. If at least there is an attempt to define the direction of the team, then there is more chance to make some forward progress.

Planning. It will actually make life easier in the long term. There is nothing more wearing than having to make up lessons at a moment's notice with no real purpose; constant

---

(1) *Modern Languages in Comprehensive Schools*, HMI Matters for Discussion, 1977, p 18.

'ad-hoc-ery' is the surest way to a nervous breakdown.

Publicity. A scheme of work will enable staff to defend more coherently the position of modern languages from the constant assault of the 'disbelievers' who are all around — pupils, parents, governors, other colleagues, employers, all of whom at some time 'see no point' in learning a foreign language.

Induction. The helping of students, new colleagues and part-time members of the team will be easier and they will be seen as part of a coherent pattern.

Satisfaction. It will make you think about what you are trying to do rather than simply reiterate last year's routine. The very exercise will involve research, questioning and problem-solving — all of which can be easily put aside on a busy year. Thinking out the rationale of the team will raise job-satisfaction.

The ideal scheme of work will then be an *agreed* statement of policy and as such it will focus the minds of individual teachers and ask them to listen to the ideas of others. All the issues must be openly discussed and debated in order to reach a consensus; only then will the head of department have the authority and the right to ask for loyalty from his or her colleagues. But beware — such loyalty does not mean slavishly following the document such that it will stifle personal initiative. On the contrary, individual teachers, by reason of open discussion, will be better able to appreciate the contribution of their colleagues and evaluate their initiatives as well as their own in the context of the work of the whole department.

Who should have access to the finished document?

- The head.
- The deputy or deputies, pastoral coordinator, curriculum coordinator.
- Other heads of department. This is good propaganda value!
- Assistant teachers, not forgetting part-timers and those

members of staff shared with other departments. Such colleagues need special help if they are to feel part of a team.

- The assistant.
- Student teachers on practice.

Copies should also be available to:

- the school governors;
- inspectors and advisers;
- teachers in feeder schools — especially if a foreign language is begun in the primary or middle school.

What will it look like?

The format of the scheme of work is important. If properly drawn up, it will be a lengthy document and its very size may discourage reading. More importantly, the wealth of detail may militate against updating. The single continuous document may mean that it will never be revised, since the idea that to change one section may very well entail the alteration of whole pages or even the whole scheme will ensure that it is fixed for evermore.

The most useful and practical format would seem to be a looseleaf file, with index, so that it is easy to replace individual sections with newer versions as the need arises. A contents section should be followed by lettered and numbered sections, in order to make it easier to grow, correct and adjust.

What follows is an example of a scheme of work in order to provide a starting point for discussions in the department. It is important not to try to do all the work in one session and not to consider that the complete tome has to be written by the head of department. Given the sectional nature of the document it is easy to ask other members of the department to do some of the spade-work and then to bring discussion documents to the departmental meeting.

HOLMEFIELD HIGH SCHOOL, NEWTOWN
SCHEME OF WORK
MODERN LANGUAGE DEPARTMENT

Section A   Aims
Section B   Courses provided by the department
Section C   Departmental policies
Section D   Syllabus and scheme of work for each language
Section E   Resources

Section A   Aims
This section should contain a brief statement of the aims of the department, answering the question 'Why are languages taught in the school?':

1   *Utilitarian reasons:* communication; future needs of pupils; foundation for future study.
2   *Intellectual reasons:* awareness of language; learning how to learn a language.
3   *Cultural reasons:* broadening horizons; combating insularity; civilization.
4   *Enjoyment:* it can (and should) be enjoyable to learn a new language.

Section B   Courses provided by the department
In this section we must address ourselves to the following questions:

1   *Which languages?*
     In most schools the first foreign language will probably be French — *though this must not be regarded as inevitable.* The local conditions — LEA policy, neighbouring schools (primary and middle), the availability of staff, etc., will have to be taken into account. Consideration could be given to alternating the first foreign language in different years, to providing a parallel foreign language in each year and other schemes. It is to be hoped that a second modern language (and even a third) will be included in the school programme.

     Among the reasons to be advanced are:
     (a)   opportunity for the more able linguist and/or gifted pupil;
     (b)   broadening the curriculum (three sciences are unquestioned);

(c)   a challenge to the traditional place of French;
(d)   widening of linguistic horizons;
(e)   cultural awareness;
(f)   career requirements;
(g)   the possibility of a fresh start for some pupils.

2   *Starting age*
This may not be entirely in the hands of the school, let alone the department, because of LEA policy which provides for (say) French in feeder schools, or, sadly, today because of restrictions on staffing. However, if there *is* a choice, this is clearly a matter over which the head and the department should come to a rational agreement. What should *not* be in dispute is the fact that *all* pupils should have the opportunity of beginning a foreign language at some time in their school career and they should be encouraged to continue with their study for as long as they can derive benefit.

3   *Length of course*
The ideal departmental policy will allow all pupils to pursue their study as long as possible. There will be in all schools, pupils of varied linguistic ability, motivation and maturity — and all deserve consideration. For a considerable number of pupils the course will last until the end of compulsory schooling. However, in a comprehensive school, this may not include all pupils and proper provision must be made for different needs. Each school will have to provide courses of various lengths, each complete in itself and possibly with its own certification. Such courses must not be merely truncated versions of the traditional five-year course, but planned in their own right. (It is worthwhile here being closely involved with your own area Graded-Test group).

4   *Examinations*
A statement should be made here indicating the various examination targets of the courses, e.g.:
    Graded Test Level;
    CSE (Mode 1, 2, 3);
    'O'-level;
    GCSE (16 +);
    A/O;
    'A'-level;
    RSA, IoL, etc.

5 *Option courses*
Departmental policy in respect of the various "options" offered at fourth-form and sixth-form level should be stated.

Section C Departmental policies

1 *Differentiation of objectives*
A policy must be discussed and agreed, to take into account the different needs of various pupils (as in (3) above). Given the staffing resources of the school it must be decided how many courses can be offered and with what objectives.

2 *The use of the foreign language in the classroom*
A consistent policy is important with the encouragement of meaningful, purposeful use of the foreign language for real communication at all times. The target language should be seen as the medium of communication for real transactions and not just as a game to be played for forty minutes between the reality of maths or biology.

3 *Assessment and record-keeping*
Assessment is a vital part of the work of the department and all members of staff will be called upon to measure and record pupil progress at various times. The head of department must ensure that an agreed policy is set up and operates. Regular monitoring of progress by the classroom teacher should be underpinned by a departmentally coordinated system of testing and sampling of pupil understanding. At certain times of the year, it will be appropriate to set tests and examinations across a group of sets or classes in order to give guidance at, say, option time. School-policy will have determined the timing of set-piece examinations, but that will mean that the department must elaborate a policy consistent with the school norm.

Record-keeping, appropriate to the aims of the course is primarily the concern of the department as a whole. Agreement is needed as to the form of the record, the range of skills to be recorded, etc.

4 *Marking*
This is also a vital part of teaching and is seen as such by the pupils. Departmental guidelines on a positive, encouraging scheme are

needed. Advice will be needed for clear, prompt and regular marking of pupils' work and of the necessity of looking at "corrections". A policy on analysing and dealing with error is worthwhile.

5   *The foreign language assistant*
This section should deal with the department's use of the FLA. It is probable that it will necessitate a separate document, with suggestions and ideas.

6   *Day-to-day administration*
The departmental handbook should contain an outline of the duties allocated to various members of staff as well as information which will allow the smooth running of the affairs of the department — issue of books, repairs to machinery, stock, duplicating, etc.

Areas of responsibility which can be allocated to staff may include:
(a)   helping staff new to the school;
(b)   the assistant;
(c)   minuting of meetings;
(d)   stock; requisitions;
(e)   rooms; displays;
(f)   foreign links; pen-friends, visits, exchanges, etc.
(g)   links with other establishments; middle schools, HE/FE, etc.
(h)   particular year groups;
(i)   examinations, internal and external entries;
(j)   audio visual aids;
(k)   reprographics;
(l)   the library.

Section D   Syllabus and scheme of work for each language

Objectives. Specific objectives should be set out for each stage of the course. These language-specific objectives should be stated in "behaviourist" terms, i.e. stating what the learner will be able to do, using specific language skills. For example the simple heading "object pronouns" is not sufficient. It is necessary to add: "Pupils should be able to answer simple questions in the present and perfect tense using the direct object pronoun instead of the noun."

The balance between the four skills should be made explicit for different ability groups and different ages. This section is usually the most difficult and complex to write for it will reflect genuine language use in the classroom. A communicative syllabus, however, needs to take into account factors other than structures and vocabulary lists, since the ability to make grammatically correct sentences is not the only ability we need to communicate. An indication of communicative strategies is useful here.

Methodology. Guidance must be given to staff on appropriate methodology. At the same time it is important that the syllabus document should not restrict individual initiative or enterprise. There will be no one "right way", and this is why discussion must be open so that ideas may be used with confidence within an agreed framework.

Section E Resources
Detailed lists of tests are not required here. However, there must be some guidance as to the suitability of materials for particular groups. It may be wise to restrict certain materials to nominated groups or year groups so as to avoid frustrating repetition.

Postscript

With the coming of the new GCSE examinations in 1987 schools have had to be involved in redrawing their teaching syllabuses in order to take account of the demands of the examinations.

Over a number of years, various working parties have been establishing aims and objectives for examinations and courses in modern languages and thus each school, following the long period of national consultation, must now consider its courses in the light of these nationally agreed criteria.

The national criteria for modern languages are as follows:
1   To develop the ability to use French/German/Spanish effectively for purposes of practical communication.
2   To form a sound base of the skills, language and attitude required for further study, work and leisure.
3   To offer insights into the culture and civilization of French/German/Spanish speaking countries.

4 To develop an awareness of the nature of language and language learning.
5 To provide enjoyment and intellectual stimulation.
6 To encourage a positive attitude to foreign language learning and to speakers of foreign languages and a sympathetic approach to other cultures and civilizations.
7 To promote learning skills of a more general application (e.g. analysis, memorizing, drawing of inferences.)

The emphasis throughout must be on practical communication and the skills tested are to carry equal weighting. It must be noted however that aims 2–7 above are not in any order of priority and are not all to be tested in the examination since they cannot all be translated into measurable objectives. They are, nonetheless, all considered to be essential aims for any language course and as such should be closely followed by all those concerned with syllabus construction.

It is essential that each school consult the published aims of the GCSE examinations for their areas (details from the Examination Boards in Chapter 30). It is also important to note that if a school wishes to set up a *Mode 3* type scheme for their pupils, then this also *must* conform to the national criteria as laid out above.

20 Keeping records

Pupil records

Good record-keeping is vital in a well-run department for the benefit of pupils, parents and staff. What we are concerned with here is the recording of pupil progress. Other areas requiring monitoring — the syllabus provision, staff, stock levels, etc., are dealt with in other chapters.

The most important starting point is a clear assessment policy which will provide:
- evidence for consideration;
- information that is useful;
- feedback to those concerned.

Any such policy must be in line with the policy of the school in general and this is particularly important at the times in the school year when departments come into contact — for example when pupils compare their performance in several subjects when they are required to make 'option choices'. Is the department, for example, consistent with the geography department? Did Wayne Brown choose geography (with his 'A' grade) because the German colleague only rarely gives 'A' grades? Children do make that sort of judgement — and it can lead to disappointment. Within the department, comparisons are made between staff and pupils. Does all the departmental team assess to a common standard? If not, then promotion/demotion are problematical.

These are some of the consequences resulting from the departmental assessment policy. As a result, teachers must be provided with a clearly stated assessment programme, which will provide correct information to all those who have a legitimate need to know — pupils, parents, colleagues, careers staff and certain outside agencies such as HE/FE institutions and prospective employers.

Of course the general school policy on reports and assessment will influence the nature of the departmental record-keeping and the head of department should see that deadlines are met — and this will involve planning and cooperation. As well as end-of-term or end-of-year examinations, the department may well be involved in some form of continuous assessment of pupil progress. This may very well be considered important in the context of the language department, since pupil progress is often dependent on the mastery of the previous stages. Furthermore, appropriate testing and monitoring, if carried out in a positive manner, reflecting the aims and objectives of the course, can be a valuable aid to teaching and learning — providing opportunities for remedial action as necessary at the various stages in the course.

Records should ideally reflect the full range of the course and sample all the skills being mastered.

Setting the tests and examinations

All members of the department should be involved and agree on the style and content of the tests and examinations. It cannot be stated too strongly that the tests should flow out of the aims and objectives decided upon by the staff. The tests and examinations should not *be* the aims and objectives of the course as this perspective will distort the teaching.

In order to ensure proper coverage of the syllabus it is very useful to establish a checklist arising from the work covered. There are various ways of producing such a checklist — for example in a way which highlights settings and topics, or

Checklist of topics/settings for Year

Settings	Topics	Personal Identification	Family	House/home	Geography	Travel	Food/drink	Money	Free time	Education	etc.
Home											
Home town											
Transport											
Restaurant/café											
Place of entertainment											
School											
etc.											

Figure 8

which sets out structures or perhaps even lists vocabulary. It is a difficult job to do but is an essential part of devising the syllabus.

Thus, if the syllabus for the particular year in question specifies certain *settings* for the language work and certain *topics* within the settings, then the checklist may look like that in Figure 8. Such a list can serve many purposes — for example, checking on progress through the course. Checklists of this sort help to ascertain if the sampling in the test is fair and appropriate.

It is also a good idea, if using any form of continuous assessment, to build up a battery of tests of various types to use throughout the year. It is difficult in a busy term to constantly remake tests each time one is called for; but there is also a positive good in retaining (in security) tests that have proved to be reliable instruments, and in refining them over a period of time. Such a refining can be seen as a form of 'pretesting', for it is difficult to have reliable 'home-made' tests in school other than by building on accumulated experience.

There is clearly no point in setting up a testing and monitoring process which makes no difference to the pupils or the teacher. Assessment will imply making changes in methods, arrangements of sets/classes, etc. *Thus the reporting and recording of the assessment must be clearly understandable and lead to departmental discussions.*

As the pupils move up the school, it is likely that they will meet different teachers. To increase their effectiveness, teachers facing a class for the first time can be helped a great deal by the passing on of adequate records. *Ease of access is therefore essential.* Several methods may be used: the individual file-card; the class record sheet; and the school computer. These will now be dealt with in turn.

The individual file-card

One for each pupil, pre-printed, allowing the teacher to fill in test results, assessments, dates, etc. This is then kept in a departmental file-box. It can follow the pupils during their

NAME			YEAR: 19 .... –19			
Date	Rdg.	Lstg.	Wrtg.	Spkg.	Staff	Comment
23/10	8/10	9/10	7/10	6/10	DM	Improving
22/12	7/10	7/10	9/10	8/10	DM	Now less shy

Figure 9

career and can be 'reshuffled' according to the pupil-grouping in use at the time.
   Advantage: Flexibility.
   Disadvantage: Across-group comparisons are not easy to make. See Figure 9.

The class record sheet

A record-sheet is maintained for each class or group. This is also pre-printed and made readily accessible in a file.
   Advantage: Enables across group comparisons. Easier to read at a glance.
   Disadvantage: Needs writing out each time the group changes. See Figure 10.

The school computer

Give serious consideration to using the school computer in order to keep records. Most schools now have access to computing facilities and even moderate machines such as the BBC 'B' micro with a disc-drive and a printer can store enough data to enable set-lists, examination entries, etc., to be printed and updated. Data-base software will be needed to sort, order and search the records, but once the information has been stored, it is very easy to keep it up to date. Such accuracy can be a boon when it comes to compiling external examination entries.

Good records help to give good advice

The maintenance of accurate and reliable records will enable staff to give sound advice to pupils, particularly at 'option' time, prior to entry into the sixth form and when discussing careers. Decisions of such vital importance to the future of pupils should not be based on inadequate information. Other staff and outside agencies may have a legitimate reason to look at pupils' records and thus they should be written in positive and easily understandable terms.

GREENWAY HIGH SCHOOL MODERN LANGUAGE DEPT														
Year 85-86 Language GERMAN Class/Set/Group 3A Staff DM														
Pupil Date	23/10	22/11												
Max	20	50												
J. BROWN	14	39												
P. CLARK	12	28												
D. EVANS	18	39												
M. FOSTER	17	40												
Average:														
Test name:	LIST. COMP	WTG TEST												

Figure 10

Collecting records and moderating standards

How should one collect the information? In a large
department, it is not always easy to bring together the
standards of a variety of teachers; some mark more leniently
than others, while some pride themselves on their 'harsh'
reputation.

1   There must be a departmentally agreed policy on such
    matters as whether the marking is positive — rewarding
    communicative use of the language, or negative —
    deducting penalties for inaccuracy, or a mixture of the
    two.
2   Coordinating marking at crucial times is best achieved
    by say, one teacher being allocated a whole test (or
    section of a test) across the range to increase consistency.
    The head of department should try to share out the work
    fairly over the year.
3   Make sure that the mathematics involved are accurate.
    Decisions should not be made on the basis of compu-
    tational errors!

Interpreting the results

First of all it is unwise to throw away the pupils' scripts as
soon as they are marked, because this will waste valuable
information. A perusal of the scripts should be an additional
aid to providing remedial action for pupil benefit.

Secondly 'chart' the results to help visualize the wealth of
information, instead of simply looking at a mass of figures.
For example one could draw up a 'histogram' of the marks to
check the distribution. (See Figure 11.) From this we can see
if the test has discriminated well, if it was norm referenced
(i.e. did the better pupils perform better than the weaker
ones, and were the marks spread out in an appropriate
way?). On the other hand, if the test was criterion referenced,
did the majority of pupils satisfy the criterion laid down
beforehand?

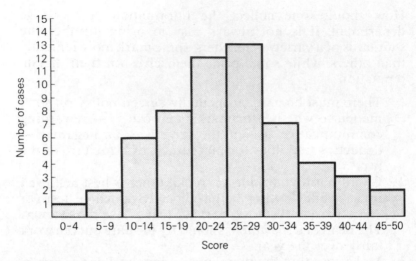

Figure 11

A visual display of the results can help departmental discussion afterwards.

Maintaining records of external examinations

As well as keeping good records of internal tests and examinations, it is important to file records of external examinations where appropriate. A well-run department will keep a systematic record for consultation for several reasons:

1   Schools are frequently asked to provide information on past pupils — by FE and HE establishments, prospective employers, etc. Memories are fallible and accuracy fades away with time.

2   The recording of such results from external tests will enable the department to monitor success on a public yardstick.

3   When called upon to give course assessments and

estimates for pupils, one may look at previous results as an extra dimension, and the accumulated 'wisdom' of the years is a valuable balance to 'gut-feeling'.

4   When making up the 'annual report' to the head on the year's work in the department, include the examination statistics and results.

Accurate records help in making accurate entry lists for examinations

The administration of public examinations can be very time-consuming, but accuracy at *all* stages is vital. The process begins *before* the course starts and ends only when results are received and duly recorded. It is not the place here to discuss the effects of the examinations on the syllabus, or the choice of examination board or type of scheme, but rather to outline the administrative procedure which leads up to pupils being entered for the right papers at the right time. Of course details vary from board to board, but the principles are the same.

There are two stages to go through.

Before the course begins
As soon as the syllabus and any reading list is issued by the board, read it through carefully, highlighting any changes from previous practice. Make sure that all staff involved have access to copies of the syllabus and that they have noted any changes. It is well worthwhile having external examinations as a topic on the departmental meeting agenda.

Making the entries
At the beginning of the examination year (fifth form and upper sixth), talk with the member of staff in charge of entries about the key dates and note them in the departmental diary.

The key dates will be:

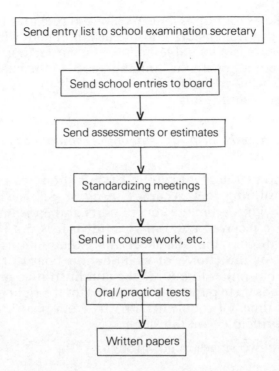

Around these key dates the department must arrange its work and be prepared in advance.

Finally, in the departmental filing system it is helpful to have a section devoted to publications from the examination boards. Keep these documents in a 'year-dated' system and discard superseded copies as soon as new ones are published. Confusion can be avoided by careful planning.

School reports

Most schools, if not all, have a system of school reports which permits the teaching staff to pass on to parents and possibly to future employers the opinions of the school on the work done and the progress — or lack of it — made by each pupil.

Over the last few years reports have come in for a fair amount of criticism from the press and from educational pressure groups. The main points have been that the reports convey very little useful information. A mark, possibly a grade, for effort plus a brief comment in traditional schoolmaster's jargon has sufficed for many years: '56% C — fair work and progress.' Since the report did not actually say the pupil was pretty awful and likely to fail his O-level this, presumably, satisfied the majority of parents.

Despite the bland nature of most reports, schools have usually made a fuss about the way they are done in the belief that the report is the school shop window. Heads and deputy heads usually spend many hours checking what their staff have written and how they have written it.

In some instances reports have to follow a very precise pattern. Each member of staff must use every pupil's name once. No report may begin with a pronoun and so we get the monotonous, not to say ludicrous 'Jennifer has done well... Jennifer could do better . . . Jennifer is getting better . . . Jennifer may fail...' Some heads refuse to allow a comment that is not a full sentence — 'Has done some excellent work this term,' being unacceptable. Other heads will not allow reports to be written in ball-point pen.

General points about reports

1 It is a good idea to give a two-part comment, the first half commenting on work this term and the second half indicating what aspect of the work needs special attention in order to improve the standard.

2 It is important to watch how the report is presented.

Parents scrutinize them closely and make comments on handwriting and spelling. If a report looks as though it could be made up at the chemist's, neither head teacher nor parent is happy.

3 Think carefully before making any comment that could be misunderstood. 'This is quite good progress for a girl of her ability.' Does it mean that the girl's standard was already so high the teacher did not imagine further progress possible . . . or is she beyond the pale?

4 At all costs avoid the 'funny' remarks of the 'Trying . . . very' kind. 'He may think his French is good but Mitterrand and I have decided otherwise.'

5 It is wise to avoid being too technical: 'In her spoken French her uvular R has improved greatly.'

6 A record of past comments should be kept so that comment can be made on progress since the previous report.

7 The school report is not the place to make criticisms of the school, e.g. 'It is a pity she has not been allowed to start a second language this term.'

8 Ensure that comments are fair and that they really do reflect the whole period a report is intended to cover. It is all too easy to be influenced by one extra good or bad piece of work.

9 Parents often seek out staff on parents' evenings to ask for clarification of a comment. Be prepared to substantiate remarks put on a report two months or more previously.

10 It is a mistake to make firm predictions about expected progress and especially dangerous to forecast the outcome of public examinations.

Changes, however, are in the wind. Profile reporting is coming in both for school reports and modern language examination results. The DES has already made it clear that 'reports' are to become 'records of achievement'. To do this it will be necessary to 'cover a pupil's progress and activities across the whole educational programme of the school, both in the classroom and outside, and possibly activities outside the school as well' (DES Statement of Policy, July 1984). To bring this about it will be necessary to compose a document which young people will take with them when they leave school and it will have two main components:

- Information, other than academic successes, which throws light on personal achievements and characteristics.
- Evidence of attainment in academic subjects and practical skills, including any graded results in public examinations. (*DES, Statement of Policy*)

The term 'profile reporting' has been used to refer to the type of report described above and also to results within the context of individual examinations. Here too the modern linguist is going to have to sharpen his tools since it is generally agreed that the present system of recording results in public examinations is a blunt instrument in so far as the pass certificate gives no indication of what the successful candidate is good at. The proposal here is that candidates' examination results in any subject should be recorded by means of statements of performance in the different components of the examination. In addition a single overall grade would be awarded as at present.

21 How to survive administration

Departmental meetings

For the department to run successfully, regular consultation is vital. It is to be hoped that informal consultation will take place in the staffroom and that such discussion will be lively and informed, but it is also vital to have a structure for staff meetings to make sure that all staff are involved in the decision-making process, and that clear lines of communication are established from the department in all directions. It is well-known that long rambling meetings 'after hours' are not liked, and therefore it is important to see that all such meetings are businesslike and worthwhile. In order to allow more time to discuss matters of real importance it is a good idea to deal with routine, admininstrative details by circular and then mention them at the departmental meeting.

Running the meeting

1   Have no more meetings than are necessary — but not too few either!
2   Note the dates well in advance.
3   Publish an agenda in advance, and make sure it is relevant.
4   Appoint someone to take the minutes.
5   Circulate the minutes to senior colleagues as well as to the members of the department.
6   Invite the head or the deputy to meetings if appropriate. A good piece of psychology!

7   Follow up all suggestions and ideas — and report on progress.
8   Occasionally use the meeting as 'in-service' training. If you know a colleague in your school (or elsewhere) who has a particular expertise or who has an interesting and appropriate research interest, this could be the place to share in the experience.

Administration

Very few heads of department receive training in the day-to-day management of paperwork. Yet much frustration can be avoided by attention to detail and the setting up of a routine. But do not let systems of administration take over the real task of leading a team.

1   Have an in-tray and a 'pending' tray.
2   Deal with all matters as soon as possible and in strict order of priority.
3   Keep file copies of all important documents.
4   Have separate files for the various areas of responsibility, for example:
    — entries, syllabuses, set-book lists, results, and circulars from the boards;
    — internal examinations;
    — schemes of work;
    — stock and requisitions;
    — pupil records;
    — school policy file;
    — staff records — references, etc.
    — publishers' brochures;
    — careers;
    — departmental minutes.
5   Make sure that other members of staff have copies of all necessary documents.
6   Discard material that is out of date.
7   Specify action needed on departmental matters and ensure that all other staff are informed as necessary. Include a 'circulation' list.

8 Specify agreed dates for action and see that they are adhered to.
9 Have a regular tidying up session every week.
10 File documents as soon as possible to avoid loss.
11 Have an agreed system for filing tapes, worksheets, etc., that all staff can understand!
12 Make sure that at least your 'number two' understands your filing system.

Delegation

The head of department cannot be expected to do everything in the complex organization of today's schools — nor is it advisable to try. It is particularly short-sighted in terms of administrative efficiency and also from the point of view of one of the most important tasks of the head of department — that of ensuring staff development.

Delegation of responsibility should lead to greater stuff involvement and is good for individual development even when additional financial rewards are not as freely available as before. It is also wrong to assume that our colleagues will always be with us and we must look to their career advancement. Nor must we assume that the head of department will be in the post for ever and it is therefore professionally correct to plan for continuity.

Delegation must therefore be seen as a healthy process, but any tasks so delegated must be *real* tasks and not merely thought up for the sake of it. Furthermore it is a good idea to redefine and reallocate responsibilities from time to time: staff will then have a variety of experience, both routine, clerical as well as creative.

Particular schools will provide areas of personal initiative: for example in a split-site school, a second-in-charge may have day-to-day responsibility for a section of the buildings. When the language staff have several languages to teach, particular responsibility for one of the languages may be devolved onto a particular teacher within the overall framework of departmental strategy.

The following are examples of which tasks could be devolved, subject to the final responsibility of the head of department:

1 *In connection with particular year groups*:
— liaison with feeder schools;
— examinations for a section of the school;
— arrangements for option-choice and guidance;
— 'setting'.

2 *In connection with departmental resources*:
— care and maintenance of audio-visual aids;
— stock and requisitions; review and inspection copies;
— production, storage and copying of home-made materials, worksheets, etc.
— displays in the language area.

3 *In connection with administration*:
— external examination entries;
— oral/practical examination arrangements;
— Mode 3 submissions;
— meeting agendas and minutes.

4 *General*:
— visits, exchanges, pen-friends;
— 'Language club';
— careers information;
— library: suggestions for books;
— departmental staff library;
— students in the department.

Delegation will only lighten the administrative burden if properly planned. Too often we hear the complaint 'I could have done it better myself,' when all that was needed was proper discussion beforehand.

The departmental diary

An invaluable tool for efficiency will be an 'academic year' diary. At the first possible opportunity, mark up in that diary the important deadlines of the school year. Events to be included are:

— external examinations;
— internal examinations;
— pupil reports and assessments;
— external examination entries;
— parent/teacher consultations;
— requisitions;
— major staff and departmental meetings;
— PTA functions;
— university and college open-days;
— sports days;
— holidays (not just to anticipate relief from pressure, but because holidays do vary from year to year and this variation can affect the cycle of work in the school).

Even if all the ideas suggested in this chapter are put into practice, things may still go wrong on occasions. Help *within* the school will probably be largely administrative, but help in terms of subject expertise is also required and can usually be found without much difficulty.

What to do when things go wrong

Within the school, it is helpful to be honest and open with the head and deputies, discussing problems as they arise in an atmosphere of trust. If you need to go beyond the school, there are several organizations and individuals ready to help in different ways.

The language adviser

Make a friend of the local LEA advisers — both the subject specialist and the particular adviser who is assigned to your school. In most authorities there is an information bulletin sent to all schools giving information about the services offered, courses run by the LEA advisory service, etc.

The adviser can help in three main ways:

1   By individual visits to schools to discuss specific problems and ideas.
2   By organizing courses and seminars on topics of interest. Attendance at such gatherings is always valuable, not only for the topics and ideas discussed but also for the opportunity afforded to meet colleagues from other establishments.
3   By being the 'link-man' between individual schools and many other agencies who may be able to solve the problem.

The Teachers' Centre

Most authorities maintain a Teachers' Centre within the LEA area, and facilities will usually include a library, resources area (films, videos, tapes, etc.), exhibition area, reprographic facilities and, above all, rooms for meetings. The personnel will have the job of keeping teachers informed on a variety of matters and their collective expertise can be used most profitably.

The Centre for Information on Language Teaching and Research (CILT)

This organization publishes a vast amount of material which is invaluable for teachers and students of languages. Publications include reports and papers from conferences, annotated lists of teaching materials, selected reading lists, information guides and so on. The library at its headquarters (see Part 4) has a large collection of material for consultation including over 25,000 titles and a repository of over 1,000 samples of language courses.

Modern language subject associations

The MLA is the oldest and largest of the language

associations in the UK, and was founded in 1892. It has an active branch network throughout the country. Along with other language-specific associations, local events are organized by and for members and these include talks, workshops, films, seminars, demonstrations, sixth-form days, etc.

All associations publish journals such as *Modern Languages, treffpunkt, Vida Hispanica, ATI Journal, Journal of Russian Studies, British Journal of Language Teaching*, etc. (See Part 4.)

All associations are a valuable source of information to members and in addition they also channel members' opinions and ideas to the DES, research bodies, examination boards, etc. Teachers can join as individuals and also as 'institutions'. For a full list of such bodies see Part 4.

The Central Bureau for Educational Visits and Exchanges (CBEVE)

This national organization is responsible for the development of all kinds of exchanges and contacts with foreign countries, including:

— teacher exchanges — long- and short-term;
— study visits
— pupils exchanges, pen-friends, school 'twinning';
— the 'assistant' scheme.

Full information can be obtained from its several publications.

The examination boards

Questions about external examinations can be addressed to the various boards — they all keep research and development units and produce various publications of interest as well as their regular examiners' reports, etc.

Information services of foreign countries

A lot of use can be made of these services and a list of such bodies is printed in Part 4.

PART THREE

Beyond the School

22 School links, pen-friends and exchanges

Links

There are many ways of organizing a school link and one of the most useful and effective ways is to build a scheme into a local town twinning arrangement. Anyone who is unsure about town twinning arrangements or who considers trying to persuade local councillors to investigate possibilities should first obtain detailed information of procedure from:

The Joint Twinning Committee
65 Davies Street
London W1Y 2AA

This body was set up by the local authority associations, the British Council and the Central Bureau for Educational Visits and Exchanges. The Secretariat publishes twice-yearly *Twinning News*, which is distributed free to local authorities. It contains ideas based on reports of successful twin town events and also lists towns in many countries seeking to establish a twinning with a British town.

Pen-friends

Once a link with a school is established it is then the stimulating task of someone in the modern language department to organize the development of correspondence between pupils. Failure rate is high for many reasons but the successes make the enterprise worthwhile and no one ever loses by it. Nonetheless it takes active staff participation to ensure even a moderate success rate for a pen-friend scheme. The staff themselves need to be good correspondents on both sides to pass on messages that X has not yet replied to Y's letter this term. It could become just too much in a busy term. Yet it is worth doing and certainly we should encourage pupils to bring to school individual letters they have received and perhaps even to read extracts to the rest of the class. It does help if the teacher fairly regularly gives suggestions on what to write about next because this is one of the main problems — 'I don't know what to put, Miss.'

Some schools have found pen-friend schemes work much better if they are done as a class or group effort with the teacher taking the initiative. With this sort of scheme no individual pupil is heavily committed because it is only in the later stages that links between individuals begin. Initially it is a letter contributed to by the whole class and often written in English. The letter goes off to the foreign school in the form of a small parcel with photos of the school, school teams, plays, carol concerts, etc. After a while the exchange of tapes can be introduced — recordings made in both English and the target language describing school events, holidays and local events. From this point anything becomes possible. Individual links arise naturally from the class link. The class link itself can continue side-by-side with personal correspondence. Barry Jones of Homerton College has described some fascinating exchanges of parcels between schools — swap your rubbish even — which give a valuable insight into the everyday lives of foreign pupils. (See *Using Authentic Resources* Ed. B. Jones.)

Exchanges

Once a good link is established teachers can think seriously about extending the scheme to include exchanges. A private scheme between two schools means that everything can be tailor-made to suit local needs. Sometimes an exchange scheme is run on a larger scale involving a number of schools on both sides. There are several advantages to this — cheaper fares, simpler arrangements and more likelihood of pairing-off every pupil who wishes to take part. The disadvantage is that at the start it is more impersonal but this is soon overcome when pupils are put in contact with each other.

Who goes? Not every pupil is ready to take part in an exchange at the same time. Before there can be any hope of success teachers should look carefully at applicants to decide whether their language has reached 'survival level' and whether they are sufficiently mature to cope with a separation from home for a two- or three-week period. Experience has shown that the most vulnerable children are girls, under the age of fifteen who are quiet, even withdrawn, at home and amongst friends. They have often never been separated from their parents. Their language is at a primitive level. They often show very little curiosity about their surroundings in the foreign home. Teachers who feel they have a pupil who falls in some measure into this category should beware of thinking that a fortnight away is just what she needs. It could be a very miserable fortnight for all parties concerned. The trouble is that once back home this kind of pupil tends to lay the blame for the failure at anyone's door and this can have disastrous consequences for future exchanges. Far better, then, suggesting the pupil wait a year until a suitable partner can be found. An exchange which confirms prejudices, strengthens insularity and undermines self-confidence obviously does far more harm than good.

Preparation for the exchange

For an exchange to stand a chance of success some careful preparation of the participants is essential. Such an exercise falls into three sections:

1 fostering the right attitude;
2 providing the necessary survival language;

3   familiarizing the pupil with the region to be visited.

Where time is limited and teacher energy widely deployed it is the first two areas which must be accorded priority.

The right attitude

All pupils are bound to have some apprehensions about going to live with an unknown family and it is sensible to recognize this, to stress the short time that is involved and the excitement of going. The most important single quality we should encourage is curiosity — find out about ... It will in fact help if all participants are given a list of things to find out about. It will give them something to talk about in the early days while relations are still being established. The list can cover any aspect of daily life — how much is a 'baguette', what time is the TV news on, how much does it cost to post a letter, what is the dog/cat called, etc.?

It is also reasonable to point out to pupils that they can occasionally feel homesick. It is normal and will pass and they can expect their partner to have a similar experience in England.

Finally it is most important that our pupils go abroad with the right attitude to foreign customs and manners, i.e. they are not better or worse but different. Unless this is clearly put we do run the risk of strengthening prejudices and of undoing any good that might otherwise come of the exchange.

Survival language

We do not suggest here that extra lessons will be called for but simply that if we commit these children to a foreign home it is our duty to ensure they have the minimum *bagage linguistique* to handle the most basic of situations. The foreign assistant can be of immense value here (if there is one!). Without this basic provision our pupils run the risk of being considered uncouth, ill-mannered and uncoopera- tive, and that is when trouble starts. The simplest way of dealing with the situation is to equip every pupil with a basic word-list containing all appropriate conversational lubricants: I don't understand; What does that mean? Will you say that again, please? I'm not well; I enjoyed our visit to...; I come from Exeter; my father is a postman; I do not like this, etc.[1]

In addition to words some attention should be given to 'body language' — the importance of shaking hands, kissing and to the ordinary phrases of polite society — saying 'good morning' to every one, saying 'good night'.

Knowing the region to be visited
It would be wonderful if a detailed regional study could be undertaken by a whole group but such a project is unlikely. Nevertheless the least we should do is to indicate the books available, ensure they are in the school library and, at the same time, organize a display of photographs, etc., sent by the twin school. Naturally the English school reciprocates to enable the partners to do similar preparation.

(1) 'What do I say now?' and 'What do I say next?' Nuffield (Schools Council) *Guide de la Communication* by Alan Chamberlain and Ross Steele, Didler, 1985.

23 How to organize a foreign visit

If we are to bring the learning of a foreign language alive, then it must be obvious that the trip abroad is essential and as such will be part of the work of a modern language department. Such visits can be varied — ranging from the one-day 'Boulogne Flyer' to the exchange visit extending over several weeks. All have their own merits and their own purposes. The one-day visits are excellent for the younger pupil, particularly as a taster, to complement the work done within the four walls of the classroom. On the other hand it is better to reserve the extended exchange scheme for more 'mature' pupils who are better able to cope with longer periods away from home both from the point of view of the personality and the linguistic maturity.

These days it is possible to participate in all kinds of foreign visits — ranging from the traditional week away with a school party, to special interest holidays (for example with football teams) — but all have one thing in common — the need for very careful planning beforehand. Taking a group abroad is a great responsibility — from the educational organizational and legal points of view and should not be taken on lightly, and particularly should not be the sole responsibility of the first-year teacher.

Planning

The following are the major steps in planning a school group visit abroad:

The first steps

1   Obtain the permission of the head and if necessary the LEA.
2   Ask your colleagues to join you. Make sure you have the correct ratio of men to women for the composition of the party. Check on the staff/pupil ratio required.
3   Scrutinize carefully the brochures sent by the tour operators.
4   Choose carefully the centre and the dates.
5   Obtain a quotation (in writing). Make sure you know what the quoted price includes: is insurance included? Are the excursions extra? What accommodation is offered? What food is included? How many free staff places are offered? Does the price include travel from the school or from another starting point such as a port?

Making up the party

1   Decide which year-groups will be eligible to participate. There are arguments for keeping the age-range to, say, two year-groups, making for greater homogeneity of interest. On the other hand a wider range can make the group easier to handle. Make up your own mind.
2   Let all eligible pupils have a letter setting out the details — place, dates and cost. Invite parents to reply by means of a tear-off which has the following formula:

I wish my son/daughter.................. of form.................. to be considered for the school trip to Germany during the Easter holidays 19...... Signed...................... Date......................

You are not thus *obliged* to accept all applicants if you or the other staff feel that it is not appropriate.

Choosing the members of the party

To some extent this depends on the purpose and the nature of the visit. Consult as widely as possible. Excluding children is very difficult and not to be taken lightly but if there are likely to be problems for whatever reason, it is wise to consult even the head. Remember that if problems occur while the group is abroad, it is the teachers who eventually have to sort them out.

It is wise to have a reserve list in addition to the list of selected members, particularly if there is a minimum number stipulated by the tour company. Once the selection has been made, send a letter home with the following details:

1   departure date and time;
2   return date and time;
3   total cost, and details of what the cost covers;
4   request for a deposit (make it clear if this is non-refundable);
5   dates when further payments can be made, and date for the final payment;
6   tear-off acceptance/medical slip on the following lines:

I agree to my son/daughter................ taking part in the school trip to Germany from................. to................. I also agree to make the full payments by................... I declare that there is no known medical condition to prevent him or her from participating in all activities.

Signed:............................ Date................................

This does not mean that one should exclude a pupil with a known medical condition, but rather that parents should inform the group leader.

Managing the finances

1 Open a bank account called 'The X School German Holiday Account'. Make sure that there are two signatories.

2 Make arrangements for the participants to pay by instalments but be careful to make it known that money will be accepted only on fixed days and in a fixed place. Do *not* accept money casually on the corridor and certainly not without making an entry in your cash book and also in the pupil's payment record.

3 Insist that the final payment is made at least ten days before you are due to settle the account with the operator.

4 It is wise to have quoted a price slightly above the actual cost (say £1 to £1.50 per head) for emergencies and the unused part can be refunded at the end of the holiday.

5 Pocket money. This is a difficult question but the age of the pupils may well decide the best course of action. It is certainly wise to stipulate the maximum amount a pupil can take and to suggest in what form it should be taken (notes, travellers cheques, etc.). For the younger groups it is possibly better for the teacher to dole out the money in daily instalments to prevent the all too frequent case of the pupil who, not realizing the value of the strange looking coins, spends up within three hours of landing on foreign soil.

Preparations for the holiday

1 Although a holiday, the trip should be a holiday with a difference. The aim will be 'educational' but not restricting. Parents (and pupils!) will want to get good value for money and so adequate preparation is essential.

2 It is good to hold regular meetings according to the aim of the trip. Various facets of the holiday should be explored in a way which stresses the holiday as well as the educational nature of the tour. If the trip is to Berlin,

for example, then there should be some input about the historical, geographical and political significance of the city. Help should also be given with the linguistic aspects of the holiday. Basic 'survival' language should be known by all pupils.

3 It is also a good idea to have some sort of workbook or 'project' for the pupils, depending on their age. A prize at the end is a good incentive!

4 Involve the pupils too in this preparation — get them to write to the tourist office for brochures and information.

5 Mount an exhibition in school about the area to be visited — using posters, maps, slides, etc. (The geography department may help).

6 Just before going have a meeting for parents and pupils to explain the final details such as the amount of luggage, the need for packed lunches for the journey, etc. Give parents the opportunity to ask questions.

7 Prepare a 'tour brochure' for all the participants. It should contain at least the following information:

- List of participants.
- Map of the journey and sketch map of the area to be visited.
- Address of the hotel, centre or hostel.
- Telephone numbers with instructions on using the international STD.
- Details of the itinerary.
- Daily programme of events, excursions, etc.
- Basic rules of behaviour; meal times; 'bed times', etc.
- Basic expressions in the appropriate language (directions, shopping, etc.)
- Comparisons of distances, money system values, etc.
- Appropriate details of a geographical or historical nature according to the age of the pupils and the aim of the holiday.
- The holiday quiz and project work.

Official forms etc.

Passports. You may decide to have a collective passport. You should apply in good time — several months before departure — in order to complete all the formalities. This is particularly important if the party has pupils whose parents were not born in the United Kingdom. The complicated procedures are explained on the application form and these must be followed precisely. The application form should be obtained from the Passport Office serving the town where your school is situated. In case of difficulties write to the main passport office in London.

If the pupils are to have their own passports, make sure that they obtain them in good time, have a physical check that they have them on departure from school and at various times during the holiday.

Insurance. Make sure that the party is insured. This will usually be arranged by the tour firm, but if not, then make sure you are covered sufficiently for third-party liability, luggage, illness and accident. The local office of the national insurance companies will supply details specially for parties and it is also possible that the LEA has negotiated special rates. Whatever happens, never go away uninsured.

Sickness insurance. Now that the UK is part of the EEC it is advisable to contact the local office of the Department of Health and Social Services (DHSS) to obtain the European Claim Form E111. This must be filled in by the individual family of each pupil and enables medical treatment costs abroad to be reimbursed.

'Credentials'. It is a good idea to obtain from your own school a statement from your head, on official notepaper, saying that you are a *bona fide* school party. By showing this to officials it is possible to obtain entrance to museums etc., free or at reduced cost.

The journey

1   Put pupils into groups of no more than ten, in the charge of a member of staff. When checking in at ports and on transport it will be a simpler task.
2   Provide each teacher with a register.
3   When using boats, decide firmly on a time and place to meet before the party breaks up.

At the centre

1   Make sure all pupils know the fire drill.
2   Explain each day the routine and programme for the day.
3   Never leave pupils unattended in the hotel or the centre — especially in the evening. Arrange a staff rota and some activities for the pupils.
4   Insist that pupils do not wander around on their own — particularly in the evening. Remember you are responsible!

Returning home

1   Warn pupils about going through the customs — duty-free goods are *not* allowed for people under seventeen.
2   Arrange a parents' evening to see the slides, projects, etc.

A do-it-yourself trip abroad

Today a large number of schools have their own minibus and it is perfectly possible to arrange a school holiday abroad using the school's own transport. This is particularly convenient when taking the football team on a 'European Tour' or when taking, say, the Upper Sixth French class to Paris or to the 'twin' school for a week's lessons in France or Germany. The preparations needed are more or less those outlined above but, in addition, there will be some important matters to deal with in connection with the vehicle and the drivers.

1   Make sure there are two drivers.
2   Obtain correct insurance cover for the vehicle (The Green Card).
3   Obtain permission from the vehicle's legal owner to take the minibus out of the country.
4   From one of the motoring organizations (e.g. the AA or the RAC) take out insurance to cover breakdown,

vehicle repatriation, etc. This is usually negotiated in a package.
5   Make sure you have the vehicle documentation with you — log-book, etc.
6   Check up on the regulations regarding permitted hours of driving, the 'tachograph', etc. (Consult the motoring organization.)
7   Book the sea-crossing in good time. There are often special terms for groups and minibuses.
8   Plan the journey with plenty of spare time. Don't overtax the drivers with the risk of accidents.

By taking on the responsibility of arranging the holiday like this, especially when the numbers are small, you can save a great deal of money, though you must be aware that there is a lot of work involved.

24 Cooperating with parents

Parent power is increasing and will continue to do so. That is 'a good thing'. 'A good thing' that is if teachers and parents can work more closely together for the benefit of the children each party has an interest in.

It goes without saying that parents are the original VIPs of this world. Without them there would be no schools and hence no teachers. In short, we need them around and we should welcome their close cooperation and involvement. And, let it be understood, even if teachers don't want parents around they are going to get them, for on the new governing bodies of schools parents are to have much more than the token representation that they have at present. In fact in the years to come we can expect parents to have a very substantial say in the way the curriculum takes shape and the sort of curriculum that is offered to different groups of children.

Language teachers need to give this some thought for not every parent is convinced of the value of language learning. Too many, in fact, are living proof of the lack of success of earlier generations of teachers now perhaps writing out their verb conjugations on the great blackboard in the sky. Teachers will have to convince such parents that modern languages as a school subject have a clear and attainable aim. Parents will have to be convinced that there is real benefit to be derived from five or even eight periods a week being spent learning the language of countries which, very often, speak excellent English.

The sort of arguments that teachers will need have already been referred to in Chapter 12 'Answering the Difficult Questions'. Here we simply make suggestions for strategy which, in the first place, will ensure that the teacher does a thoroughly professional job and which, in addition, will convince parents of the validity of the modern language teachers' claim that they have a great deal to offer children who opt for their subject. In other words it is vital to have parental backing. If the parents support what the teacher does there is a very good chance of success. The following points will further contribute to the development of understanding between parents and language teachers:

1 It is important to stress at all times to pupils that teachers and parents work together to help them as much as they can. It will, therefore, pay teachers not to play into the hands of pupils who from time immemorial have enjoyed exaggerating school teachers' eccentricities with the consequent alienation of parental sympathies.

2 The need to involve parents when the department is on show has already been emphasized (Chapter 15). Open days and open-nights are the ideal time to demonstrate the value and the success of the work of the language teachers.

3 On parents' evenings when they attend to discuss their children's progress it is important to convince them of the efficiency of the languages team. Mark books up to date. Notes made on pupils who are having particular difficulties. No slip-ups about talking to the wrong parents. Check if there are two with similar surnames. It is very important to let parents see that the teacher knows their child well. Parental confidence increases enormously.

4 When it is necessary to complain about a child (bad work, bad behaviour) it is a good practice to make sure the parent is sympathetic to the teacher by, first of all, speaking of the child's good qualities. He may then go on 'However...' When such criticism is necessary the teacher must show that he has some kind of remedy to propose, some positive help which will need parental backing.

5 It is important also to avoid making open accusations against a child. If there is a suspicion of truancy a naive comment about absence may well bring out the truth almost by accident. Parent and teacher can then cooperate for the child's ultimate good.

6 Discussions between parents and teachers are professional duties that can, on occasions, verge on the confidential. Teachers should show parents that they can have confidence in the teacher and that there is no danger of their own child being discussed with another parent. This can easily happen if a parent starts to complain about the influence of X in the same form. Teachers must make it quite clear that they do not discuss other people's children, nor do they talk about their own affairs and still less about colleagues on the staff.

7 If, in the course of a five-minute interview on a parents' evening, a substantial issue emerges, e.g. an accusation of incompetence or worse, the teacher should rapidly bring the discussion to a close and insist upon an interview being arranged for a later date at which some senior colleague can also be present. It is unprofessional, undignified and time-consuming to get into argument at what is really a public session.

8 Parents will occasionally criticize school policy. Teachers should bear in mind that this is not the time to seek allies and that the best thing to do is to state clearly what the school policy is and advise the parent to approach the head or deputy head or parent-governor if he wishes to make an issue of the matter.

9 Most teachers want to see satisfied parents going home at the end of an evening but they must beware of making promises they cannot possibly keep if the circumstances change. So we say 'I hope she will pass O-level next year.' and not 'I will see she passes O-level.'

10 Even if a child is weak at languages the teacher must avoid giving the impression that she is some kind of pariah. In fact it is a good thing to find out which areas of the curriculum are the ones she does best in for the

teacher who begins 'I wish I could say her German was as good as . . .' has already obtained a sympathetic hearing.

11 Even on ordinary parents' evenings it is a good idea to put out some evidence of the work in the department — a few posters, a few library books on display and most useful, a small display of 'books you may like to buy for presents'. Parents could be looking at them while waiting to speak to the teacher. Such a display again stresses the concern in the department for the success of languages.

12 For open-evenings or parents' evenings it is occasionally possible to run a ten-minute beginners' class in Spanish or German. To let the parents see the teacher in action is to convince them of the quality of the contribution modern languages can make to the well-being of their child.

13 In the past we have failed to make enough of parental expertise. Here is an area that all teachers would do well to explore and teachers of languages would be particularly well advised to seize the opportunity of inviting a parent into the school to describe experiences in other countries particularly if languages are closely involved.

25 Careers for linguists

The sad thing is that we cannot offer a wide choice of career for the 'pure' linguist. In almost every case skill in foreign languages is seen to be an adjunct, highly desirable perhaps, but still an ancillary. In other words we should be telling our pupils that if they wish to use their languages in a career they must at some time acquire other marketable skills as well.

A second important point we should make plain at school level is that on the whole we are not short of experts in the commoner languages of Western Europe. In addition, native speakers are easily obtained. However, when it comes to the less well-known languages there are more openings. Since Greece has joined the Common Market modern Greek will be in greater demand. As contacts with the Middle East and Far East develop there is likely to be a greater need for Chinese, Japanese and Arabic. These ideas should be put before sixth-formers before UCCA forms are to be completed so that at least some good linguists will be tempted to consider beginning one of the more exotic languages. The great advantage is, of course, that all such languages can be done *ab initio* in many universities and polytechnics.

Some career possibilities

Translating

There are very very few such posts in firms. Most translators work through agencies who normally expect translations to be done into the mother-tongue. To stand a chance one needs a range of languages, at least one exotic language and a good knowledge of certain specializations — the textile industry, medicine, the law. In other words most translation work is technical and you need to understand what you are talking about. Translating of literary work is much more limited and much of it is done freelance. Publishers often have their contacts and seldom buy a translation from an unknown source.

Employment for translators is to be found in the international organizations (United Nations, EEC) and in the Civil Service. In commerce there are possibilities for linguists with high-level office skills, e.g. a post-graduate diploma. Such people tend to become personal assistants who can use their languages as they are needed.

Interpreting

Much of what was said above applies to interpreters — except that there are even fewer openings. Conference interpreting is a highly skilled job and very few are required. Other organizations which are dependent on staff being able to translate usually require staff to undertake many other duties, e.g. air hostesses, airport staff, travel agents, couriers.

Teaching

Nowadays entrants to the profession are advised to have at least two languages they can teach to a high level. This is one job where skill as a linguist is the main qualification though all teachers will point out to pupils considering this possibility that other personal qualities are necessary to be successful. One possibility for the languages graduate is to qualify afterwards in TEFL and to seek a post teaching English abroad.

Commerce and Trade

The so-called bilingual secretary has been referred to above. Skills in foreign shorthand and typing are essential. A good telephone manner in several languages is also a sought-after skill in some firms.

Language graduates are taken on by many firms dependent on exports but such graduates are not necessarily being trained to sell their products abroad. They may be on a management course. Much selling abroad is done by agents resident in the country concerned. They are often native speakers. Yet the agents themselves have to be appointed and this does involve employees of the British firm.

Broadcasting

There are the external services and the monitoring services. The actual broadcasting in foreign languages is almost always done by native speakers in thirty-nine language sections. Cuts are being made in this area. In addition to needing a native knowledge of the language, applicants have to be able to show familiarity with the social and political institutions of the country concerned and have a good 'Microphone' voice.

Monitoring requires first-rate comprehension ability of at least one language, good English, ability to condense and basic office skills. There is a test for applicants — translating, listening and general knowledge. The Monitoring Service is at Caversham Park, Reading.

Travel agents, couriers and tourism

Again much local work is conducted by native speakers resident in the country concerned. Nevertheless there is a small demand for representatives to negotiate terms with foreign hotels, etc.; couriers, in the main, are in contact with the English customer. Airports have information staff, and cabin staff are needed by all major airlines. The languages needed will be relevant to the routes flown by particular companies. Airlines tend to recruit from their own native speakers. Hotels do need receptionists who speak several languages but again the languages are an ancillary skill. Some jobs for English people abroad are possible in the tourist industry. British Telecom also recruit some language speakers for the overseas telephone service.

Librarianship
For this the linguist has to take appropriate post-graduate qualifications in librarianship. An alternative route offered by some polytechnics is to do a BA in librarianship and a language may be part of the course. There are public libraries (probably little scope), academic libraries where the librarian may become a subject specialist and scientific and technical libraries where knowledge of a science is often paramount.

International banking
There are openings here but the linguist has to be prepared to undergo training in banking. Some banks will sponsor hand-picked candidates through university but it is the mathematicians who are likely to be picked for sponsorships. Personal qualities count for a great deal. Since Great Britain entered the EEC British Clearing Banks have tended to open branches in Europe and many European banks are now establishing themselves in the UK.

For teachers advising pupils and colleagues in charge of careers there are some useful handbooks well worth acquiring:

- 'Careers in Modern Languages' in *The Teaching of Modern Languages*, published by the Headmasters' Conference, 1980 (see pages 107 to 140).
- Careers information leaflets published by the Institute of Linguists at 24A Highbury Grove, London N5 2EA.
- *Guide to Languages in Polytechnics and similar Institutions*, published by SCHML and distributed by CILT.

What can the department do to provide appropriate information for pupils and parents? It will be a good idea to involve all staff but to delegate particular responsibility to a colleague to coordinate the departmental effort in this direction.

Below are some ideas which can be put into operation without much difficulty.

Gathering careers material

— As is often necessary in teaching — *be a magpie!*

— From newspapers, trade journals, magazines, handouts, collect advertisements for jobs using directly or indirectly foreign language skills. These can be filed for consultation by staff and pupils and also be mounted for display in the classroom and at careers meetings.

— Collect advertising literature of all sorts even from the most unlikely places with examples of foreign languages at work — e.g. Marks and Spencer's packaging and labels, French 'Mars Bar' wrappings, etc., which will indicate to pupils that the High Street companies they are familiar with have links abroad.

— Collect as many brochures, etc., as possible from English and foreign tourist offices with bi-lingual/tri-lingual presentations. Languages can thus be seen as useful not only abroad but also on 'home territory'.

— Invite past pupils to come back to school and talk about their experience at work if they have any use for their languages — both at craft and managerial levels.

— Enlist the help of the personnel department of local companies. Not only should you find out about possible openings for your students, but also about their needs for linguistic competence and how they train their staff to meet their requirements.

— Gather, for information and display, as many brochures, prospectuses, etc., published by all agencies involved in education beyond school: university departments, polytechnics, other colleges, and government training agencies; include also the Civil Service, the armed services and the nationalized boards, who often run sponsored training schemes at various levels.

— Encourage outside speakers to address pupils and parents. Particularly important will be speakers from the training establishments, since opportunities in HE/FE do change. The introduction of new combinations of courses and the alteration of the entry requirements can cause confusion.

— Attend careers meetings when appropriate.

— Display the MLA careers posters around the school!

— Show the Rowntree-MacIntosh video on careers in languages. (See Bibliography.)

26 Spare-time earning or How the linguist earns money by moonlight

Your language as a primary skill

The obvious outlet is to deploy your skills in the area for which you trained. The following are possibilities:

— Private tuition for O-level and A-level examinations. If the parent is not an oil tycoon you have no hope of enriching yourself unless you develop 'battery teaching' methods. A minimum of four pupils is necessary before you can get a reasonable hourly rate from people who will fork out £15 to the local Gas Board for a passing annual inspection of the central heating boiler and no work done.

— Teaching languages in evening classes is no better paid but you can meet some very pleasant people who are simply wanting to learn French to go sampling the Loire Valley wines. It's the same work as in the daytime minus the hassle.

— Teach your language abroad to children on intensive courses to prepare for O-level and A-level. The children are normally well behaved and attentive and you do have the pleasure of being in the country you love.

— Deploy your skills as a language teacher teaching English as a foreign language. Some high-class institutions actually expect you to have a TEFL diploma as well. Others are less fussy. If you live on the South Coast, in London or Oxford you can probably work from home. If you live elsewhere you may have a change of scenery but what you make teaching you will spend on board and lodgings.

— Work as a TEFL teacher abroad. Pay is moderate but at least you are abroad and the neighbours think you're on holiday.

Other than teaching

If you feel you have had enough of teaching try getting your own back examining. Any of the following may appeal:

— Mark O- or A-level written papers in June and December. Very intensive work but some devoted souls manage to work for two boards at once.

— Be a dutiful and enthusiastic examiner and become a Chief Examiner. You can then set *and* mark the paper.

— If you feel that marking written papers leaves the rest of the family ignorant of what you are suffering then volunteer to mark taped oral examinations and give the whole family a treat. Unfortunately the worse the candidate is the more difficult his tape is to mark. And you do realize how much you are assessing other colleagues' work.

— If you are sick and tired of O-level exams through the school year, try marking papers for examining bodies you are less familiar with — Institute of Linguists, RSA, etc.

— If you seek a complete change but have no different skills to trade then you should look for translation work. It means getting known. Advertise indicating language(s) and special subjects. Only translate into the mother tongue. If your only language is French and your only specialization is literature you can just about forget it. If your language is Finnish and you specialize in marine engineering, you may have a marketable skill.

To stand a chance you need to become known by an agency that knows it can rely on accurate, swift translation, neatly typed at short notice.

— And the same goes for interpreting. To be successful you need a deep knowledge of the foreign language and some acquaintance with the subjects to be discussed. If a technical subject is on the agenda the minimum to do is to read the appropriate technical journals. In addition to the precision knowledge the interpreter needs stamina to sustain him over long sessions. Even at mealtimes and over drinks, when the main speakers relax, the interpreter has to go on translating and, if things flag, continue the small talk so that the foreign visitor does not feel neglected.

In addition to formal interpreting between industrialists there is a need for interpreters in police work and in the courts. Usually little more than travelling expenses is paid.

— Money can be made from writing. Ask Jack Higgins. He started from the chalk face. Few of us, however, have the qualities of a Jack Higgins and consequently we need to give little thought to choosing a tax haven in the Channel Islands. Time will be more sensibly spent doing some writing.

Writing for local newspapers is a good start. Many local papers like to receive short pieces on educational matters at topical moments. In early September a piece called 'New start, new school: new problems?' might well be welcomed. A short piece on the town your own town is twinned with in Germany, particularly if you can show firsthand knowledge of personalities in the town. Some teachers have been very successful at this kind of writing and have got themselves a weekly column on education and parents' questions. 'Examination preparation', 'What is the new 16+?', 'Can my daughter do wood-work?', 'My son hates his teacher', are examples of the sort of topic which can be developed. (See *Guide for Authors* Basil Blackwell, 1985.)

Textbook writing is another area to explore. The days of the one-man course book are gone but there is still a demand for books to meet the needs of the new examinations: multiple choice, role-playing, up-to-date books on civilization topics, new editions of old texts and readers will always sell.

As indicated elsewhere, the modern language teachers have been slow to get in on the educational technology revolution. Programs for computers are still limited in number. This is where the future lies for teachers already devising their own material. Programming is incredibly time-consuming and everything must be tested to ensure it is 'user-friendly'.

Other writing possibilities for the modern language teacher lie in the travel industry. Our languages give us access to sources denied to English-only speakers. Our interest in faraway places makes us want to write and photograph for books of travellers' tales. The photographic side of such writing is vital and anyone seriously thinking of entering this market will need to invest in a good camera and supplementary lenses and, money well spent, a proper photographer's course will give the right sort of idea. Happy snaps don't come into it.

Your language as an ancillary skill

There are the fortunate few who have developed another string to their bows and for whom their languages are an ancillary skill. The following ideas are worth investigating and may bring rich rewards:

— The wine and spirits trade. There is the possibility of importing and selling to friends and acquaintances wines not generally available in the big supermarkets. You will never manage to undercut the big boys' prices but your wines will have an appeal some of the wines bought in bulk do not have.

— Taste-a-wine parties are popular and for anyone who enjoys company a very convivial evening can end with you being in pocket as people take three or four bottles home after being primed with a couple of free tastings.

— Write about wines and their background. Again the local press may be interested in a short series related to wines sold by their advertisers.

— Run evening classes on wine-tasting. It's teaching but a very pleasant change from hammering away at strong verbs and uvular Rs. The growth in popularity of such classes in recent years has been astounding. Armed with everything Hugh Johnson ever wrote, plus 'Bluff your way in wine' and the school projector, success with a class is almost guaranteed. A year's subscription to 'Decanter' magazine is a very sound investment for anyone contemplating this possibility.

— A local wine merchant may be interested in a joint venture in which he supplies the wines and you do the background talk on the region the wines come from, the methods of production and the 'stories behind the wine'.

— Driving is an area worth looking into. Insurance companies consider teachers to be good risk drivers. Language teachers know Europe. What about touring the vineyards by minibus or even by coach?

— Interest in coins and medals has grown considerably in recent years. Look at the monthly magazine 'Coins and Medals' and consider whether your own interest in European coinage and/or stamps could not easily be transformed into a profitable sideline.

The Jake Thackerays of this world are perhaps more numerous than we know. Linguists have access to a range of songs and music seldom if ever heard on the BBC. How many Brassens songs had we heard before

Jake Thackeray (an ex-teacher) began to offer his adaptations?

— Many linguists have serious musical talents. Joining an orchestra, accompanying a singer or even singing, may offer real possibilities.

— The catering trade offers many possibilities, from working in the kitchen to waiting at table in a top restaurant. One teacher advertises his services as a stand-in butler for dinner parties and gets plenty of bookings plus an opportunity to meet interesting people in surroundings he would never otherwise see.

— People with a talent for crafts, and for designing and making costumes could well consider the 'Rag Trade' as a sideline. Again, writing about what the French have to say at the 'Salon du Prêt-à-Porter' may be attractive.

PART FOUR

Reference
Section

27 What do the specialist organizations do?

There are a considerable number of organizations and bodies who provide help of various sorts for the teacher of modern languages. They are certainly too numerous to deal with in detail in a volume of this size. There is a list of many of the organizations in Chapter 30. This section of the book is therefore selective and not exclusive. We have attempted to outline some of the services provided by the best-known bodies. If the answer to any query is not within the scope of these bodies, they will certainly be able to help you find it somewhere.

Some of the organizations mentioned are voluntary, in the best tradition of the British education service, others are official or semi-official. All are experts in some way or other.

The order of appearance in this section implies no hierarchy or favour — it is simply a choice made by the authors. You can find details of addresses and telephone numbers in Chapter 30.

The subject-teaching associations

These are voluntary bodies, concerned with the teaching of modern languages. A complete list is to be found in Chapter 30.

The Modern Language Association

This is the oldest and largest of the language associations, founded in 1892 and today having some 2,500 members. It brings together students and teachers of all modern languages in universities, polytechnics and schools, as well as others who are concerned with foreign languages and literature in their work. Its main aims are: to keep under review the content and method of language teaching; to obtain and maintain for modern languages the high place in the curricula of schools, colleges and universities to which their intrinsic interest and their educational value entitle them; and to provide members with opportunities for discussion and study at day and residential conferences.

The MLA has a central office with full-time professional support which links members around the country and maintains close contact with branches and with other professional associations and government bodies.

The strength of the MLA lies in the system of local branches which provide a lively forum for members and which are extremely active in promoting events of all kinds for the membership.

The Association publishes two journals — *Modern Languages* (quarterly) and *treffpunkt* (three times a year). Members receive these free. In addition the MLA has a strong tradition of research and publishing and is able to help the teacher in a wide variety of ways. The standing of the MLA is such that it is often asked for its views on issues connected with languages by a wide cross-section of bodies, ranging from the House of Commons committees, to the BBC, the DES and embassies.

The Association of Teachers of German

The ATG is the German section of the Modern Language Association (qv). Its aim is to provide a forum for German teachers in all kinds of institutions and operates at local level via the branch network of the MLA. The ATG publishes a lively journal *'treffpunkt'* once a term as well as occasional papers.

The Association of Teachers of Italian

The ATI provides an exchange of information and experience for teachers of Italian at all levels as well as up-to-date lists of schools where Italian is taught, details of courses and conferences, etc. It publishes the *ATI Journal* three times a year, a newsletter and occasional papers.

The Association of Teachers of Russian

The aims of the ATR are to provide information and experience concerning the teaching of Russian; to review textbooks and teaching aids, to press the case for Russian and to press for more frequent and wider exchanges with the USSR. Main publication: *Journal of Russian Studies* (twice a year) and a newsletter.

The Association of Teachers of Spanish and Portuguese

The aim is to encourage interest in and knowledge of Spanish and Portuguese and to improve the teaching of these languages in the United Kingdom. The Association's journal *Vida Hispánica* appears three times a year.

The British Association for Language Teaching

The Association brings together language teachers from all sectors of the educational scene. The aim is to develop modern methods of teaching and learning foreign languages. There are active branches throughout the country and the journal *British Journal of Language Teaching* appears three times a year.

In addition to these associations which are open for teachers to join, there are other bodies, councils and congresses which do not accept individual members, but which are very important. They usually have representatives drawn from the 'primary' associations mentioned above (and others of course) and bring together views, opinions and ideas from a wide cross-section of the language world. A selection of these bodies is listed below.

Joint Council of Language Associations (JCLA)

This is a federation of the language teaching associations to represent the whole range at national level. It organizes the annual JCLA conference which draws together all the associations in a lively forum once a year.

Council of Subject Teaching Associations (CoSTA)

This body provides a forum for all subject associations and not just those concerned with modern languages. It meets twice a year to hear views and opinions and is a forum for discussing matters of importance connected with the curriculum and education in general. Occasional conferences.

National Council on Languages in Education (NCLE)

A standing body set up in 1976 to act as a forum for continuous discussion on matters concerning languages and language education in the UK. It brings together all major associations and organizations to formulate recommendations for policy and action by central government. Between the biennial assembly, the work is carried through in working parties. There are numerous publications published via CILT (qv).

National Council for Modern Languages in Higher and Further Education (NCML)

The aim of this forum is to promote the development of modern languages in higher and further education and to keep under review the provision for research. It brings together a wide spectrum of interests ranging from associations of modern language teachers, bodies representing teachers of English as a foreign language and liguistics.

Membership of the 'primary' associations also brings contacts with international organizations which are very important in the field of language learning and teaching. There are international associations bringing together single language interests as well as those with a wider interest.

Fédération Internationale des Professeurs de Français (FIPF)

This body exists to link French teachers' associations throughout the world. It disseminates ideas, initiates research and meets in a 4 year assembly. It publishes a bulletin twice a year as well as periodic reports.

Fédération Internationale des Professeurs de Langues Vivantes (FIPLV)

This organization links associations of language teachers throughout the world, to coordinate the efforts and research of constituent bodies in order to improve methods and development of modern language teaching. A newsletter *Alsed-FIPLV* is published four times a year.

Internationaler Deutschlehrerverband (IDV)

The aim is to establish contact and collaboration between teachers of German in all countries. It publishes a newsletter three times a year, holds a triennial congress and supports working parties.

Other organizations in the United Kingdom of the utmost importance are:

The Central Bureau for Educational Visits and Exchanges (CBEVE)

The CBEVE has offices in London, Edinburgh and Belfast. It is the national agency responsible for the development of educational travel and exchanges with other countries and is under the auspices of the various Education Departments in the British Isles. It operates schemes for pupils and young people and also those specifically for teachers and administrators.

For pupils and young people in general:
Pen-friends; home-to-home exchanges; work abroad; children's holiday centres abroad; language camps; etc.

For teachers, advisers and administrators:
Post-to-post exchanges from between six weeks and one year; short courses abroad; intensive study bursaries; reciprocal study visits; specialized study visits, etc.

The third service run by the CBEVE is the Foreign Assistant scheme, but for state schools this service is administered locally by the LEA. In addition there are a number of helpful publications produced by the Bureau on all aspects of visits and exchanges. Some of these are annual and a full list can be obtained from any of their offices.

Centre for Information on Language Teaching and Research (CILT)

The Centre aims to collect and coordinate information on all aspects of modern languages and their teaching and also to disseminate this information to individuals and organizations in the United Kingdom. The organization publishes a vast range of lists, catalogues and digests on all aspects of language teaching and learning and maintains a large library which is a unique collection of over 25,000 titles and in addition a repository of more than 1,000 samples of language courses.

28 Directories and Catalogues

It is hoped that the information contained in this section will help teachers of modern languages who have a particular problem or query. There will be help at hand from one or more of the sources listed.

Please note: Addresses do change. The addresses listed were correct at the time of publication. If in any doubt, it is wise to consult the appropriate telephone directory in any reference library or main post office.

General directories

Directory of British associations and associations in Ireland. Beckenham: CBD Research. Updated every 2–3 years.
Educational Authorities Directory and Annual. Redhill: School Government Publishing Company.
Education Year Book, London, Longman.

CILT Publications

CILT publishes an excellent series of guides for teachers under the titles of:
  Teaching Materials for French
  Teaching Materials for German
  Teaching Materials for Italian, etc.
These excellent volumes provide an up-to-date catalogue of teaching materials. The French volume provides for example, 700

entries, giving full details of the publications, an indication of the level of the material and a brief résumé.

Their *Language and Culture Guides* series provide a similar service for lesser known languages (Afrikaans to Welsh). A full list of publications, guides, reports and directories can be obtained direct from CILT (see Address section.)

A very useful guide for teachers of French is the *Guide Documentaire à l'Intention des Professeurs de Français à l'étranger* published by La Documentation Française (1980) 29–31, Quai Voltaire, Paris 75340 Cedex 07, France.

No school should be without *Quid*, an annual publication by Editions Robert Lafont et Sté des Encyclopédies Quid. The 2,000 pages are packed with information and statistics on every conceivable subject.

29 Acronyms

As in many fields the language teaching world uses a large number of acronyms. The following list gives all the common ones and some less common ones:

AAPF	Association Allemande des Professeurs de Français
AATF	American Association of Teachers of French
ABH	Association of Hispanists of Great Britain and Ireland
ACE	Advisory Centre for Education
ACSET	Advisory Committee on the Supply and Education of Teachers
ADULT	Association of Dutch Language Teachers
AFLS	Association of French Language Studies
AEPE	Asociacion Europa de Profesores de Español
AFMLTA	Australian Federation of Modern Language Teachers' Associations
AILA	Association Internationale de Linguistique Appliquée
APEDAC	Association Pédagogique Européenne pour la Diffusion de l'Actualité
APLV	Association des Professeurs de Langues Vivantes
APU	Assessment of Performance Unit
ASM & CF	Association for the Study of Modern and Contemporary France
ATG	Association of Teachers of German
ATI	Association of Teachers of Italian
ATR	Association of Teachers of Russian

ATSP	Association of Teachers of Spanish and Portuguese
AUPELF	Association des Universités Partiellement ou Entièrement de Langue Française
AUPF	Association of University Professors of French and Heads of French Departments
BAAL	British Association for Applied Linguistics
BALT	British Association for Language Teaching
BELC	Bureau pour l'Enseignement de la Langue et de la Civilisation Françaises
BERA	British Educational Research Association
BIS	British Italian Society
BOTB	British Overseas Trade Board
BUAS	British Universities' Association of Slavists
CBEVE	Central Bureau for Educational Visits and Exchanges
CEG	Computer Education Group
CIEP	Centre International d'Etudes Pédagogiques de Sèvres
CILT	Centre for Information on Language Teaching and Research
CIREEL	Centre d'Information et de Recherche pour l'Enseignement et l'Emploi des Langues
CPVE	Certificate for Pre-Vocational Education
CNAA	Council for National Academic Awards
CNDP	Centre National de Documentation Pédagogique
COMAC	Comité d'Accueil
CoSTA	Council of Subject Teaching Associations
CREDIF	Centre de Recherche et d'Etude pour la Diffusion du Français
CREES	Centre for Russian and East European Studies
CUTG	Conference of University Teachers of German in G.B. and Ireland
DES	Department of Education and Science
DES	Diplôme d'Etudes Supérieures
DEUG	Diplôme d'Etudes Universitaires Générales

EAT	European Association of Teachers
EFVA	Educational Foundation for Visual Aids
ESP	English for Special Purposes
ETA	Esperanto Teachers' Association
ETML	Early Teaching of Modern Languages
FIOCES	Fédération Internationale des Organisations Correspondences et d'Echanges Scolaires
FIPF	Fédération Internationale des Professeurs de Français
FIPLV	Fédération Internationale des Professeurs de Langues Vivantes
FLAW	Foreign Languages at Work
FLIC	Foreign Languages for Industry and Commerce
FTA	French Teachers' Association, Dublin
GOML	Graded Objectives in Modern Languages
GREX	Graded Examinations
IATEFL	International Association of Teachers of English as a Foreign Language
IDV	Internationaler Deutschlehrerverband
IoL	Institute of Linguists
IPA	International Phonetic Association
IRAAL	Irish Association for Applied Linguistics
ISBN	International Standard Book Number
JCLA	Joint Council of Language Associations
LAGB	Linguistics Association of Great Britain
LMDU	Language Materials Development Unit (York)
MHRA	Modern Humanities Research Association
MICE	Microcomputers in Comprehensive Schools
MLA	Modern Language Association
MLANI	Modern Language Association of Northern Ireland
MUSE	Micro Users in Secondary Education
NALA	National Association of Language Advisers

NAME	National Association for Multiracial Education
NARE	National Association for Remedial Education
NATE	National Association for the Teaching of English
NCLE	National Congress on Languages in Education
NCML	National Council for Modern Languages in Higher and Further Education
NFER	National Foundation for Educational Research
NCMTT	National Council for Mother-Tongue Teaching
OFINES	Oficina Internacional de Información y Observación del Español
OMLAC	Oxfordshire Modern Language Achievement Certificate
PAD	Pädagogischer Austauschdienst
SALT	Scottish Association for Language Teaching
SBPF	Société Belge des Professeurs de Français
SCHML	Standing Conference of Heads of Modern Languages in Polytechnics and Other Colleges
SFS	Society for French Studies
SIS	Society for Italian Studies
SNPF	Société Nationale des Professeurs de Français en Grande-Bretagne
SODEC	Service d'Orientation et de Documentation pour l'Enseignement de la Civilisation
SUFLRA	Scottish Universities French Language Research Association
TALC	Foundation for Teaching Aids at Low Cost
TESOL	Teachers of English as a Second Language
UCCA	Universities Central Council on Admissions
UK CEE	United Kingdom Centre for European Education

Some computer acronyms

ACL	Association for Computer Assisted Learning
BASIC	Beginners' All-Purpose Symbolic Instruction Code

BIT	Binary Digit
CAL	Computer Assisted Learning
CALL	Computer Assisted Language Learning
CPU	Central Processing Unit
DOS	Disk Operating System
RAM	Random Access Memory
ROM	Read Only Memory
VDU	Visual Display Unit

30 Useful organizations for the language teacher

Alliance Française, Queensbury Place, London SW7 2DN
  1 Lillybank Gardens, Glasgow G12 8RZ
  1 Kildare Street, Dublin 2
Anglo-Austrian Society, 46 Queen Anne's Gate, London SW1H 9AU
Anglo-German Association, 2 Henrietta Street, London WC2E 8PS
Anglo-Spanish Society, for the latest address consult ATSP.
Anglo-Swiss Society, 16 Montague Place, London W1H 2BQ
Association of Teachers of German: see Modern Language Association
Association of Teachers of Italian: (Membership) consult *Italian Studies* for the most recent address
Association of Teachers of Russian: consult the *ATR Journal* for the most recent address for membership
Association of Teachers of Spanish and Portuguese: consult the journal *Vida Hispánica* for the most recent address for membership
Austrian Institute, 28 Rutland Gate, London SW7 1PQ
Austrian National Tourist Office, 30 George Street, London W1R 9FA
Belgian National Tourist Office, 38 Dover Street, London W1X 3RB
Berolina Travel Ltd., (for the GDR), 20 Conduit Street, London W1R 2DD
Great Britain–GDR Society, 129 Seven Sisters Road, London N7 7QG

British Association for Language Teaching: for details of membership consult *The British Journal of Language Teaching*
British Council, 10 Spring Gardens, London SW1.
British-Italian Society, Kensington Palace Barracks, Kensington Church Street, London W8
British Overseas Trade Board, 1 Victoria Street, London SW1
Bureau pour l'Enseignement de la Langue et de la Civilisation Française à l'Etranger. (Publishes 'Le Français dans le Monde'), 9 Rue Lhomond, 75005 Paris
Central Bureau for Educational Visits and Exchanges, Seymour Mews House, Seymour Mews, Wigmore Street, London W1H 9PE
3 Bruntsfield Crescent, Edinburgh EH10 4HD
16 Malone Road, Belfast BR9 5BN
Centre de Recherche et d'Etude pour la Diffusion du Français (CREDIF), Ecole Normale Supérieure de St Cloud, 92 St Cloud, France
Centre for British Teachers Ltd, Quality House, Quality Court, Chancery Lane, London WC2A 1HP
Centre for Information on Language Teaching and Research, Regents College, Inner Circle, Regents Park, London NW1 4NS
Centre de Documentation Pédagogique, 29 rue d'Ulm, 75230 Paris, Cedex 05
Comité d'Accueil, 166 Piccadilly, London W1V 0HH
Council of Europe, F - 67006, Cedex, Strasbourg, France
DES Publications Despatch Centre, Honeypot Lane, Stanmore, Middlesex
Educational Foundation for Visual Aids, 33 Queen Anne Street, London W1H 0AL
Fédération Internationale des Professeurs de Français, 1 Avenue Léon Journault, 92310 Sèvres, France
Fédération Internationale des Professeurs de Langues Vivantes (Head Office): Seestrasse, 247 CH-8038 Zurich, Switzerland: President, Mr E.M. Batley, Pentland House, Old Road, Lee, London SE13 5SZ
Food and Wine from France, 41 Piccadilly, London W1V 9AJ
French Cultural Delegation, 188 Oxford Road, Manchester M13 9GP

French Government Tourist Office, 178 Piccadilly, London W1V
   0AL
French Railways, 179 Piccadilly, London W1V 0BA
German Film Library, Unit B11, Park Hall Road Trading Estate,
   London SE21 8EL
German Food Centre Ltd, 44–46 Knightsbridge, London SW1X
   7JN
German Language Centre for Teachers — Mr A. Jones, Hatfield
   Polytechnic, PO Box 109, Hatfield, Herts. AL10 9AB
German Tourist Office, 61 Conduit Street, London W1R 0EN
Goethe-Institut, 50 Princes Gate, Exhibition Road, London SW7
   2PG
   Ridgefield House, John Dalton Street, Manchester M2 6HG
   The Kings Manor, York YO1
   3 Park Circus, Glasgow G3 6AX
   37 Merrion Square, Dublin 2
Great Britain–USSR Association, 14 Grosvenor Place, London
   SW1X 7HW
Hatfield Polytechnic German Centre, PO Box 109, Hatfield,
   Herts. AL10 9AB
Hispanic and Luso-Brazilian Council, Canning House, 2 Belgrave
   Square, London SW1X 8PJ
Institut Français d'Ecosse, 13 Randolph Crescent, Edinburgh
   EH3 7TT
   3 Kensington Road, Glasgow G12 9LE
Institut Français du Royaume Uni, 17 Queensbury Place, London
   SW7 2DT
Institute of Linguists, 24a Highbury Grove, London N5 2EA
International Association of Teachers of English as a Foreign
   Language (IATEFL), Membership: Mrs B.I. Thomas, 87
   Bennells Avenue, Tankerton, Whitstable, Kent CT5 2HR
Internationale Deutschlehrerverband (IDV), c/o Professor Karl
   Hyldgaard-Jenson, Eriksfältsgatan 16a, S-214 Malmö, Sweden
Inter Nationes, 53 Bonn 2, Kennedyallee 91–103, West Germany
Intourist, 292 Regent Street, London W1
Italian Institute, 39 Belgrave Square, London SW1X 8NX
Italian State Tourist Office, 201 Regent Street, London W1R 8AY
Language Teaching Information Centre, 27 Harrogate Road,
   Leeds LS7 3PD

London Chamber of Commerce and Industry, Marlowe House, Station Road, Sidcup, Kent DA15 7BJ

Luxembourg Tourist Office, 36–7 Piccadilly, London W1V 9PA

Modern Humanities Research Association, c/o Professor D. A. Wells, Queen's University of Belfast, Belfast BT7 1NN

Modern Language Association, c/o CBEVE, Seymour Mews House, Seymour Mews, Wigmore Street, London W1H 9PE

The Modern Language Centre: 26–30 Laystall Street, Rosebery Avenue, London EC1

National Association for Language Advisers, Journal Business Manager: R. Savage, 19 High Street, Eccleshall, Staffs ST21 6BW

National Association for Teachers in Further and Higher Education (NATFHE), Languages section: Hamilton House, Mabledon Place, London WC1H 9HB

National Congress on Languages in Education (NCLE), Hon. Sec.: Mr A. Moys, at CILT (qv)

National Foundation for Educational Research in England and Wales, The Mere, Upton Park, Slough, Berkshire SL1 2DQ

Pushkin Club, Pushkin House, 46 Ladbroke Grove, London W11 2PA

Scottish Curriculum Development Service (publishes 'Modern Languages in Scotland'), 69 Hilton Place, Aberdeen AB9 1FA

Service d'Orientation et de Documentation pour l'Enseignement de la Civilisation (SODEC), Centre d'Etudes Pédagogiques, 1 Avenue Léon Journault, 92310 Sèvres, France

Société Nationale des Professeurs de Français en Grande-Bretagne (founded 1881), Secretary: 38 Brooksville Avenue, London NW6 6TG

Spanish Institute, 102 Eaton Square, London SW1

Spanish Tourist Office, 57–8 St James's Street, London SW1A 1LD

Swiss Tourist Office, Swiss Centre, 1 New Coventry Street, London W1V 3HG

Embassies

Austrian Institute, 28 Rutland Gate, London SW7 1PG

Belgian Embassy, 103 Eaton Square, London SW1W 9AB
French Embassy, 22 Wilton Crescent, London SW1X 8SB
German Democratic Republic, Embassy Press Dept, 34 Belgrave
    Square, London SW1
German Federal Republic, Embassy, 23 Belgrave Square, London
    SW1X 8PZ
Italian Embassy, 14 Three Kings Yard, Davies Street, London
    W1Y 2EH
Luxemburg Embassy, 27 Wilton Crescent, London SW1 8SD
Portuguese Embassy, 11 Belgrave Square, London SW1X 8QB
Spanish Embassy, 24 Belgrave Square, London SW1X 8QA
Swiss Embassy, 16 Montagu Place, London W1H 2BQ

Examination Boards

GCE Examining Boards

Associated Examining Board Wellington House, Station Road,
    Aldershot, Hampshire GU11 1BQ
Cambridge University Local Examinations Syndicate Syndicate
    Buildings, 17 Harvey Road, Cambridge CB1 2EU
Joint Matriculation Board Manchester, M15 6EU
Oxford and Cambridge Schools Examination Board Elsfield Way,
    Oxford, OX2 8EP and Brook House, 10 Trumpington Street,
    Cambridge, CB2 1QB
Oxford Delegacy of Local Examinations Ewart Place, Summertown,
    Oxford OX2 7BZ
Southern Universities Joint Board Cotham Road, Bristol BS6
    6DD
University of London School Examinations Council 66–72 Gower
    Street, London WC1E 6EE
Welsh Joint Education Committee 245 Western Avenue, Cardiff CF5
    2YX

CSE Examining Boards

Associated Lancashire Schools Examining Board 12 Harter Street,
    Manchester M60 7LH

East Anglian Examinations Board The Lindens, Lexden Road, Colchester CO3 3RL

East Midlands Regional Examinations Board Robins Wood House, Robins Wood Road, Nottingham NG8 3NH

London Regional Examining Board Lyon House, 104 Wandsworth High Street, London SW18 4LF

North Regional Examinations Board Wheatfield Road, Westerhope; Newcastle-upon-Tyne NE5 5JZ

North-West Regional Examinations Board Orbit House, Albert Street, Eccles, Manchester M30 0WL

South-East Regional Examinations Board Beloe House, 2-4 Mount Ephraim Road, Royal Tunbridge Wells, Kent TN1 1EU

South Western Examinations Board 23-9 Marsh Street, Bristol BS1 4BF

Southern Regional Examinations Board 53 London Road, Southhampton, SO9 4YL

West Midlands Examinations Board Norfolk House, Smallbrook, Queensway, Birmingham B5 4NJ

Yorkshire and Humberside Regional Examinations Board 31-33 Springfield Avenue, Harrogate HG1 2HW *and* Scarsdale House, 136 Derbyshire Lane, Sheffield S8 8SE

Welsh Joint Education Committee 245 Western Avenue, Cardiff CF5 2YX.

GCSE Examining Groups

Northern group Joint Matriculation Board; Associated Lancashire Schools Examining Board; North Regional Examining Board; North-West Regional Examinations Board; Yorkshire and Humberside Regional Examinations Board.

Midland group Cambridge University Local Examinations Syndicate; Oxford and Cambridge School Examinations Board; Southern Universities Joint Board; East Midland Regional Examinations Board; West Midlands Examinations Board.

London and East Anglia group London University School Examinations Council; London Regional Examining Board; East Anglian Examinations Board.

Southern group Oxford Delegacy of Local Examinations; Associated Examining Board; Southern Regional Examining

Board; South-East Regional Examinations Board; South
Western Examinations Board.
Wales Welsh Joint Examinations Committee.

In Scotland and Northern Ireland
Scottish Examination Board, Ironmills Road, Dalkieth, Mid-
lothian EH22 1LE
Northern Ireland Secondary Examinations Board, Beechill
House, Beechill Road, Belfast BT8 4RS

Other national examining bodies

The Institute of Linguists, 24a Highbury Grove, London N5
2EA
The London Chamber of Commerce and Industry Examinations
Board, Marlowe House, Station Road, Sidcup, Kent DA15
5BJ
The Royal Society of Arts Examinations Board (Publications),
Murray Road, Orpington, Kent BR5 3RB

Addresses useful for career guidance

Guides and Couriers: British Tourist Authority, 64 St James's Street,
London SW1
Airport Information Staff: British Airports Authority, Personnel
Department, Mercury House, North Hyde Road, Hayes,
Middlesex
Hoteliers: for courses write to Hotel and Catering Institute, 191
Trinity Road, London SW17
Telephonists: British Telecom International Service, Caroone
House, Farringdon Street, London EC4
British Broadcasting Corporation: External Services: Bush House,
London WC2; Monitoring Services: Caversham Park, Reading,
Berks.

31 Publishers of textbooks and materials

Edward Arnold Ltd, 41 Bedford Square, London WC1B 3DQ

E. J. Arnold and Son Ltd (part of the Pergamon group), Parkside Lane, Dewsbury Road, Leeds LS11 5TD

Audio-Visual Productions, Hocker Hill House, Chepstow, Gwent NP6 5ER

Bell and Hyman Ltd, Denmark House, 37 Queen Elizabeth Street, London SE1 2RB

Ernest Benn Ltd, 25 New Station Square, London EC4A 3JA

A. & C. Black Ltd, 35 Bedford Row, London WC1R 4JH

Blackie and Son Ltd, Bishopbriggs, Glasgow G64 2NZ

Basil Blackwell, 108 Cowley Road, Oxford OX4 1JF

Bradda Books Ltd, 30 Gleve Road, Letchworth, Herts SG6 1DS

British Broadcasting Corporation (Publications), 144/152 Bermondsey Street, London SE1 3TH

Cambridge University Press, The Edinburgh Building, Shaftesbury Road, Cambridge CD2 2RU

Cassell Ltd, Educational Department, 35 Red Lion Square, London WC1R 4SG

W. & R. Chambers Ltd, 11 Thistle Street, Edinburgh EH2 1DG

Collins Educational Publishers, 8 Grafton Street, London W1X 3LA

J. M. Dent & Sons Ltd, 26 Albemarle Street, London W1X 4QY

European Schoolbooks Ltd, Croft Street, Cheltenham, Glos GL53 0AX

Evans Brothers Ltd, Montague House, Russell Square, London WC1B 5BX

Exeter Tapes, St Fagans Road, Cardiff CF5 3AE
Ginn & Co. Ltd, Elsinore House, Buckingham Street, Aylesbury
   HP20 2NQ
G. G. Harrap & Co. Ltd, PO Box 70, 182–4 High Holborn, London
   WC1V 7AX (educational list now published by Nelson (qv))
Heinemann Educational, 22 Bedford Square, London WC1B 3HH
Hodder & Stoughton, Mill Road, Dunton Green, Sevenoaks, Kent
   TN13 2YD (includes University of London Press and English
   Universities Press)
Hulton Educational Publishers Ltd, Raans Road, Amersham,
   Bucks HP6 5BR
Hutchinson Education, Hutchinson House, 17–21 Conway Street,
   London W1P 6JD
Longman Group Ltd, Longman House, Pinnacles, Harlow, Essex
   CM19 5AA (incorporates Oliver and Boyd)
Macmillan Education, Houndmills, Basingstoke, Hants RG21
   2XS
Manchester University Press, 316 Oxford Road, Manchester M13
   9PL
Mary Glasgow Publications Ltd, Brookhampton Lane, Kineton,
   Warwickshire CV35 0JB
Methuen Educational Ltd, 11 New Fetter Lane, London EC4P
   4EE
John Murray Ltd, 50 Albemarle Street, London W1X 4BD
Nelson & Sons Ltd, Nelson House, Mayfield Road, Walton-on-
   Thames, Surrey KT12 5PL
Oxford University Press, Walton Street, Oxford OX2 6DP
Penguin Books Ltd, Bath Road, Harmondsworth, Middx UB7
   0DA
Pergamon Press Ltd, Hennock Road, Exeter EX1 1AZ
Routledge & Kegan Paul, Broadway House, Newtown Road,
   Henley-on-Thames, Oxfordshire RG9 1EN
Sussex Tapes Ltd, Freepost, Devizes, Wiltshire SN10 1BR
Stanley Thornes Ltd, Educa House, Old Station Drive, Leck-
   hampton Road, Cheltenham, Glos GL53 0DN
University Tutorial Press Ltd, 842 Yeovil Road, Slough SL1
   6BZ
University of York, LMDU, The King's Manor, York YO1
Wheaton & Co. Ltd, Hennock Road, Exeter EX1 1AZ

Bibliography

AMMI, *Teaching Modern Languages in Secondary Schools,* Hodder & Stoughton, 1979

ATI, *Italian in Schools,* ATI, SIS, CILT 1980

Baer, Edith, K. (ed.) *Teaching Languages.* Ideas and Guidance for Teaching Languages with Adults, BBC, 1976

Barnes, C., *French Topic Crosswords,* Edward Arnold, 1981

Berthier, Jean-Edel, *1000 Chants,* Presses d'Ile de France, 1972

Bird Ewan (ed.) *Minority Community Languages in School,* NCLE Papers & Reports. CILT, 1984

British Broadcasting Corporation, *Catalogue of Sound Effects Records and Tapes,* The Langham, Portland Place, London 1AA

Berlitz, Charles, *Native Tongues,* Granada, 1983

Buckby, M. et al., *Graded Objectives and Tests for Modern Languages: an Evaluation,* University of York, 1981

Buckby, M. and Grant, D. *Faites vos Jeux,* University of York, 1971

Burstall, C. et al., *Primary French in the Balance,* NFER, 1974

Burney, Pierre and Damoiseau, Robert, *La Classe de Conversation,* Hachette, Larousse, 1969

Caré, J. M., Debyser, F., *Jeu, Language et Créativité.* Hacchette, Larousse

CBEVE, leaflets Nos. SDN 100, SDN 101, SDN 102

CILT, *Part-Time and Intensive Language Study: A Guide,* 1982

———, *Teaching Materials for French,* 1980

———, *New Teaching Materials for French,* (Additions 1981–82, 1982–83, 1983–84)

—— , *Teaching Materials for German*, 1983
—— , *Teaching Materials for Italian*, 1983
—— , *Teaching Materials for Spanish*, 1984
Cole, Leo R., *Language Teaching in Action*, Longman, 1973
Crawshaw, B.E. *et al., Jouez le Jeu*, John Murray, 1985
Davidson J. M. C. (ed.), *Issues in Language Education*, NCLE
    Papers and Reports 1981
DES, *Modern Languages in Comprehensive Schools*, HMI Matters
    for Discussion 1977
—— , *Departmental Organization in Secondary Schools*, Educa-
    tional Department of the Welsh Office, 1984
Doyle, N.P., *France Quiz*, Hodder & Stoughton, 1973
Fontier, G., and Le Cunff, M., *Guide de l'Assistant de français*,
    Longman, 1975
Green, P. (ed.) *York Papers in Language Teaching*, LTC, York, 1985
Green, P. S. (ed.), *The Language Laboratory in School*, Oliver &
    Boyd, 1975
Hadley, Eric (ed.), *Teaching Practice and the Probationary Year*,
    Edward Arnold, 1982
Harrison, Andrew, *Review of Graded Tests*, Schools Council
    Examination Bulletin 41, 1982
—— , *Language Testing Handbook*, Macmillan, 1983
Harding, Ann *et al.*, *Graded Objectives in Modern Languages*, CILT,
    1980
Harding, David H., *The New Pattern of Language Teaching*,
    Longman, 1970
Hares, R. J., *Teaching French*, Hodder & Stoughton, 1979
Hawkins, Eric, *Awareness of Language: an Introduction*, Cambridge,
    1984
—— , *Modern Languages in the Curriculum*, Cambridge, 1981
Head Masters' Conference, The, *The Teaching of Modern Languages*,
    HMC Modern Languages Report No. 2, 1980
Holden, S, *Drama in Language Teaching*, Longman, 1982
Hornsey, Alan W., *Handbook for Modern Language Teachers*,
    Methuen, 1975
Jesperson, J. O. H., *How to Teach a Foreign Language*, Allen &
    Unwin, 1980
Jones, Barry (ed.), *Using Authentic Resources in Teaching French*,
    CILT, 1984

Lee, W. R., *Language Teaching Games and Contests*, Oxford University Press, 1965

Lee, W. R. and Coppen, H., *Simple Audio-Visual Aids for Foreign Language Teaching*, Oxford University Press, 1968

Littlewood, William, *Communicative Language Teaching*, Cambridge University Press, 1981

Maley, A. and Duff, A., *Drama Techniques in Language Teaching*, Cambridge, 1982

Maley, A., Duff, A. and Grellet, F., *The Mind's Eye*, Cambridge University Press, 1981

Marland, Michael, *Head of Department*, Heinemann, 1975

——, *The Craft of the Classroom*, Heinemann, 1975

——, *Departmental Management*, Heinemann, 1981

McArthur, T., *Foundation Course for Language Teachers*, Cambridge, 1983

Merimet, Gérard, *La Francoscopie; Les Français, qui sont-ils? Où vont-ils?*, Larousse, 1985

Modern Language Association Handbooks

—— No. 1, *The Probationary Language Teachers' Handbook*, (ed.) Smalley, A., 1983

—— No. 2, *German in the Classroom*, (ed.) Jones, A. and Whitton, K. S., 1984

—— No. 3, *The Head of Department: A Guide to Good Practice*, Morris, D., 1984

—— No. 4, *The German Assistant's Handbook*, Holly, E., 1985

—— No. 5, *The French Assistant's Handbook*, Smalley, A., 1985

Morley, W. (ed.) *Bulletin of the ILEA Modern Language Centre*, see address list

Moys, A. et al., *Modern Language Examinations at 16+: A Critical Analysis*, CILT, 1980

Muckle, J., (ed.), *Russian in Schools*, Association of Teachers of Russian, 1982

Muir, S., *Handbook for the Foreign Assistant*, Mary Glasgow Publications, 1975

National Association of Language Advisers, *Using the Foreign Assistant: A Guide to Good Practice*, CILT, 1977

Oudet, S., *Guide to Correspondence in French*, Stanley Thornes, 1984

Perren, G. E. (ed.), *The Space Between: English and Foreign Languages at School*, CILT, 1975

Paneth, Eva, *Tapes of your own*, Longman, 1981
Phillips, D. and Stencel, V., *The Second Foreign Language*, Hodder
    & Stoughton, 1983
Pierre, J., *Comptines en Liberté*, Nathan, 1984
Radford, Colin, *Questions d'Actualité*, Edward Arnold, 1983
Rapaport, B. and Westgate, D., *Children Learning French*, Methuen,
    1974
Richardson, G. (ed.), *Teaching Modern Languages*, Croom Helm,
    1983
Rinvolucri, Mario, *Grammar Games*, Cambridge, 1984
Rivers, Wilga M., *A Practical Guide to the Teaching of French*, Oxford
    University Press, 1975
Rowlands, D., *Group Work in Modern Languages*, University of
    York, 1979
SCHML, *A Guide to Language Courses in Polytechnics and Similar
    Institutions*, CILT
Sanderson, David, *Modern Language Teachers in Action*, University
    of York, 1982
Sewell, H. (ed.) *School Travel and Exchange*, CILT, 1984
Sidwell, Duncan (ed.), *Teaching Languages to Adults*, CILT, 1984
Smith, D.G. (ed.) *Teaching Languages in Today's Schools*, CILT,
    1981
Stevick, Earl W., *Teaching and Learning Languages*, Cambridge
    University Press, 1982
Strange, D., *Language and Languages*, Oxford University Press, 1982
Susse, J., *Jeunesse qui Chante*, Editions Ouvrieres, 1984
Trainaud, A., *Des Jeux pour Apprendre*, Hachette, 1983
Trim, J. L. M., *Minority Community Languages in School*. NCLE
    Papers and Reports, CILT, 1980
Walker, R. and Adelman, C., *A Guide to Classroom Observation*,
    Methuen, 1975
Webb, David, *Teaching Modern Languages*, David and Charles,
    1974
Weiss, François, *Jeux et Activités Communicatives*, Hachette, 1983
Wringe, Colin, *Developments in Modern Language Teaching*, Open
    Books, 1976
Wright, A., Betteridge, D. and Buckby, M., *Games for Language
    Learning*, (new edn), Cambridge University Press, 1984
Wright, A., *1000 Pictures for Teachers to copy*, Collins, 1984

Computers now deserve close attention in the field of language teaching. The choice of books and guides is increasing rapidly. Below is a small selection for the beginner.

It will reward the interested teacher to consult first of all:
Davies, G. and Higgins, J. J., *Computers, Language and Language Learning*, CILT, 1982

Others include:
Bradbeer, R., *The Personal Computer Book*, Gower, 1982
Bishop, P., *Introducing Computers*, Nelson, 1981
Evans, C., *The Making of the Micro*, Gollancz, 1981
Shelley, J., *Microfuture*, Pitman, 1981

A miscellaneous collection of useful material:
Carelman, *Catalogue des Objets Introuvables*, Ballaud (now available in English)
Education Year Book, (yearly), Longman
Mail Order Catalogues from:
    La Redoute, Roubaix 59 France
    Les Trois Suisses, Roubaix 59 France
A Treasure Chest for Teachers, The Teacher Publishing Company, 1981
Whitaker's Almanac, Published at 12 Dyott Street, London WC1A 1DF
Fairbairn, Kerry, *Foreign Languages in Secondary Schools*. A Supplementary Report: a collection of comments by students on their experiences with foreign languages. From the Research Services Branch, Department of Education, Queensland
Marder, Joan V., *Acronyms and Initialisms in Education*, published by the Librarians of Institutes and Schools of Education (LISE 2nd edition 1984). Obtainable from the University Library, Lancaster LA1 4YH
Service Compris, Mary Glasgow Publications, (termly)
CBEVE, *Working Holidays Abroad*
CBEVE, *Volunteer Work Abroad*

A new service to teachers of languages: a facsimile digest of foreign newspapers can be obtained on subscription from: *Authentik*, c/o CILT, Inner Circle, Regents Park, London NW1 4NS and also

Actualquarto, Le Monde par la Presse, details from 20 Allée des Bouleaux, 6280 Gerpinnes, Belgium.

Two new video tapes are well worth acquiring:
Oral Activities for the language assistant, 1980. 58 mins, B & W. from
    ILEA Centre for Learning Resources, 175 Kennington Lane,
    London SE11 5QZ
Using Languages in the World of Work. Colour. Made by Cadbury-
    Schweppes, 1984. Distributed by CILT.

Two audio tapes:
Comment ça va? and *Quand tu sera grand*. Matt, Muffin Record Co.,
    Toronto. Distributed in the UK by K. F. Coles, 2 Vale View, St
    Bees CA27 0BP

Index

THE MODERN LANGUAGE ASSOCIATION

(incorporating THE ASSOCIATION OF TEACHERS OF GERMAN)

APPLICATION FOR MEMBERSHIP

Name in Full: Mr./Mrs./Miss/Ms. ....
(Block capitals please)
Academic qualifications ....
(Please give full details)
Professional position and status ....
If a teacher, languages taught or qualified to teach ....
Official Address ....
(Block capitals please)
Private Address ....
....
(Address for all communications: Official/Private – delete as appropriate)
Do you wish to be attached to the German Section ATG? ....
Branch (if any) to which you wish to be attached ....
If you claim entitlement to membership at a reduced rate of subscription,
please give full details, indicating the estimated duration of such
entitlement ....
....
....

I hereby apply to become a member of the Modern Language Association
and enclose the appropriate subscription of £ ....

      Signed ....
      Date ....

Communications should be addressed to:
The Gen. Secretary, Modern Language Association,

Cheques etc., should be made payable to:
THE MODERN LANGUAGE ASSOCIATION

FOR OFFICE USE

Receipt ....   Branch ....
Card : ....   Section ....
Stencil ....   Mag. back Nos ....
Letter ....